DEAR MR GORBACHEV

DEAR MR GORBACHEV

Edited by Lloyd S. Fischel

Chapter Introductions by Professor Bill Wallace

CANONGATE

First Published in 1990 by Canongate Press,
16 Frederick Street, Edinburgh, Scotland

Introduction and Chronology © Lloyd S. Fischel
This collection © Progress Publishers and Lloyd S. Fischel
Chapter Introductions © Professor Bill Wallace
The Letters © the letter writers

British Library Cataloguing in Publication Data
Letters to Gorbachev
        1. Governments. Policies
        I. Fischel, Lloyd
        351.0072

ISBN 0–86241–331–1

Typeset by Falcon Typographic Art Ltd, Edinburgh & London
from discs supplied by Street Level Publishing Services
Printed and bound in Great Britain by
Butler & Tanner Limited
Frome, Somerset

DEDICATION

To all the letter-writers who have written to President Gorbachev in the name of Peace and Freedom.

ACKNOWLEDGEMENTS

This book would not have been possible without the tens of thousands of people who chose to take time to write to Mr Gorbachev. For the most part their work was done in the spirit of concern not only for themselves and their children but for the future of our planet. It is because of these people that Dear Mr Gorbachev came into being, whether their letters were finally selected in this book or not. I thank you all and I hope this compilation will encourage you to continue to believe in a better future for the world. To President Gorbachev, words can not express my heartfelt admiration for your efforts in your job which some say is the most difficult one in the world.

The dynamics necessary to obtain various permissions were made possible by several individuals, some of whom encouraged me to go forward when the possibilities looked bleak, and others who lent their advice. Several other persons spent their time in quite different arenas. Of these I would like especially to thank Lucy Anisimova, Oleg Benyukh, Ted Fujioka, Lawrence Grobel, Diarmid Gunn (GB/USSR Friendship Association, Scottish Branch), Derek Hart, Ed Johnson, Arnold Kawasaki, Peter Matson, Lt Col. Scot McMichael (Department of Defence Studies, Edinburgh University), Hidosuke Mochizuki, Igor Preferansky, Joe Procopie, Alexei Pushkov (Novosti Publishing, Moscow), George Riches (past chairman of the Musterlin Group Plc), Linda Robbins, Alina Stanciu, Professor Bill Wallace, Ed Vega, Richard Yakota and Daisaku Ikeda for permission to use part of his poem 'Arise the Sun of the Century'.

Due to the great distances between the United States and the Soviet Union I experienced numerous problems of communications, travel, and matters of daily living. My appreciation goes out to the many people who helped me through a seemingly endless stream of adversities. Particularly I offer great thanks to the Afanasieva family for their efforts to do whatever they could to help make my stays in Moscow warm and safe; to the people at Intertorg-Moscow who offered a smile and a place to hang my coat, and to Russ Solomon, founder and President of TOWER RECORDS, whose desire to spread peace through music to the people of the Soviet Union, and his trust in my firm, is typical of his spirit and enterprise.

As in any work of this nature, many supporters are needed. In this connection, I would like to extend my deeply felt appreciation to Eve Brody, Carolyn Donato, Carlyn and Patrick Duffy, Karen Falcon, Monet Fischel, Armasha and Mariana Hammer, Carolyn Jones, Brian and Karen Potter, Marina Samsonova, Mendi Schilit and Amy Smith.

All of the translators who contributed their time and effort at such short notice were crucial to the completion of this book. They are Xinying Li (Chinese), Alena Linhartova (Czechoslovakian), Sylvia Furness (Danish and German), F.E.J. Carroll (Dutch), Y. Al-Khatib (Egyptian), Dr Maija McKinnon (Finnish), Dr Keith Aspley (French), Werner Kittell (German), M. Tabatabai (Iranian), Liz Potter (Italian), Iroko Ise (Japanese), Kirsti M. Dinnis (Norwegian), Grazynka McAinsh (Polish), Vasile Toch (Romanian), Veronique Nelson (Spanish), Dr David Guild and Diarmid Gunn (Russian).

The publishers involved in making this collection a reality were Canongate in Scotland and Progress in Moscow. The collaboration was truly international. The vision, stamina and courage of Stephanie Wolfe Murray and her staff at Canongate, especially Richard Ayles and Andrew Young, are most remarkable in this age when publishers are more often interested in making a quick buck. Stephanie's keen sense to reach the essence of things has made the job of choosing the present collection a most enjoyable, if arduous, one.

I can never fully repay the encouragement and trust given me by Alexander Avelichev and Alexei Ershov of Progress Publishers. Without their help and cooperation this whole project would have been impossible. V. Kachianov's desire to achieve the impossible in his search for many of the letters and photographs and his attempts to convince various authorities to release them is much appreciated. Nancy Donohue and Lorri Weiss's devoted help in the editorial process to which they contributed so much was only possible because of the compassion they feel for humanity. To all of you I offer my heartfelt respect, gratitude and thanks.

Lastly I would like to thank the Gireyev family, and Hirmoi, Hana and Maya for continually reminding me through their love of their families that if I could do something which might make an improvement in this turbulent world, it would be worthwhile.

CONTENTS

FOREWORD

I have long felt rather guilty as regards those who write to me from abroad. I do indeed try to find time to read all the letters addressed to me, but please believe me when I say that I am unable to reply to them all.

For me these letters are more than a sign of belief in perestroika, more than a sign of deep interest in what is taking place in our country. They are also a constant reminder of my share in the responsibility for the present and the future.

I am convinced that the nineties will determine the kind of world we have at the beginning of the next millennium. That is the measure which everyone involved in politics should use to assess his actions and concepts.

My meeting with President Bush in Washington confirmed our common choice in favor of co-operation, trust and mutual understanding between the USSR and the USA, and this is also of importance for the whole world.

In many of your letters there is a note of anxiety about the future of perestroika. There are indeed difficult changes ahead, and a great deal of work to be done. Nonetheless, the decisive fact is that the anchor which kept us moored to the past has been raised, and the Soviet Union in the process of renewal is now sailing for new shores. We shall not abandon the new course we have taken. We shall build a truly democratic and humane society in which the universal criterion is the interest of the human being.

I am deeply grateful to those who write to me for this is evidence that they are not indifferent, but take a friendly interest in our affairs and our concerns.

With best wishes,
Mikhail Gorbachev
July 4, 1990

The intellect of progressive minds knows no stagnation;
For they do nothing but earnestly seek
The radiance of truth and wisdom;
The eye of the progressive mind
Knows no dint of darkness;
For they never lose sight

Of the rainbow of hope, far and distant;
The progressive mind knows no hesitation,
For action to take initiative,
Itself is our supreme honor.

'Arise the Sun of the Century', Daisaku Ikeda

'. . . the only genuine backbone of all our actions, if they are to be moral, is responsibility – responsibility to something higher than my family, my country, my company, my success'.

President Vaclav Havel of Czechoslavakia to a joint meeting of the United States Congress, February 21, 1990.

INTRODUCTION

While riding the New York subway in early 1988, I read an article in The Wall Street Journal which reported on the large amount of mail which had been sent to Mikhail S. Gorbachev from all over the world. I was curious to know what was being said and by whom. Perhaps some of these letters sent to Gorbachev were having some impact on his foreign policy and the socio-economic restructuring of Soviet society. Furthermore, it seemed to me an unprecedented occurrence that so many people from around the world had sent correspondence to the leader of a foreign country.

Some time later I was acting as an advisor to the first US-Soviet Youth Summit in Moscow, so I took advantage of the occasion to pay a visit to the Kremlin's official publishing house, Novosti, to talk about the letters to its director, Alexei Pushkov. Pushkov was aware of the fact that many letters had been received by the Kremlin. Initially he was astounded by the idea of turning such confidential matters over to a foreigner and it took prolonged discussions to convince him that we shared common ground, with regard to the letters, and that a published collection of the letters might influence the American public to voice concern over the great appropriations the US Congress had been making to fund the Strategic Defence Initiative, commonly known as Star Wars. Pushkov agreed to help me to gain access to the correspondence. I returned to the United States and over the course of several months sent many telexes asking if the necessary permission had come through, but it had not. On a subsequent business trip nine months later, I once again visited Novosti and Pushkov informed me that in order to proceed the matter must be discussed with the directors of a different publishing firm, namely, Progress.

A bit exasperated and feeling the pressure of Soviet bureaucracy, but undaunted, I met with Progress Publishing's director, Alexander Avelichev, and deputy director, Alexei Ershov. After being informed of my inquiry, they had taken a serious look at some of the correspondence in advance of our meeting. Within the last few years, the opening of the Soviet Union to the West has made business meetings between the Soviet nomenclatura and foreigners much more conciliatory but until very recently it was illegal for Soviets to even talk 'business' with foreigners. Even after legislation opened the door to many Soviets, they were extremely reluctant to have unsanctioned contact with businessmen from non-socialist countries. Therefore, I was not surprised when I was told by the directors that they were unwilling to put themselves at risk by pursuing permission for me, an American, to have access to Gorbachev's mail. However, if a western publisher had made a firm commitment to publish the material, they would think about it. I did not want to spend time finding a western publisher unless there were guarantees that the Soviets would keep their side of the bargain. They did not appear to be concerned that some of the letters might be derogatory to the Soviet Union, but were more apprehensive about the possibility of malicious editing. It took six months of persistence and persuasion to gain their trust and secure an agreement.

While attending the annual convention of the American Booksellers Association in May 1989, I approached the executives of the Musterlin Group Plc and found them to be very receptive to this idea. Stephanie Wolfe Murray, Managing Director of Canongate Publishing, one of Musterlin's companies, wholeheartedly shared my enthusiasm. After I showed her only a dozen photocopied sample letters, we began discussing a publishing contract which when finalised I then took back to Moscow for the approval of Gorbachev's office and the Progress executives. It was agreed to and signed. Trust between the Soviets and myself had been established, a publishing contract entered into, and now I was finally in a position to take a look at the letters.

Ershov helped me locate a Moscow flat which doubled as an office, and there, in what my Soviet friends called 'a real Russian winter', an American assistant and I began the task of organizing and reading the letters. Within a relatively short period of time it became clear that the one-hundred-and-twenty-thousand-plus letters did indeed represent something of a phenomenon and that amongst them were many thoughtful, interesting, and inspiring letters.

For the most part, once received and partially translated or summarized in the Russian language, letters sent to the Kremlin are channelled into various departments of the Central Committee, as is the case in many government bureaucracies, allotted to accomplish it. Therefore, it is not surprising that many letters sent to the Soviet leader were in various stages of review. Some letters were on desks waiting to be acted upon, others were elsewhere pending decisions, or were filed in a variety of places – ostensibly for posterity.

Often, and for no apparent reason, certain letters were selected for a full translation and were then channelled to a different department. Notations on many of the letters and attached memoranda indicated that a particular letter had been assigned to Gorbachev's office, or to other government leaders. I could discern no pattern as to which letters were sent up, down, or sideways within the labyrinthine offices of the Kremlin.

In his book Perestroika, President Gorbachev requested that readers write to him to express their ideas. Thousands of people around the world took him to heart: however most references to this have been deleted in order to make the book less repetitive. As person after person sent their thoughts to Gorbachev, I began to get the feeling that they were participating in the creation of a powerful process of world democracy. The letter writers often stressed a heartfelt appreciation of the current Soviet political and economic situation. For example, Cynthia Kang wrote that she supports his policy, '. . . but I do not know that it may present some problems for you. For instance, in my hometown of Pittsburg, many people used to work in the steel mills, but due to the concept of free economy, the steel industries closed down and many people were left unemployed. How will you handle cases like this? Do you think you will be able to control unemployment?'

Letter writers often offered personal invitations to the President and his wife to stay in their homes and share in the life of their families and communities. Large numbers of letters contained photographs of everything from family members and friends to homes and offices, as well as published articles of all sorts, money, gifts, and original poetry. The letters were both typed and handwritten, simple and complicated, suggestive and forthright. Many are filled with pure passion which overflows into a variety of topics and often they espouse political beliefs which differ from the government policy of the writer's country.

In selecting the letters I tried to choose those which are most representative of what was made available to us. It should be noted that letters of a political nature, sent by persons in an official capacity dealing with especially sensitive issues, were understandably not released to me. There are many letters which discuss business proposals and nothing else, most of which I left out of the final selection.

An undeniable indication that letters sent to Gorbachev have had some affect on his government's policy can be found in Gene La Roque's correspondence located in the chapter 'People of Peace'. La Roque, a retired Rear Admiral of the United States Navy, wrote several letters in an unofficial capacity. On January 18, 1985, La Roque wrote suggesting that the Soviet government stop the testing of nuclear devices, intimating that the United States might follow suit. Shortly after, the Presidium of the Supreme Soviet of the USSR announced that it would enter into a unilateral moratorium to stop the Soviet testing program. In an article published by the official state Soviet newspaper Isvestiya on April 21, 1985, the Soviet government stated that La Roque, in his letter had '. . . appealed for a declared moratorium on the testing of all nuclear weapons from 6 August, 1985 – the 40th anniversary of the atomic bombardment of Hiroshima. The Soviet Union greeted this initiative and announced its consent to take this step of goodwill'.

In the last month of 1988, the fourth Gorbachev-Reagan Summit was unexpectedly curtailed due to an unusually destructive earthquake in Armenia, prompting Gorbachev to return immediately to his country. This catastrophe precipitated a flood of letters which contained messages of condolence and, often in the same letter, praise for the Soviet leader for his historic speech to the United Nations General Assembly, which he delivered in New York the day the earthquake struck. Among other significant ideas, his speech called for a new world order in which the superpowers' actions for world hegemony which has characterised the post war years would be replaced with a new spirit of co-operation. Along with the humanity expressed in his speech, there was a practical recognition that the world could no longer support such rivalries either economically or politically. Thousands of letter writers expressed their support.

The year 1989 was one in which great historical changes occurred particularly in Eastern Europe, at such a rapid pace that we all had a difficult time understanding the implications. Many of the letters are like a stop-watch on those events. The unsigned letter from 'Friends of Romania' in the chapter 'Eastern Europe' prompts us to recall the storm of the Romanian Revolution of Christmas 1989 which occupied our attention for such a short time-span. Reports have documented that the Romanian leaders of the uprising believed that Gorbachev would not send in tanks and soldiers. He indeed kept the promise he had made to the world not to get involved in other countries' internal affairs.

Letters written in the early part of Gorbachev's tenure as leader of his country often demonstrate people's desire to question his authenticity and suggest his media exposure was calculated. However, I found that as time passed, increasingly letters conveyed a sense of humility, as though acquiescing to the historical significance of the man. They became an indicator of public opinion. Time and again people around the globe made reference to viewing Gorbachev on television, often confessing that the Soviet leader's television image was the most important factor motivating his or her to write.

Obviously a great volume of correspondence is directed towards the abolition of nuclear weapons. There is the ever-present spectre of annihilation created by what are among the most advanced technological achievements of our age – a stockpile of weapons so powerful that their very existence threatens our survival. Among the thousands of passionate pleas addressed to Mr Gorbachev, there are cries of hope that the Soviet leader will want to and be able to exercise his powers to help alleviate this greatest single threat to our future. Tamme Bergsma of the Netherlands summed up this general perspective when she wrote, '. . . We don't want Europe to become the battlefield of the future. We don't want to live in fear any more, but want to see the USSR and the USA negotiate from a positive basis and feeling. Although certainly there are still many people who put all their trust in America, and who distrust everything Russia is doing, I thing we should learn from you. . . '.

The fact that so many individuals have taken a moment from their lives to reach out to Mikhail Gorbachev, the foremost representative of what has been one of the world's most repressive governments for three quarters of the twentieth century, is indicative of humanity's common wish for a peaceful world, one that is stronger than the doubt and suspicion which has become commonplace amongst us. Recently, Daisaku Ikeda, a leader in the international world peace movement declared: 'Today whether we like it or not, the world's civilisations and cultures are being globalised; we must strive through the inevitable clashes we face to forge our cultures and values anew, enduring the often painful remaking of ourselves'.

The letters in Dear Mr Gorbachev illustrate how appropriate this viewpoint really is and that people throughout the world are voluntarily facing this process. While governments may eternally argue about the differences between them, the common man has a gut level understanding of what is fundamentally important to his own survival. I'll never forget the sparkle in the eyes of the Russian taxi driver the morning after the Congress of Peoples Deputies elected Gorbachev as the first President of the Soviet Union to be voted into office. I had just picked up a few more boxes of letters from an office near the Kremlin and I asked the driver how he was doing. He turned to me and answered with a smile on his lips, 'You know. . . we have a President now'.

Lloyd Fischel
Santa Monica
California
United States of America

NUCLEAR DISARMAMENT
Annihilation or Conciliation

WITHIN A FEW YEARS of becoming General Secretary of the Soviet Communist Party in March 1985 Mikhail Sergeivich Gorbachev did so much to change the direction of Soviet policies and consequently of international relations that it is difficult to think back to the state of extreme tension that existed between East and West before his time. Yet in order to understand why countless people in many different parts of the world subsequently felt moved to write to him, it is essential to recall just how close the two superpowers and their allies were to becoming embroiled in what would have been the third and worst world war, a nuclear war.

In Afghanistan since December 1979 Soviet troops tried to quell the Afghans and the West poured in arms to help them. In 1983 the Soviet Union had moved its SS20 intermediate nuclear missiles into Czechoslovakia and East Germany in response to the stationing of America's equivalent Cruise and Pershing II missiles in Western Europe. Nuclear testing continued apace on both sides; and while President Reagan was developing the so-called Strategic Defence Initiative, President Brezhnev was threatening to follow suit and thus fuel a nuclear arms race in space. Quite apart from the terrible destruction that would result if a war did break out, there was the immense economic burden of maintaining large and increasingly well-equipped armed forces in East and West.

Gorbachev's accession to power did not seem to promise immediate release from the growing threat of a nuclear war. His selection by the Politburo was quicker and more decisive than any of his predecessors. But although he had made brief visits to Canada in 1983 and Britain in 1984, he was relatively unknown in the West, was not thought to be well-informed about it, and had made no special study of arms control, nuclear or otherwise. He therefore appeared to offer little fresh hope.

In addition, although open-minded and quick to learn, he did not instantly turn his attention to the moral or even just to the survival issues presented by a possible nuclear conflagration. The immediate issue as he saw it in the spring of 1985 was the Soviet economy. It was in a worse state than even the most hostile observers had realised. The whole military-industrial complex, therefore, not just its nuclear component, was too expensive to sustain. It was also politically entrenched and opposed to change in general. So arms spending had to be reduced. Accordingly, Gorbachev's first pronouncements on the nuclear question were down-to-earth and practical, lacking the fundamental rethinking that much of the world's public wanted to hear.

In April 1985 he announced a unilateral freeze on the further deployment of SS20s and in August a unilateral moratorium on underground nuclear tests. In January 1986 he proposed arms talks that would culminate in a nuclear-free world by the year 2000. This certainly aroused widespread interest in the West. But his motivation seemed to remain economic. At the 27th Party Congress in March he imprinted on the minds of his fellow communists the need to put recovery before all else if the Soviet Union was to have the kind of prosperity and welfare that the Revolution had promised. Gorbachev's initiatives also had a simple element of tactical manoeuvring common to both sides in diplomatic exchanges.

But things changed virtually overnight with the disastrous explosion and fire at the Chernobyl nuclear power station in April 1986. Most people, inside and outside the Soviet Union, took the disaster as a pale imitation of the terrible things that would happen on a large scale should there be a nuclear war, and no one more so than Gorbachev. He was converted to the humanitarian case for nuclear disarmament, showing his sincerity in the open and honest way in which he dealt with the aftermath of the tragedy. This not only influenced his handling of foreign policy. It made an enormous impact on world opinion, anxious to see an end to the nuclear threat.

It was a new and refreshing experience. Gone at last was the Brezhnev-style Soviet leadership, inflexible, inhumane, and bent on asserting supremacy by any means, even by the use of nuclear weapons. Gorbachev emerged as a human being, firm and hard-hitting when necessary in presenting the Soviet case, but above all concerned to find a peaceful solution to East-West disagreements.

He had already taken steps to restart the East–West dialogue. The last Soviet-American summit had taken place between Brezhnev and President Carter as long ago as 1979; and President Reagan's hostility to everything communist had made another such meeting unlikely. But Gorbachev indicated his willingness to have an exchange of views with Reagan, and the two men sat down together at Geneva in November 1985. This proved successful in creating a friendly atmosphere for further negotiations on the whole range of East-West problems and in putting purpose into the Geneva arms talks that had been limping along on the side for more than six months. But it took Chernobyl and its aftermath to breathe real life into the mix of high level summitry and official talks that rapidly produced the first big step in nuclear disarmament.

3

In June 1986 Gorbachev announced new proposals on strategic weapons which drew a positive response from Reagan in July. In September he made concession on intermediate-range nuclear missiles. And carried forward by the post-Chernobyl spirit, the two superpower leaders held their second summit at Reykjavik in October. At one moment it seemed as if Gorbachev would get what he wanted, a major reduction in all nuclear weapons and an end to the Strategic Defence Initiative. But giving up SDI proved too much for Reagan at that stage; and officials all round wanted to discuss the finer points of verification as well as the many other technical questions determining successful arms control.

The world was disappointed and began to apportion blame. The fact was, however, that agreement had been reached on two targets - reducing strategic weapons by 50 per cent and cutting intermediate missiles to 100 on each side. With his economy still not recovering and the nuclear threat not diminishing in the course of 1987, Gorbachev saw no alternative but to make a crucial concession earlier in the year by ceasing to insist on an end to the American SDI programme. World pressure for agreement was maintained; and great strides were made in methods of improving on-site verification to ensure that an agreement would be observed. The Intermediate-range Nuclear Forces (INF) Treaty was signed at the third summit in Washington in December of that year. As if by a miracle, Gorbachev and Reagan decided to dispose of all their INF weapons, in Asia and the US as well as in Europe.

It was not a miracle. It followed from the exigencies and imperatives of Gorbachev - and, in all fairness, from Reagan's change of heart. At the INF summit the two men also went so far as to accept the principle of a 50 per cent reduction in long-range nuclear missiles.

Gorbachev was by now a kind of international folk-hero. In 1987 he had published his book on *Perestroika* which was aptly subtitled *New Thinking for Our Country and the World*; and following the INF Treaty it was widely read and interpreted as proof that Gorbachev was a statesman who wished to change the course of international history - and could do so. He was therefore someone worth writing to. That does not mean to say that outside opinion was uncritical. Whether justified or not, the Soviet resumption of underground nuclear testing in February 1987 was not popular. Setting high standards, Gorbachev was occasionally judged by them, to his disadvantage. But perhaps heeding the criticisms, and certainly responding to the many pressures for further arms control, he continued the dialogue he had started with Reagan into the presidency of George Bush. The long-range issue proved a particularly difficult one, despite summits in Moscow and at Malta. But in June

1990, at yet another Washington summit, the two men - as well as signing an accord on reducing their stock-piles of chemical weapons - initialled an outline agreement on cutting by half their respective long-range nuclear capabilities. And what still stands as Gorbachev's objective is the one he put to the UN General Assembly in New York in December 1988 after Chernobyl, converting 'the armaments economy into a disarmament economy'.

Bill Wallace

Center for Defense Information
Washington, DC
USA

18 January 1985

Dear Mr Chairman,

We note that you have repeatedly affirmed your personal commitment and that of the Soviet Union to the conclusion of effective arms control agreements with the United States. Toward this end we wish to suggest a first step which is readily achievable and would be of great value in slowing the pace of the nuclear arms buildup. It would completely bypass the current disagreements in INF and START issues and demonstrate your leadership as a man of peace.

This first, essential step is to propose a moratorium on nuclear testing and early resumption of negotiations on a Comprehensive Nuclear Test Ban. Based upon their Tripartite Report of 31 July 1980 (attached) the United States, the Soviet Union, and the United Kingdom are already in substantial agreement on the elements of such a Test Ban. Dr Herbert York the chief US negotiator, has stated that the negotiations ties were sincerely committed to concluding a treaty consistent with the terms outlined in the Tripartite Report, including provisions concerning on-site inspections.

We have enclosed a recent Defense Monitor which explains the importance of an early end to nuclear testing. Since publishing this report in August, more than 100 organizations have already pledged their support to a world wide campaign to end all nuclear weapons explosions. The proposal will be considered soon by appropriate agencies at the UN. We are certain that you will be applauded and strongly supported by a great majority of people around the world if you take the lead to bring about an end to nuclear explosions forever. We encourage the Soviet Union to announce a moratorium on all nuclear weapons testing effective on and after 6 August 1985.

It is impossible to conceive of a more dramatic and constructive way in which to move now to lessen the danger of nuclear war. By taking this bold initiative, you will earn the approval of the citizens of the world for your service to the cause of peace.

Respectfully,
Gene R. La Rocque
Rear Admiral, USN (Ret)
Director

This letter to Soviet President Chernenko was written before Gorbachev became his successor in March. Please refer to the Introduction for an explanation of the letter's relevance to the moratorium on the Soviet nuclear testing program initiated by Gorbachev later in the year 1985.

Hatfield
Pennsylvania, USA

18 October 1985

Dear Mr Gorbachev,

Many of my American scientific colleagues and I sense that you represent a reformation of Soviet repression and an unusually strong proponent of arms de-escalation towards peaceful coexistence. Scientists are used to deriving truth through their observational powers, which does not exclude the press, and then acting upon those truths derived. This simplistic pursuit of truth ignores political complexity, which ignorance oftentimes does not win us many favours in political circles and in fact arouses suspicion.

In many ways we scientists are like Samantha Smith, the naive yet intelligent and gifted young girl invited to the Kremlin by your predecessor. Negotiations over the arms race, star wars and a proper agenda for the upcoming summit would do well to imitate Samantha Smith's simple pursuit of world accord rather than the present subterfuge and descent into bombast.

So we are sensitive to your peace initiatives. We are listening and suggest another more direct method to attract further curiosity and potential support from the American scientific community: To free some of your more eminent scientists from their house arrests and captivity as a goodwill gesture that you do not fear truth. The list of those Soviet colleagues now so oppressed is long, but contains in part the following distinguished scientists: Sakharov, Schrachansky and Koryagin. There are many others whose voices deserve to be heard and for whose freedom we are hopeful, but if you could just release these three from their house arrests and detentions, an enormous swell of American support from the scientific community would immediately follow.

Do not underestimate the strength of the American scientific community. These actions on your part will be as significant as your good suggestion to reduce present nuclear stockpiles by fifty per cent. We are listening!

Yours sincerely,
Bruce Molholt PhD

Andrei Sakharov was forcibly exiled to the closed city of Gorky in January, 1980, after he publicly condemned the Soviet regime for invading Afghanistan. He was allowed to return to Moscow in December, 1986, after a telephone call from Gorbachev during which Gorbachev invited him to return home to resume his 'patriotic' activities.

Natan Scharansky, a computer scientist, has been a leading spokesman for the Jewish emigration movement in the USSR and was arrested by Soviet authorities in 1977 for dissident activities. He received a 13 year prison sentence on charges of treason in 1978. Following a worldwide campaign, the government released him in exchange for Soviet spies held in the West and he took up residence in Israel in 1986. His book, Fear No Evil (1988), received critical acclaim.

Anatoly Koyagin, M.D., as a Soviet psychiatrist, studied fifty-five dissidents being detained in psychiatric confinement between 1977–1981. He could find nothing psychiatrically wrong with any of them and furthermore chronicled the political rather than medical causation of their internments. After Koryagin published these findings in 1981 in the British Medical Journal 'Lancet' (Vol. 1, p.821), he was sentenced to seven years hard labor followed by five years internal exile for 'anti-Soviet activities'. In 1987 Koryagin was released from prison and emigrated to Switzerland.

Reno
Nevada, USA   5 June 1987

Dear General Secretary Gorbachev,

We can't expect God to write the ten commandments of nuclear and conventional disarmament on the side of the UN building for us, can we? We have to plan to disarm if we are to disarm. The first phase of my five-phased plan is the American Initiative, which introduces the concept of bilateral doubling reduction. We Americans would place twenty of our obsolete warheads at Andrews Air Force Base under the joint custody of the UN Disarmament Committee and the US Air Force. We would ask that you Soviets immediately match the move, placing twenty of your obsolete warheads under the joint custody of the same UN committee and your military at a base near Moscow. You could, of course, move first while we Americans debate it, and we would then match your move. As soon as both superpowers had placed a set of twenty warheads on the table, they would then bilaterally dismantle a set of forty, this time active-duty warheads. That would be followed by a set of eighty and so on through seven sets: 20, 40, 80, 160, 320, 640 and 1,280.

Perhaps you fear that whipping up a souffle of bilateral doubling reduction while a Euromissile cake is in the oven would be regarded as grandstanding. Or that initiating in grand style an untested idea of an utterly unknown would be regarded as foolhardy both at home and abroad. It is certainly true that my ideas have not been tested, but then whose have? If you decide not to initiate bilateral doubling reduction, will you at least publish 'Solving Problem Number One' in Pravda, perhaps complemented by an interview and a brief story about how thoroughly I have been ignored by American and European media. By doing so, it would seem that at least European media, and eventually Third World and American media, would pick it up. The ideas could be discussed and debated, and perhaps some could even be tested.

Sincerely,
Ed Cowan

Philadelphia
Pennsylvania, USA   30 September 1987

Dear Mr Gorbachev,
    I am writing to you to express my thanks and appreciation for your continued efforts to lessen the nuclear arms threat. As a member of the health care provider system, I am very concerned about the arms race. Many of us in the nursing profession consider the nuclear threat to be the greatest threat to the public health and welfare. Indeed, our nursing association drafted a resolution that proclaims this, and declares that it is our collective professional responsibility to address this issue. I have enclosed a copy for your information. *
    Please know, Mr Gorbachev, that many Americans are aware of the new approach you have brought with you to your leadership role, and share in respect and admiration for you. You bring hope to the West, as well as to your own people. My best wishes to you, your administration and your family. May you be well, and prosper in your efforts.

Sincerely,
Donna Gentile MSN, RN

* ANA RESOLUTION ON DANGERS OF NUCLEAR WAR
Whereas the immediate effects of a nuclear war would include deaths and injuries in excess of the response capacity of any health system or civil defense plan because of the destruction of food, shelter, water, medical supplies and transportation and communication systems needed to assist targeted populations; and
    Whereas such destruction could not be limited to nations participating in nuclear war, but would affect surrounding areas, and no country could escape the effects of such disaster because of its impact on the biosphere, the world economy and culture; and
    Whereas the long-term effects of nuclear war would include

9

radioactive contamination, infectious diseases, social breakdown, economic collapse, and genetic and environmental damage affecting surviving groups for generations; and

Whereas historically, the nursing profession has participated in the planning and delivery of emergency nursing care in times of disaster, and is qualified to speak to the response capacity of the nursing profession in case of nuclear disaster; and

Whereas the ANA Code of Ethics states, 'The nurse participates in the profession's efforts to protect the public from misinformation and misrepresentation . . . ' and 'collaborates with members of the health professions and other citizens in promoting community and national efforts to meet the health needs of the public'; and

Whereas the ANA Statement on Social Policy attests to nursing's social responsibility and affirms that 'For nursing, the public good must be the overriding concern'; and

Whereas the American Medical Association and the American Public Health Association have stated categorically that no adequate medical response is possible to a nuclear war;

Now therefore be it

Resolved that the American Nurses' Association acknowledge that there is no adequate response to a nuclear war or its aftermath; and be it further

Resolved that the American Nurses' Association support efforts for peace and disarmament, beginning with a verifiable bilateral nuclear weapons freeze between the United States and the Union of Soviet Socialist Republics as a first step toward nuclear disarmament; and be it further

Resolved that the American Nurses' Association encourage educational programs by state nurses' associations and curricula development by schools of nursing on the public health impact of nuclear arms on a community and a nurse's ethical responsibility to alert the public of this ultimate threat to public health; and be it further.

Resolved that the American Nurses' Association not support or endorse activities which imply that nuclear war is survivable; and be it further

Resolved that this resolution be distributed to state nurses' associations, schools of nursing, nursing and health organizations, to appropriate local, state and national government leaders and health departments; to the International Council of Nurses for distribution to constituent members with recommendation for adoption of similar resolutions, and for support of negotiated international disarmament; and to the media.

SPRINGFIELD COLLEGE IN ILLINOIS
Springfield, Illinois, USA   28 October 1987

Dear Mr Gorbachev,

Along with many people throughout the world, I was disappointed when the American Secretary of State George Shultz, back from Moscow, reported that you were uncertain about coming to the United States for a summit. He told us your hesitancy seemed to stem from President Reagan's continued commitment to SDI.

I meant to write you to urge you to reconsider – if indeed the source of your uncertainty was correctly reported.

Our fast-moving world is full of both nasty shocks and pleasant surprises. In particular, this morning's paper brought me the pleasant surprise that you had apparently reconsidered.

Nevertheless, I decided to write you, for I'm not sure that my earlier letters to you on SDI were sufficiently clear or eloquent.

As a physicist, I believe the chances that SDI developments can produce a shield for the cities of the world sometime this century are very slim. However, there is no clear way to make progress on strategic defense without threatening to undermine the deterrence that relies on the potential for retaliatory strikes. Therefore, secret, unilateral SDI efforts on either side are extremely unsettling to the other side.

I believe that President Reagan's 'SDI open laboratories' suggestion can offer a way out – but only if it is carried even further.

Picture an SDI effort which is an open and international effort. To direct such an effort, imagine that the concerned governments created a Board of Directors whose members were of unquestionable integrity and scientific stature. Andrei Sakharov, Roald Sagdeyev, Carl Sagan, and Bernard Feld come readily to mind. Imagine further that not a dollar or a ruble would be allocated for SDI efforts by the American Congress or the Soviet government except in response to the specific recommendations of such a Board, and even then, only for a joint, open effort.

We would then not be spending money or resources on nonsense. In fact, we would probably spend very little. At worst, SDI efforts would be harmless. At best, the Board of Directors and the joint enterprise might come up with actual missile defenses useful to people everywhere in this highly armed world.

I do not intend these ideas as naive suggestions. Here in the United States, in Russia, and elsewhere, people are likely to think, 'What's to prevent secret, unilateral SDI efforts also . . . perhaps even on a major scale?' I would have to answer that there is no absolute way to guarantee against such efforts, but that we could write into our treaties (and, in fact, should write into our treaties) powerful mechanisms to protect and encourage 'whistleblowers'.

My best wishes,
Samuel Olanoff
Professor Emeritus, Physics;
Independent Peace Activist

Sabadell
Spain   8 December 1987

Dear Sir,
   As a simple Spanish citizen, it gives me great pleasure to congratulate you from the bottom of my heart for the Reduction of Arms Treaty signed by you, for the USSR, with the President of the USA, as the first step towards universal peace and understanding.
   The history of the world will ascribe this event in your favour and humanity will always thank you for this gesture and your high intentions.
   With the joy of such a magnificent occasion, I am delighted to send you my sincerest regards,

Augustin Alonso

Whitmore Lake
Michigan, USA   12 December 1987

Dear General Secretary Gorbachev,
   Over the past several years, watching the Soviet Union declare a unilateral moratorium on nuclear testing, propose cuts in conventional forces in Europe, a fifty per cent reduction in strategic nuclear weapons, etc., it has become clear that there is a real chance for an end to the madness and waste of the arms race. Having grown up in a world that has always been on the brink of self-destruction, this is still hard for me to believe. I can remember very clearly being eleven years old during the Cuban missile crisis, listening to a transistor radio and wondering if the world would blow up before I went to school the next day. Disaster was narrowly averted then, but every year the chance of a war becomes more likely, as the number of weapons grows larger and the time available to stop them from being used grows shorter.
   What irony for the human race to evolve and develop over millions of years if the net result is only a kind of mass suicide . . .

12

We seem to be at a turning point in human history: the decisions made by world leaders like yourself today will in large part determine the fate of the five billion men, women, and children alive today and their untold billions of heirs in the future. This is truly an awesome responsibility.

What a shame to see the vast potential for good of science and technology being made to serve the most primitive impulses of our species, and enormous amounts of talent and resources being wasted so stupidly while fifteen million children die needlessly every year in the Third World. If someone came here from another planet and observed what we were doing, they would have to conclude that we were insane.

Sincerely yours,
Nicholas S. Stuteville

The US Congressional Research Service reported in 1990 that arms sales to the third world from industrialized countries totalled $38.4 billion in 1988, and $29.3 billion in 1989, the lowest figures since 1983. Soviet arms sales to the third world in 1989 amounted to $11.2 billion while American arms sales reached $7.7 billion, the report said. In the same period, British sales totalled $3.2 billion, Chinese sales of $1.1 billion, and the French signed contracts worth $300 million (down from $3.1 billion recorded in 1988).

The report observed that arms delivered to Libya in the period were valued at $3.5 billion in 1986-1989. Deliveries to Iraq totaled $27.7 and Syria received $5.5 billion in shipments during the same period.

Saudi Arabia purchased $4.9 billion worth of arms in 1989 and Afghanistan $3.8 billion the most purchased by any two countries that year.

The United States military spending since 1951 totals over $9.3 trillion (adjusted for inflation).

The Soviet figures for this period have never been totally available. However, during the Twenty-Eighth Communist Party Congress in July 1990, Foreign Minister Eduard Shevardnadze reported that during the past 20 years $1.17 billion was spent on weapons beyond what was needed to reach parity with the West. He concluded, "Squandering a quarter of our budget on military expenditures, we have ruined the country."

18 December 1987

Dear Mr Gorbachev,

At a time when the process towards disarmament is likely to be greatly facilitated by the signing of the agreement to ban intermediate nuclear weapons by the United States of America and the Soviet Union, we believe it is opportune to seek to strengthen the Treaty of Raratonga.

It is our view that this treaty, while deficient in its military aspects, has great political significance. The more so because the pattern for disarmament in the Pacific region as a whole is likely to be a series of regional treaties rather than one covering the entire area.

Further, we do not view the Treaty of Raratonga as an end in itself but rather as a beginning.

Consequently, we believe that the next step in strengthening the treaty might well be negotiations to add three protocols as follows:

1. That all missile tests be banned in the region of the treaty;

2. That the passage of nuclear-armed and/or -powered ships and submarines and nuclear-armed aircraft be banned from the region of the treaty; and

3. That the parties concerned declare not to use or threaten to use the region of the treaty to launch or threaten to launch nuclear weapons.

In proposing these additional protocols we are encouraged by the knowledge that some island states, such as Vanuatu and the Solomon Islands, have called for strengthening the treaty along these lines.

Further, as to our proposal number two we would point out that the Law of the Sea states that the high seas be used 'exclusively for peaceful purposes'. Our proposal fully accords with this concept both legally and morally.

Yours sincerely,
Rev. Richard Wootton
Executive Chairperson

Lansdale
Pennsylvania, USA   December 1987

Dear Mr Gorbachev,

Thank you for appearing on our television recently with Tom Brokaw of the National Broadcasting Company and clearly

14

answering precise questions posed to you. I hope that our country will soon have a leader similarly inclined to enlighten your people of our views and problems. We must learn to communicate, understand and adapt for we have but one atmosphere and one world. Protecting ourselves from solar radiation is apparently of urgent importance as we pollute our natural habitat. Of course radiation from weapons must be abolished. A far better use of those funds and energy would be to develop a world language, a road from Europe to China, a cure for cancer, a greening of the Sahara, and many other more sensible projects. I have enclosed a copy of an article comparing in picture form the present firepower of the world with that of World War II. To me the horror truly questions the common sense of human beings today!

Very truly yours,
C. Craig Rife

Bracken Ridge
Queensland, Australia   24 January 1988

Dear Sir,

The phenomenal spending on arms is keeping the peoples of the Soviet Union tied to a standard of living which is disappointingly low. Even the once vibrant US economy has now slid down the scale – no doubt attributable partly to that country's massive military budget. The entire US economy is so intertwined with the munitions industry that very real fears are held for employment levels should there be any significant reductions in expenditure for the armed forces.

If military spending could be progressively re-directed to increasing the living standards of countries like Ethiopia, The Sudan, parts of India and numerous others nearly as poor, in a very short time these regions would become markets for the overproduction of the OECD's factories, for the Americans' grain surplus and the EEC's 'butter mountain'.

We, as trade unionists are always told that we must try not to take too big a share of the 'cake'. True enough, of course, but we see the overall picture in much the same way. Even the most wasteful countries are coming to realize that most of what we consume – even the air we breathe – is not in endless supply. Our resources are all finite, and must be managed, not squandered. Surely then, it is also mankind's duty to ensure that the unforgivable excesses of military spending are curtailed, to be re-directed into needy areas so that the people of the world all reap the benefits, not just the merchants of death.

We urge you, in the name of humanity, to use every resource at your disposal to reduce military spending; to remove the threat of annihilation that hangs over us all; to work for peace and mutual prosperity by seizing every opportunity and making the most of it.

We know you share our concerns in these matters and want you to know that we support the cause of world peace, freedom and justice regardless of nationality, race or creed.

Yours fraternally,
R. J. Steel
Secretary

Ф. ТГ-22

МЕЖДУНАРОДНАЯ

МИНИСТЕРСТВО СВЯЗИ СССР　　ТЕЛЕГРАММА

ПРИЕМ __ го __ час __ мин.	ПЕРЕДАЧА: __ го __ ч. __ м.	Адрес: __
Валяж № 660	№ связи __	
Принял:	Передал: __	

TMB411 VIA ITT. QIB107. 4-013056S067
SUMS CO UIAX 080
FRS TDBN WASHINGTON DC 80/75 07 1218P EST

SECRETARY GENERAL MIKHAIL GORBACHEV
THE KREMLIN
MOSCOW

PLEASE HOLD YOUR POSITION, NO RESEARCH OR TESTING ON SPACE WEAPONS.
DO NOT ALLOW FOR RESEARCH, DEVELOPMENT OR TESTING OF ANY KIND OF
STRATEGIC DEFENSE INITIATIVE EXPERIMENTS. LEGISLATION TO BAN ALL
WEAPONS FROM SPACE WILL SOON BE ANNOUNCED IN THE HOUSE AND SENATE.
THIS IS CRUCIAL TO OUR WORK.

DR. CAROL ROSIN
THE INSTITUTE FOR SECURITY AND COOPERATION IN OUTER SPACE
8 LOGAN CIRCLE
WASHINGTON DC 20005
202-462-8886

In 1983, Dr Rosin founded the Institute for Security and Cooperation in Outer Space (ISCOS), a non-profit educational think-tank based in Washngton, DC. She travelled to the Soviet Union extensively in the mid-1970's pursuing these ideals. 'Rosin is regarded to be the original political architect of the move to stop the SDI and ASATs.' (Military Space, July 1984)

16

12 February 1988

Dear Mr Gorbachev,

The Medical Association for Prevention of War (Australia) notes with great disappointment the performance of a nuclear test by the Soviet Union on 6 February at Semipalatinsk. This test represents the continuation of the most dangerous arms race ever seen. It is an arms race which must be stopped. The first step in that process is a Comprehensive Test Ban Treaty.

International Physicians for Prevention of Nuclear War, with which MAPW is affiliated, aims to stop all nuclear tests by 5 August 1988. This is the twenty-fifth anniversary of the signing of the Partial Test Ban Treaty which banned nuclear tests in the atmosphere, outer space and underwater, and which was seen as a step towards the complete cessation of all nuclear tests and an agreement on general and complete disarmament. The promise of that treaty will be realized only when all nuclear testing is permanently ceased.

MAPW (Australia) and IPPNW applauded the unilateral moratorium on nuclear tests by the USSR from 6 August 1985 to 31 December 1986. This move was regarded with great hope, and as a very positive step. We strongly encouraged the USA to reciprocate. The fact that the USA regarded your moratorium with disdain dismayed us, and represented an opportunity lost. However the need for such a moratorium, leading to a Comprehensive Test Ban Treaty, is still just as urgent. The world needs another such act of supreme statesmanship. Now, as then, a nuclear test moratorium would not in any way threaten the security of the USSR. Your country has sufficient weapons for any conceivable purpose.

The medical consequences of a nuclear war (accidental or intentional) are completely beyond human experience. No adequate medical response would be available in the event of such a catastrophe. To prevent this, and to instead use the world's rich resources to alleviate human misery and to build trust and goodwill, must be our highest priority.

Millions of people throughout the world continue to be outraged by the hostage situation imposed on them by the nuclear balance of terror. Such a situation erodes hope for the future, builds fear, and perpetuates the myth that there are irreconcilable differences between East and West which can only be addressed by the threat of utter destruction. In the nuclear age our common enemy is fear and the weapons which arise from it.

The negotiation of a Comprehensive Test Ban Treaty is imperative. Such a treaty would:

17

— halt the nuclear arms race
— be verifiable
— increase, not decrease, each nation's security
— build hope and trust.

As medical practitioners, with responsibility for maintaining and improving world health, and as world citizens, we urge you to again take the lead by ceasing all nuclear tests forthwith. Your nation and the world have nothing to lose and everything to gain.

Yours sincerely,
Dr Susan Wareham
ACT Coordinator for MAPW Australia

International Physicians For The Prevention of Nuclear War (IPPNW) was formed in 1980 as a result of an exchange of letters between Dr Bernard Lown of the Harvard School of Public Health and Dr Evgueni Chazov of the USSR Cardiological Institute. IPPNW favors the complete abolition of nuclear weapons and prudent interim measures designed to slow the arms race or engender the trust needed for its cessation. There are IPPNW affiliated groups in 55 nations, representing more than 170,000 physicians worldwide.

IPPNW holds annual world congresses which are attended by its members and affiliates, the largest being the Physicians for Social Responsibility (USA) and the Soviet Committee of Physicians for the Prevention of Nuclear War, with over 28,000 and 60,000 physicians respectively. The congresses generate documents which are widely distributed to world leaders in government and medicine. IPPNW, along with the Soka Gakkai International - a non-governmental organization of the United Nations - is sponsoring the exhibit, 'Nuclear Arms: Threat to Our World.' The exhibit has been shown in 16 countries including the United States and the Soviet Union.

NATIONAL COUNCIL
THE REPUBLICAN ASSOCIATION OF EX-SERVICEMEN
AND WAR VICTIMS
Paris, France

2 March 1988

Dear Secretary General,

Our Association sent you, 24 March 1985, a letter telling you of our dearest wish to see the nuclear disarmament negotiations – entered into by the USA and the Soviet Union – end in positive agreements for the future of our planet.

That is why, together with many men and women throughout the entire world, we rejoiced at the treaty signed in Washington last December agreeing to the destruction of medium and short range missiles. Today, we are delighted that we can observe the first concrete steps to dismantle them and we hope that the other implementations of the treaty will quickly follow the initiative of the two co-signatories.

At the same time we look forward to a positive outcome to the Geneva negotiations (on the suppression of fifty per cent of strategic nuclear weapons) and the other negotiations that are taking place between America and Soviet experts about the feasibility of a plan to reduce and verify nuclear testing.

All these initiatives demonstrate that the analyses and declarations made in December 1986 in Vienna by the representatives of the four international organisations of ex-servicement were not utopian and are beginning to be put into operation at the level of states.

We thus ask you to continue resolutely your policy on this path to peace and disarmament, to intensify it and to accelerate the process as far as the total elimination of nuclear, chemical, biological and conventional weapons, the sole situation capable of guaranteeing the survival of mankind and of commencing at last an age of international solidarity and fraternity between peoples.

The new logic that you have inaugurated with the treaty of Washington must lead all the countries of the world to embark likewise on the path to disarmament in a spirit of negotiation and we ask you to help this universalisation of the process.

The final document of the second worldwide gathering of Ex-Servicemen's Associations indeed declares with good reason 'the breathtaking and ruinous stockpiling of weapons is less conducive to guaranteeing the independence and the integrity of states than to reinforcing the dangers of conflict through mutual reactions of fear and suspicion.'

Mr President, Mr Secretary General, history already remembers the positive act you signed in Washington last December. We ardently desire that it likewise remembers this date as the start of a permanent process of disarmament that will cease only with the definitive establishment of a new era of peace, solidarity and fraternity between peoples.

We are certain that, with this end in view, you will continue to receive the support of ex-servicement and men of goodwill throughout the world.

Yours respectfully,
Georges Doussin
National Secretary of ARAC

NATIONAL FEDERATION OF INDIAN WOMEN
16 Kasturba Gandhi Marg
New Delhi, India

8 March 1988

Your Excellency,

Women who give birth to life, who nurture life, are particularly concerned about world peace. They know through their own experience and through history how deep and agonising is the suffering when sons and daughters fall victims to armed aggressions and war. Therefore women, regardless of their nationality or creed, throughout the world, express their deep concern to build a world free of danger of nuclear war, a world where resources can be utilised for peace and development, not for war and destruction. They know only too well that today with the unprecedented arsenals of nuclear arms, with the threats to extend the scope of these arms to space that there is no question of a 'limited'or 'winnable' war – a nuclear war will mean the total annihilation of all humankind. Women realise only too well how resources which should and would be used for human development, their development, are today being diverted for the use of making nuclear weapons.

According to estimates, only a small portion of the money that the world spends on nuclear arms would be sufficient to eliminate hunger, eradicate several dangerous diseases and provide medical care, sanitation and safe drinking water for everyone. Thus the dream for a nuclear-free world is based on the present cruel reality of huge unprecedented wasteful expenditure. We know that peace and development are indivisible.

It is in this background that we welcome as a most important first step the INF Treaty signed between the Secretary General of the CPSU and the President of the United States of America in December last which for the first time eliminates missiles of the medium range. We join the world peace movement in its demand for immediate ratification of the Treaty by the respective Governments and concerned Parliaments in both the countries. There may be forces who are unhappy with this first step towards disarmament and want to reverse the process and sabotage the Treaty. We, therefore, deem it of utmost importance to immediately ratify the treaty and to take the process forward to the next step which should cover an elimination of both short and long range missiles. We are also extremely distressed that while a distinct possibility has opened up for elimination of such weapons on earth, the attempt by some to build these weapons in space.

Yours sincerely,

Suman Krishan Kant	Vimla Farooqui
President	General Secretary
Vimal Randive	Ivy Khan
Vice-President	General Secretary

Camden
New Jersey, USA   8 April 1988

Dear Secretary General Gorbachev,

Nuclear war has become the ultimate threat to mankind. Its growing probability, consequences, and inextricable linkage to other growing problems are such that the reduction of the threat of nuclear war by the INF Treaty has been greeted with enthusiasm on both sides of the ocean. Nevertheless, an invention once made, cannot be disinvented. The nuclear weapon is here to stay; it has become part of the human condition. Man will have to live with it permanently: not only through the next decade or century, but for ever – that is, as long as mankind survives.

I think that the West can cooperate with the East where we share common ground and dispute with you constructively on other grounds. If we can control the motion of satellites orbiting distant planets or leave the earth and land on the moon, then surely, we can reach across the conference table and become friends. As Einstein eloquently stated, 'Shall we choose death, because we cannot forget our quarrels? We appeal, as human beings to human beings; remember your humanity and forget the rest.'

Sincerely yours,
Hollace Okevia Bluitt
Associate Professor
Department of Political Science

Binghampton
New York, USA   14 April 1988

Dear General Secretary Gorbachev,

Enclosed are copies of two letters: one from United States Senator Alfonse D'Amato, the other from United States Senator Sam Nunn, both received by me on 11 April 1988. Senator D'Amato is one of two Senators representing New York State in the United States Senate in Washington, DC. United States Senator Alfonse D'Amato is a conservative Republican, member of the same party as President Reagan. United States Senator Sam Nunn is a conservative

Democrat, Chairman of the US Senate Armed Forces Committee, and one of two Senators representing the State of Georgia, one of the American states located on the eastern seaboard.

The enclosed are for your information. I am forwarding the enclosed to you in the hope they will elucidate the US arms policies and make a common agreement between the USSR and the United States on arms control an achievable reality.

Thank you for your time, attention and consideration of the enclosed. Thank you! I remain,

Respectfully yours,
Mark Porteus

UNITED STATES SENATE
Washington, DC, USA

4 April 1988

Dear Mr Porteus,

Thank you for contacting me and please excuse the delay in replying.

I strongly support our attempts to secure fair, stable and verifiable arms-reduction agreements with the Soviet Union. We have engaged the Soviet Union in negotiations to reduce strategic nuclear weapons in the Strategic Arms Reduction Talks (START), to reduce theater nuclear weapons in the Intermediate Nuclear Forces (INF) talks, both in Geneva, and to reduce both tactical nuclear and conventional forces in the Mutual and Balanced Force Reduction (MBFR) talks in Vienna.

At present, the US negotiators are attempting to salvage the tentative agreement hammered out in Reykjavik. The key elements of this initiative are as follows:

Terms United States & Soviet Union
Total SNDVs   1,600
Total RVs   6,000 warheads
Sublimits   4,800 on ICBMs/SLBMs
                     3,300 on ICBMs
                     1,650 on heavy ICBMs
                     or ICBMs w/more
                     than 6 RVs

ALCMs   1,500 RV limit outside START ceiling

22

ABM Treaty	Adherence to the ABM Treaty for 10 years with no RDT&E restrictions added followed by option to deploy unilaterally Adherence to the ABMT for 10 years with added restrictions on RDT&E followed by mutual decision to deploy
Mobile ICBMs	Banned unless definitely verifiable Designated deployment areas have been discussed
ASAT	No test moratorium Test moratorium
SLCMs	No limits unless verifiable Banned on surface ships
INF	100 RVs (deployments limited to CONUS and Soviet Asia; SRTNF to be folded in either by way of a freeze (SU) or a ceiling and build-up (US))

A hindrance to negotiations is the Soviet's insistence that agreements on SDI, strategic arms, INF, and a test ban must all be linked into a single package. So far, this position is unacceptable to the US. A further complication is the tandem offer made by the US to eliminate all ballistic missiles within a ten-year period. This proposal has been tabled at Geneva, and is considered an alternative to the more modest SALT-like follow-on embodied in the framework outlined previously.

The new terms, were they accepted, would require a major revamping of both sides land-based deterrents. The 'Midgetman', heralded as a solution to the problem of America's long-standing ICBM vulnerability, would be stillborn. Similarly, both the Soviet SS-24 and SS-25 programs would have to be dismantled. The Soviets would also have to make major reductions in their force of the SS-18s. SSBN covertibility to Cruise missile carriers is problematic.

I am optimistic that the arms-control talks between the US and the Soviet Union will lead not only to reduced world tensions, but also to a verifiable, fair and enforceable arms-reduction agreement. I believe the US is negotiating from a position of strength that will result in an operable agreement that will significantly reduce the cost of a nuclear defense and the threat of a nuclear war.

I welcome the opportunity to address your concerns.

Sincerely,
Alfonse D'Amato
United States Senator

7 April 1988

Dear Mr Porteus,

Thank you for contacting me about the proposed Intermediate-range Nuclear Force (INF) Treaty. While my initial reaction to the treaty is positive, I believe there are many substantive questions which need to be addressed during the Senate hearings and floor debate on the treaty. How I come down on this treaty will depend in large measure on how the administration answers these questions.

As you are aware, NATO has relied to a large extent on the threat of an early use of nuclear weapons to deter Soviet aggression in Europe for the past forty years. This means that the Alliance has focused on the cheaper, nuclear deterrent without adequately investing in the more costly area of conventional defense. Over this period, the Warsaw Pact has made considerable improvements in its conventional capabilities and in some areas enjoys significant quantitative advantages over NATO.

This conventional imbalance underlies many of my concerns about the INF Treaty. It disturbs me that the administration has not fit the treaty into an overall conceptual or strategic framework. During its hearings, the Armed Services Committee will look at the overall conceptual framework in which the treaty should be viewed and will focus specifically on the requirements for maintaining and strengthening NATO's deterrent posture in the new environment brought about by the attainment of an INF Treaty. This will include adjustments which will be necessary in NATO strategy, conventional force improvements, conventional arms control policy, and theater nuclear weapons modernization. The Armed Services Committee will also coordinate with the Foreign Relations and Intelligence Committees on specific issues related to the details of the treaty and its verification.

By any logic, NATO should have started negotiating on conventional arms and proposed bold and innovative conventional arms control agreements which would effectively deny to Soviet ground forces forward deployed in Eastern Europe their current ability to threaten NATO with a short warning conventional attack. This necessarily would entail significant reductions in Warsaw Pact tanks, artillery tubes, maneuver battalions, and other land-based weaponry. I also believe the administration should have been more successful over the last seven years in getting more defense capability out of each defense dollar it has been given to spend.

In light of the highly favorable conventional force imbalance, I have said that I would favor attaching a declaration to the INF Treaty which would serve notice that the United States might exercise the supreme national interest clause in the INF Treaty and withdraw from the agreement prior to the removal of the last US missiles if NATO fails to make substantive improvement in the conventional force balance prior to that time.

On a more positive note, the INF Treaty does have several meritorious features if it is viewed in isolation. For example, the treaty represents important continuity between successive administrations in planning and deploying the Pershing IIs and Ground Launched Cruise Missiles (GLCMs). It is evidence that NATO can be a cohesive alliance and that the Alliance's two-track policy to deploy INF forces and simultaneously negotiate arms control proved successful. The treaty also establishes the important precedent of disproportionate Soviet reductions, which would be a very significant principle in any conventional arms control agreement. In the INF Treaty, the Soviet Union agrees to destroy four times as many INF assets as the United States. The treaty's on-site inspections also represent an important psychological precedent for future verification agreements, such as would be required in a strategic arms reduction treaty.

I appreciate your allowing me to share some of my thoughts on this matter with you. You may be assured that I will keep your views in mind as the Senate continues preliminary ratification hearings concerning the INF Treaty in preparation for its floor debate.

Sincerely,
Sam Nunn

Upper Beaconsfield
Victoria, Australia   26 April 1988

Dear Mr Gorbachev,

I am writing to you to protest in the strongest terms about the nuclear test explosion carried out by your country on 22.4.88 at 0930 (universal time) in East Kazakhstan. It had an estimated body wave magnitude of 4.6, equivalent to a yield of 3 kt TNT.

It is widely understood that the major purpose of nuclear test explosions is to assist in design of new weapons. This continued planning for nuclear war is a moral outrage. Nations that continue to test atomic weapons cannot expect that their avowed commitment to avoidance of nuclear war will be taken seriously by the peoples of the earth.

This year makes the twenty-fifth anniversary of the partial Test Ban Treaty – the promise of that treaty will only be realized when nuclear testing stops completely.

As a physician, I am acutely aware of the catastrophic consequences of nuclear war. Even without nuclear warfare (intentional or accidental) atomic weapons tests continue to poison the biosphere. There is no possible effective medical response to the horrors of a nuclear holocaust.

I respectfully urge you to use the power and goodwill of your office to press for an end to nuclear weapons testing, and the negotiation of a comprehensive test ban treaty.

Yours sincerely,
Dr R. W. Anderson MBBS, DRCOG

Torbay,
England   18 May 1988

Gentlemen,

Re: *This dear planet Earth – the best piece of real estate in the system*

Further to my letter to you both on the occasion of your third summit in Washington I am now happy to see that substantial progress is being made in the process of missile diminution though I am still concerned at the psychological effect on those of this world's population who continue to live in fear and worry, particularly the women who carry us for nine months and bring us into it.

Get rid of more of these obscene weapons.

Sort it out (all the political, territorial and human rights issues are glaringly obvious) and negotiate a substantial reduction in the number of land-based BMs at this stage.

Do it and do it now.

One day (it maybe two generations or so when men have regained respectability) people will look back and laugh at all this and I hope they will.

Do not let them laugh at you.

Yours truly,
Ronald J. Law

CENTER FOR DEFENSE INFORMATION
Washington, DC, USA

26 July 1988

Dear Mr Gorbachev,

The Second Conference of Retired Generals and Admirals of the Soviet Union and the United States met in Moscow and Leningrad this month. A report of their principal findings and recommendations is attached for your information.

The most notable characteristic of this report is the insistent theme that positive action is urgently needed to reduce the level of military confrontation between the US and the Soviet Union in order to reduce the risk of war.

It is remarkable that this theme does not come from naive pacifists but from knowledgeable and experienced military officers. The twenty participants in the Conference served a collective total of 748 years of active military service, spanning the period from 1921 to 1988. It is with this broad perspective that they recommend the positive measures included in the report.

In the nuclear age continued military confrontation is unnecessarily expensive and unacceptably dangerous. We respectfully urge your active support to promote progress on the recommended measures so that both our great nations may enjoy the benefits of a peaceful, cooperative relationship.

Sincerely,
Gene R. La Rocque
Rear Admiral, USN (Ret)
Director

FINAL DOCUMENT OF THE SECOND CONFERENCE OF
SOVIET AND US ADMIRALS AND GENERALS
(July 18–24 1988, Moscow-Leningrad)

This document represents a consensus of the participants which was achieved through active, constructive debate on how best to lessen US-Soviet military confrontation and reduce the risk of war.

1. The participants in the conference welcome the Soviet-American INF Treaty as a major achievement in arms reduction.

They believe that the INF Treaty will serve as a catalyst to begin a process of nuclear, chemical and conventional arms reductions. The modernization of existing nuclear systems and the development of new, even more destructive types of nuclear armaments should be prohibited.

2. The next important objective is to reduce strategic offensive weapons, starting with a fifty per cent reduction of such weapons, while respecting the 1972 ABM Treaty.

3. All nuclear weapons except strategic weapons should be removed from land, sea and air forces, beginning with those deployed at sea in US and Soviet warships. All removed weapons should be dismantled.

4. A complete nuclear test ban, plus an end to tests of nuclear delivery systems, are essential steps to end the competition in nuclear weapons technology. A cessation of nuclear testing by the nuclear states is also essential to restrain nuclear proliferation.

5. Conventional forces must be reduced through elimination of military units and their armaments in order to make it impossible for either side to launch a surprise attack or to conduct offensive military operations successfully against the defense forces of the other side.

6. The US and the USSR should take the lead in substantially reducing the sales of arms to developing nations and military training and military advisors in these countries. It is recommended that the UN should obtain relevant reports from all countries supplying arms to developing nations.

Reduced military spending by the US and USSR, as well as other NATO and Warsaw Treaty countries, would contribute to a decrease in military tension.

7. Public disclosure of all relevant details concerning armed forces is an essential ingredient of successful arms control negotiations. All such information should be fully verifiable through cooperative measures, including on-site inspection.

8. As you can see from consensus number six, we rely heavily on the United Nation's organizations to achieve the goals we wish to obtain. The participants in the Conference agreed to establish a working group to develop a program of studies and consultations to address a phased disarmament program, a joint space program and other cooperative ventures. Members of the Conference reaffirm their readiness to provide informed military comment on current security issues in the US and USSR as well as in other countries.

Vancouver
Washington, USA   25 August 1988

Dear Sir,

The continued presence of huge masses of Soviet troops and armor in the 'satellite' countries of the Warsaw Pact would seem to be a continuing threat to peace. It is inconceivable to the average citizen of the USA that Russia could seriously consider the NATO nations to be a threat – obviously, it seems to us, all of them together plus US forces would not stand a chance against Russian power in conventional weapons. These huge Russian conventional forces, infantry, tanks, and air power, could obviously get to the English Channel in a day or two, NATO notwithstanding!

Therefore, it is not surprising to us that Mrs Thatcher and the Europeans are reluctant to abandon the nuclear deterrent, the 'pax atomicum'.

You say, 'Ridiculous – we will never attack first!' Yes, but while we tend to believe your intent, you are one, mortal, political person. What might happen if the (Italian/French/Dutch/??) Communist Party loses a close election and calls for help to Mother Russia? How easy to say, 'We must help our fellow communists/socialists and protect them against those evil capitalists/fascists!!'

Many of us would like to see a bilateral agreement on conventional forces; the USSR move troops and tanks back into Russia and significantly reduce the size of your standing armies; we bring our own troops back to this country and NATO disarm proportionally for Russian/Warsaw Pact reductions. Mistrust your Warsaw Pact satellites? – should they not be able to have self-determination as per perestroika?

Yours very truly,
Heyes Peterson MD

The member countries of the North Atlantic Treaty Organization (NATO) are Belgium, Britain, Canada, Denmark, France, Greece, Iceland, Italy, Luxembourg, the Netherlands, Norway, Portugal, Spain, Turkey, the United States and West Germany.

NATO was created in 1949 to give Western European countries, whose power had been sapped by World War II, confidence that the United States would defend them from Soviet aggression. A main NATO strategy has been "forward defense" by its forces against any Soviet invasion from Eastern Europe. Another key doctrine has been "flexible response", under which the alliance reserved the option of using nuclear weapons against conventional attack.

A study published in 1989 by the International Institute for Strategic Studies gave NATO's strength in active ground forces stationed in Europe as 2,243,000. Its ground forces in reserve units in the area total 4,136,000. The study said NATO had 21,000 main battle tanks in Europe, along with 34,000 armored combat vehicles and 1,100 armored helicopters.

Jersey City
New Jersey, USA   August 1988

Dear Secretary Gorbachev,

Enclosed please find a copy of a letter I have been sending to US senators about the so-called 'Star Wars' program which you know is abbreviated using the term SDI.

There is no defense against nuclear weapons and the SDI program is just wishful thinking.

The pursuit of SDI by either side makes the hope or belief of the military men stronger that they can survive.

Neither side can survive nuclear war.

Sincerely,
Joseph Cunningham

Dear Senator McCain,

In regard to the SDI system:

I believe both sides will agree that nothing works 100%. Therefore, the controversy centers on what percentage of the nuclear warheads will pass through the SDI shield.

If 10,000 warheads are launched against the SDI shield and only 10% (1,000 warheads) pass through the shield, then the United States is totally annihilated.

SDI does not work at all against low flying cruise missiles. The East, West and Gulf coasts will be turned into dust by cruise missiles launched from Russian submarines. And more cruise missiles will be sent by Russian surface vessels. In addition, the center of the United States will be turned into dust by the warheads that pass through the SDI shield.

Once again, the SDI shield will allow each and every one of the cruise missiles to pass through to its appointed target.

Most of the people I talk to do not realize the awesome destructive force of a one megaton nuclear explosion. The device which destroyed Hiroshima was a very, very small bomb – 20 kilotons. The warheads which will reach their targets here in the United States are going to be fifty times more powerful. I invite you to review the photo of Hiroshima which appeared in your high school history book. Then picture fifty times that power.

Then picture the landscape after twenty, thirty or forty of these devices which have been dropped in place over your favorite city. What you have are very large craters surrounded by dust.

Why then are the Russians so afraid of SDI? Because SDI will cause the White House and the Pentagon to believe that nuclear war is survivable. Thus, we will enter into a nuclear war with the Russians resulting in the annihilation of both sides.

The false promise of SDI will lead us into war with the Russians which will result in our own annihilation. But it will also result in the annihilation of the Russians which is why they don't want it.

Sincerely,
Joseph Cunningham

Bergen
The Netherlands   15 September 1988

Dear Sir,

It came to my attention that your country did a nuclear test on 22 August, 16.20 GMT in NW Siberia, with a power under 55 kt, being the eighth test this year.

Testing for reliability is, as scientists tell us, nearly always possible by testing the non-nuclear part of the weapon.

Development of new weapon systems brings about the necessity of nuclear testing. That development itself is contradictory to the spirit of a test ban. Why are the Threshold Test Ban Treaty (1974) and the Peaceful Nuclear Explosions Treaty (1976) still not ratified? Money to spend on verification must be given priority in relation to money for development of new weapons, being a shorter way to final disarmament.

The report of the World Health Organisation 1987 pictures us the presumable situation after a 'restricted' war. Many of the factors mentioned in this report are applicable to defense-related conditions which you can not really discriminate from war preparation. Poverty, pollution, hunger, fear and distress lead to a disadvantage in the relation of T4 and T8 white blood corpuscles as found in AIDS.

Most of the weapon trade is directed to the Third World, where it helps to make increased inequality by way of the 'oppression hierarchy'. This inequality, between the rich who control the weapons and the poor, will prove to imply a much greater threat of war than inequality of [nuclear] weapons.

So, as a healthworker, I urge you to ratify the '74 and '76 treaties and to work towards a comprehensive test ban.

Yours sincerely and respectfully,
Akke Botzen-Gramsma Arts
Member of the IPPNW

Similar letters were sent by IPPNW (International Physicians for Prevention of Nuclear War) to other World Leaders.

Houston
Texas, USA   30 November 1988

Dear General Secretary Gorbachev,

Of all the arms limitation proposals being considered between our two countries, I feel the 'Tritium Factor' is the one which holds the most promise for the Soviet Union, the USA, and mankind in general. Because the tritium in these modern weapons decays at such a rapid rate, stockpiles of these weapons are being created. These large numbers of weapons complicate the formulation of an East-West arms limitation agreement. It is general knowledge that the political welfare and peace of the planet lie in the hands of our two countries. Both our nations, however, are causing increased strains on the global political state and jeopardizing the insurance of world peace with the production of nuclear weapons.

Both our countries have stockpiles of plutonium that are sufficient to maintain our current surplus of these already existing warheads, and even enough to modernize them, should this be desired. Plutonium, unlike tritium, lasts for thousands of years. Why then, is it necessary for us to continually manufacture tritium warheads which will only require constant labor and maintenance to ensure and rebuild their strength? The tritium in these weapons declines by half in 12.3 years. Should the Soviet Union and the USA start an agreement now to halt the production of these somewhat 'temporary' weapons, it is conceivable that within twelve years we would experience a fifty per cent cut in warheads. It is my belief that without these deadly forces, existing relations between our two nations would strengthen and grow dramatically.

I would like to close by praising you for the work you have done in creating more openness within your country and for the advances you have made in your exchange student program.

Sincerely yours,
Jolie Jones

Tritium, a component of the thermonuclear or hydrogen bomb, is a radioactive isotope of hydrogen, three times heavier than ordinary hydrogen. It is used to release nuclear energy through fusion as a bombarding particle in accelerators.

Desford
Leicestershire, England   8 December 1988

Dear Comrade Gorbachev,

The substantial unilateral cuts in conventional arms announced by you in your 'era of peace' speech yesterday are a significant contribution to world peace. The cuts represent a historic move that is worthy of a serious response from those who have hitherto regarded the Soviet Union as a threat to their security.

Significant though the cuts are, I found your speech disappointing in one very important respect. There were no proposals, in that speech, for the much-needed reform of the UN itself. Should we wait for the UN to fail, like its predecessor, before applying perestroika to it? The UN, if it is not to follow the fate of the League of Nations, is in need of urgent reforms in many areas. Let me mention two:

1. World security today perilously hangs in the hands of the permanent members of the Security Council who were chosen in 1945 as the 'big five' world powers then. Of these 'big five' with the all-important 'veto' powers, two, namely Britain and France, can hardly be called 'world powers' in 1988. Today's 'big five' will surely include India. I, as an Indian, find the exclusion of India from the Security Council's permanent membership a grave injustice to a sixth of humanity. It certainly diminishes the credibility of the UN itself. As India's friend, the Soviet Union should be the first to try to put that right. (The whole question of 'veto' needs to be looked at but, if some countries are having a 'veto', surely India is important enough to have one, too.)

2. The UN headquarters urgently needs a permanent home in a neutral country as the recent 'Yasser Arafat' controversy clearly shows.

These are not the only reforms which the UN urgently needs to grapple effectively with the daunting world problems of the 1990s and beyond. We should also consider radical ideas like 'fixed-term' for the UN constitution (say, for a fifty-year period at a time) which will take on board changes and reforms much more easily in future.

Yours sincerely,
Ram Harijan

The Security Council was established to promote international peace and security in all parts of the world. The Council investigates disputes and juridical issues, recommending ways and means for peaceful settlement of them. Its five permanent members are China, France, the Soviet Union, the United Kingdom, and the United States.

The current, non-permanent members are Algeria, Brazil, Nepal, Senegal, Yugoslavia, Canada, Columbia, Ethiopia, Finland, and Malaysia. The ten non-permanent members are elected for two-year terms by the General Assembly.

Pass Christian
Mississippi, USA   12 January 1989

Dear Premier Gorbachev,

I write to congratulate you on your recent offer to unilaterally reduce Soviet conventional arms in Europe. Hopefully, our two countries will evolve this first step into a meaningful reduction that eliminates the threat of war. I particularly hold this hope as my son is in the United States Army and though I am proud of his service for his country I dread the thought of his being committed to unnecessary combat.

As a physicist, I have spent over two decades in competition rather than cooperation with Soviet engineers and scientists. Wouldn't both countries have been better served if we had cooperated?

In contrast, my father, now seventy-six, was always fond of the Soviet Union. After graduating from Yale University in 1934, he visited your country as a student at the Anglo-American Institute in Moscow and later worked for a time as an employee of the Sovkoz at Podolsk. He remained in the Soviet Union about a year traveling to many areas including the White Sea, Kharkov and Kiev. One memorable moment was paying respect to the great Sergel Kirov at his bier in Leningrad. He attended Maxim Gorky's lecture in Moscow also. Later in 1971 Father returned as a summer student for special courses in the Russian language, initially at Soche and then at Dyuny above Leningrad. His courses were taught by teachers from Moscow and Leningrad Universities. There, with students from European countries and Japan, he won the only prize for his good work. Wouldn't our contries be better served if our peoples act as my father did, than as myself and my son?

Respectfully,
Michael Scott

WOMEN'S INTERNATIONAL LEAGUE FOR PEACE
AND FREEDOM
Fairfield County Branch
Connecticut, USA

19 January 1989

Dear General Secretary Gorbachev,

The Women's International League for Peace and Freedom, Fairfield County Branch, USA, wishes to thank you for your numerous peaceful overtures in meetings with President Reagan and in your impressive speech at the United Nations in December.

Our organization (founded in 1915), as you may know, is devoted to issues of peace and freedom, economic justice, and protection of the environment. We are concerned for the health and well-being of both our own citizens and all the people of the world.

Over the years we have become increasingly alarmed at the serious dangers posed by nuclear weapons production facilities in the United States: the contamination accidents involving workers in the nuclear plants, the widespread harm to people living nearby to these facilities, and the consequences for human health of long-term releases of radioactivity into the environment. People are suffering in many ways from the nuclear arms race; human error and malfunctioning of facilities are already taking their toll.

We are writing to you and to President-Elect Bush to ask that you confer as soon as possible about closing all nuclear weapons production facilities. On-site verification can provide the security required.

The peoples of the world would greet such a decision with profound relief, gratitude, and enthusiasm. And history would record such a decision as one of those great times when statesmen and world leaders used their power to truly serve the needs of the world's peoples and to help preserve the safety of the planet.

Sincerely yours,
Helen B. Donner

On September 9, 1988, Soviet and United States officials watched as two Pershing missiles were destroyed at an Army ammunition plant in Karmack,Texas. The INF (Intermediate-range Nuclear Forces) Treaty provides for the dismantling of all US and Soviet land-based missiles with a range of 300 to 3,400 miles. On September 15, US officials witnessed and measured an explosion of a powerful nuclear device in the Soviet Union at the Semipalatinski Test Range. These two events marked the first destruction of nuclear weapons under a treaty between the two countries.

Columbus
Ohio, USA   16 February 1989

Dear Friends,

You would earn the admiration and gratitude of all people on this planet if you could follow the suggestion of Nobel-Laureate George Wald (Letter to the Editor, the New York Times, 5 February 1989, Section E, page 24) and arrive at a mutually beneficent agreement to cease permanently the production of tritium and plutonium, as the first step toward the elimination of the production and storage of nuclear weapons. This could be the first step to a mutually verifiable agreement on the destruction of the arsenals of nuclear weapons.

Actually, even in the absence of such an agreement, the country that would take the initiative to refrain from preparations for nuclear warfare would gain financially and morally. It is quite obvious that a first strike with nuclear weapons would make no political, economic, or moral sense, and could not possibly bring any benefits to the attacking side. Therefore, why accumulate nuclear weapons, and in the process, add dangerous environmental contaminants?

Thus, the shutdown of the three nuclear reactors at Savannah River could be considered as a blessing in disguise for the US and for the entire planet. This would offer an excellent opportunity to President Bush and Secretary-General Gorbachev to come to the rescue of humanity and arrive at a mutual agreement to stop the further production of nuclear weapons and of materials required for their production and maintenance.

Sincerely,
Dr Samuel A. Corson

To the editor

An extraordinary idea that I think deserves serious consideration has come to my attention. A few months ago, the production of nuclear warheads in this country virtually ceased when safety precautions forced the shutdown of the three nuclear reactors at Savannah River, near Aiken, SC, on which our entire production of plutonium and tritium depends. We have plenty of plutonium in stock, and it is very stable (its half-life, the time for half of it to decay, is 24,000 years), but tritium is in short supply, and with a half-life of only 12.3 years, must be replenished in warheads periodically.

For those concerned with our pursuit of the arms race, to lack the means of making nuclear warheads while the Soviet Union can go on doing so might seem a formidable threat. For those who, on the contrary, look towards the early demise of the arms race, this situation might offer an opportunity. Both factions should welcome the following possibility, in which Mikhail S. Gorbachev could make a move in line with his earlier unilateral initiatives of halting Soviet nuclear explosions for 19 months (1986-1987) and his recent announcements at the United Nations of sending home some 500,000 Soviet troops and destroying 10,000 Soviet tanks:

If the Soviet leader were now to announce the complete cessation of tritium production in the Soviet Union, open to verification by the United States or neutral observers, and to continue this as long as the United States refrains from resuming tritium production, such an initiative should allay at once any American fears that the Soviet Union might forge ahead with warhead production while ours ceased.

To those who hope for an early end to the arms race and not too distant elimination of nuclear weapons, this would bring nuclear warhead production to a halt on both sides, and the hope that our government might be persuaded to continue forgoing tritium production as long as the Soviet Union refrained from it.

This should also block in this country overreaction to a situation that is not militarily threatening. It would take more than 10 years to halve the tritium in our warheads. That would not put them out of business, though decreasing their explosive yields. They would fulfil their function as deterrents as well as ever, but no longer be as effective as first-strike weapons.

To say this another way: halting tritium production, even on both sides, is not the most effective way to get rid of nuclear weapons. That can be done much more rapidly, effectively and verifiably by mutual agreement to destroy them.

New York Times
Feb. 5, 1989

George Wald, Professor of Biology Emeritus at Harvard University, won the Nobel Prize in Physiology in 1967. His research was on the chemical process that allows pigments in the retina of the eye to convert light into vision.

Genemuiden
The Netherlands   13 June 1989

Dear Mr Gorbatsjov

Although I know that you are visiting Bonn and the rest of West Germany at the moment, I write to you now anyhow, because I expect that this letter will take a lot of time before it reaches you.

The Dutch people have always been a very special kind of people. A few years ago we had very much discussion about putting forty-eight Cruise missiles into our country. I was one of the thousands and thousands who demonstrated in Amsterdam and The Hague for banning all nuclear weapons, not only out of our own country, but also out of all the countries all over the world. We wanted the world to change and wanted the politicians in America and Russia to think about their own madness to build more nuclear weapons than anybody could ever need. It was a race beyond all normal sense. I still believe that we and millions of others in Europe have succeeded in what we wanted to achieve. Although there are still far too many nuclear and other weapons in Europe and in the rest of the world, we have reached the conclusion that both political world leaders take more notice of the peace movement. We don't want Europe to become the battlefield of the future. We don't want to live in fear any more, but want to see the USSR and the USA negotiate from a positive basis and feeling.

Yours sincerely,
Tamme Bergsma

THE ENVIRONMENT
A Plea For the Future

WHEN GORBACHEV CAME TO POWER, concern about the world's environment was less widespread and intense than it has since become. Global warming, for example, was something of a fringe notion. If there was an issue, it was the testing and possible use of nuclear weapons. So in his early months in office Gorbachev was under little pressure to refer to environmental concerns.

The Soviet Union is also the largest country in the world, and in terms of natural resources the best-endowed. So it has more possibilities than most to do environmental damage without regretting the consequences. Or at least, it had. The proposition is now much less tenable. This is partly because scientists are more aware of hidden dangers, and partly because some of the adverse consequences are tragically obvious.

When Stalin industrialised the Soviet Union and collectivised agriculture in the 30s, he had little regard for people and less for material resources. The speed of change and the size of output were all that concerned him. Enormous enterprises swallowing coal and iron and spewing out smoke were characteristic of his urban complexes, thick with unwilling migrants from the countryside. His successors did little better. Khrushchev opened up the so-called virgin lands of Central Asia and turned half of them into a dust-bowl. The demands of irrigation virtually dired the Aral Sea. In his and Brezhnev's time pollution seeped into Lake Baikal, the largest fresh water reservoir in the world. Brezhnev pressed ahead with the costly Baikal-Amur railway despite the ecological threat it posed to unexplored areas of the Soviet Union and built a spiders web of leaking oil and gas pipelines. He also backed the proposal to divert the rivers of Siberia to irrigate the south, irrespective of the deprivation it would mean for the north.

No-one dared protest, at least not publicly. Senior scientists could; and they had some success, for example in reducing the damage to Lake Baikal. One environmental decision Gorbachev did make in his early days was to veto the Siberian rivers project. Significantly, however, he seems to have done so on economic grounds: the cost would have been prohibitive and the return doubtful. It was this kind of mundane consideration that gradually aroused his support for environmental protection. There are many reasons for low labour productivity in the Soviet Union; but one is respiratory illnesses resulting from air pollution - a fact which incidentally puts an additional burden on already over-expensive and inefficient health service. But the most significant diseconomy is the prodigal waste of energy. Coal, oil and gas are increasingly difficult to produce and market but are the Soviet Union's most valuable hard-currency goods. Yet Soviet industry greatly damages this export trade by using some two and a half times the energy per unit of production of most Western countries.

In theory, one of Gorbachev's earliest economic innovations ought to have had a useful environmental spin-off. Enterprise self-accounting was intended to show up waste and eliminate it. But low prices regulated by the state almost defeated this objective. In any case, reducing waste initially costs money - to introduce new practices or technology - and reducing industrial and agricultural pollution is certainly expensive. Who provides the air-filters and purifies the water? In fact, Gorbachev allowed a specialist debate to develop concerning environmental economics but, in practical terms, he found himself unable to do anything significant; he first had to develop an acceptable overall economic policy, still a distant dream.

Not altogether surprisingly, it was the nuclear issue that once more forced him into activity. There had been minor accidents to power stations in the United States and Britain that had undoubtedly caused widespread disquiet. But the Soviet Union went on building regardless; the energy was essential, and nuclear power was an excellent symbol of progressive socialism. But the Chernobyl disaster changed this. What happened to the land and the people in the immediate vicinity was bad enough. The surrounding villages and grasslands are still radio-active, and the deaths attributable to radiation will multiply. Of all places, the accident had to happen in the Ukraine. There the soil was rich but the water scarce and already polluted by industrial effluent and agricultural chemicals; and there, too, a large manufacturing concentration needs nuclear energy. Other areas were serviced by similar stations - or at least by power stations manned by equally careless crews.

More importantly, the radio-active dust spread to neighbouring Hungary and Poland, and to Northern Scandinavia and the United Kingdom. They became part of the Soviet problem, which meant that Gorbachev could no longer consider the Soviet environment in isolation. No doubt he would have been moved to take action simply on the basis of his own country's suffering. However, the international dimension seems to have been the clinching factor. He could not advocate nuclear disarmament and disregard peacetime pollution. He sought international advice and voluntarily subscribed to the accepted international rules for nuclear energy.

It was the accident and his reaction to it that won him his reputation as an environmentalist as well as a nuclear disarmer. For all that, he still put disarmament first. He saw it as the more essential and the more immediately economically rewarding. In any case, he succeeded in founding a State Committee for the Protection of Nature in January 1987.

It was a full year after the INF Treaty before Gorbachev felt able to take a strong international stand on the environment. Public pressure groups were active at home and formed links abroad. The Soviet authorities sometimes lent support to international appeals, though they also drew fire from their neighbours for continuing to build nuclear power stations near their foreign borders. At last, in his UN speech in December 1988, Gorbachev nailed his colours to the mast, publicly recording his 'awareness of the global threat to the environment' and proposing among other things an environmental aid centre and a manned space station to monitor the environment. Ironically it was while he was in New York that Armenia was hit by the devastating earthquake that sent him home with a great deal of public sympathy for his country's predicament as well as support for his new environmental approach.

Bill Wallace

Sävar
Sweden   7 April 1988

Dear Sir,

In the speech given by you in Murmansk on 1 October last
year you brought forward the proposal on the need for a closer
interrelationship between the countries situated round the Arctic
Sea. Amongst other things you suggested in the speech interaction
in the exploitation of natural resources, such as oil and natural gas.
We understood that you are proposing an increased exploitation
of the territories in the north which hitherto had been almost
untouched by man.

The surroundings in the tundra zone are more sensitive than
others located further south. The species of living organisms
which are being destroyed by man are increasing in number
and once again spreading out in the tundra very slowly, while the
rotation of ecological systems here is very long. In some cases the
wounds inflicted by man on the nature of the tundra may remain
unhealed.

Last autumn we met the Soviet writer Valentin Rasputin, who
told us about the protection of nature in the Soviet Union. We
asked him among other things which economic system – command or market – was best at looking after the environment. He
answered that in practice it did not really matter since industrial
development everywhere was identical and that only a change in
this relationship could improve the environment and help in its
preservation.

We are very glad that you should speak of the necessity of
international interaction in the preservation of the environment.
But we are convinced that your concern will have only limited
effects while industrial production takes place at the expense
of natural resources being squandered by man. If we want to
preserve life on this planet, we must change our attitude to nature.
In the first place it is necessary to develop the technology of the
application of renewable resources in our industrial enterprises
and bring into use the principle of economy in the use of energy.

We and many others in Sweden consider it our duty to preserve in
particular the natural environment of the northern territories. For that
reason we propose that there should be mutual dealings at all levels
between all the peoples situated round the Arctic Ocean to preserve
the natural resources of the Arctic and the tundra zone along with
international interaction in the exploitation of these resources.

Yours very sincerely,
Stig-Olov Holm, Biologist
Karin Holm, Physician

COOPERATION FOR PEACE
Haninge, Sweden

7 April 1988

Dear Sir,

The Soviet Union and its people has been close to my mind a large part of my lifetime. At the age of seventeen I read Leo Tolstoy's War and Peace, followed by other Russian classics. During the Second World War, I followed the hardships and victory of the Soviet forces.

When I worked in the USA during the 50s and 60s, I joined a local peace movement, working for a pull-back of US troops from Vietnam, and of the naval blockade against Cuba.

Back in Sweden I have worked with, and helped sponsor the Swedish peace movement, acting for nuclear disarmament and a nuclear-free zone in and around Scandinavia.

In 1983 I wrote an appeal and delivered it to several peace organisations in various lands. I tried to point out the importance for the world peace movement to go together in a number of syncronised efforts, urging the superpower leaders to meet, and meet again, and again until they felt confident to take real steps in the hard but necessary task of real nuclear disarmament.

I am very happy that this is going on now, 1987–88.

Before 1985 I did not have any hope of being able to do anything worth while by trying to contact the Soviet leaders of that time. By now, however, I too enjoy riding on the great wave of optimism and confidence sweeping around the world. This optimistic posture was gaining by your fine work Perestroika, and also by your cooperation with other world leaders, even if your growing domestic and East European difficulties put a damper on any high hopes.

Your excellent book Perestroika has, I believe, been of great importance to the world, and to me. Your several invitations to us readers to send you our comments have gone to my heart.

I did make extensive notes about problems, treated in your book. But I refrained from completing those as I felt sure you had already received too many hints from readers by that time.

Instead, I have gone outside Perestroika, trying to complete the picture by a few questions I believe are important to the future of the Soviet Union, and its neighbours.

I have named my contribution 'A Soviet Union Fit for Life'.

By 'fit for life' I mean healthy, safe, peaceful, a good place to live. This will take place by a long-term and profound changing of the mind, coupled with a reorganisation of your vast country, its many nationalities, many levels of government, bureaucracy, its domestic and foreign policy, its military and police force, and its economical, ecological and social life. The long-term result is to make the Soviet Union a good place to work and live for several future generations.

We Swedes as close neighbours to the large and powerful Soviet Union of course wish to live in peaceful cooperation with your people. So there is also a 'selfish' motive to my efforts: a chance for Sweden to develop better by a better trade with a richer Soviet Union, and to do more by being able to disarm sooner and move along with the rest of the world, using the gains thereof to improve the conditions for the poor and needy also in other countries, and do a lot more to save environment and resources.

Yours sincerely,
John A. Hummerhielm

A SOVIET UNION FIT FOR LIFE

A good portion of the cake

The Soviet Union (SU) has about 5.4 per cent of the world population and 15 per cent of its land mass. It is the largest of our nations, containing many riches yet to be surveyed. Still, it is in some ways an ailing country. The world itself needs extensive changes to become and remain a reasonable place to live for its present large population, and the still larger amount expected in the generations ahead.

So also does the SU which is, of course, an important participant in the making of the global future. If the Soviet peoples and their leaders find good ways to solve domestic problems together, improving their lot and realising their hopes for appeasement and disarmament, for a rational economy and production, meaningful jobs, a better life, good care of environment, nature and resources, more freedom and contentment; the sum of all this will obviously add a lot of impetus both to the SU and to the rest of the world.

The best way to reach these goals would be for leaders on various levels to be more diplomatic, to overcome scare, and dare to trust people both at home and abroad, now and in the future.

Is the human being an unsuccessful experiment?

The above was the title in a recent debate between the renowned philosopher G. H. von Wright from Finland and some Swedish counterparts. This debate was based on Wright's book Vetenskapen och förnuftet (Science and Reason, 1986). It begins with Francis Beacon's (1561–1626) observation: 'Mere power and mere knowledge exalt human nature but do not bless it.'

45

Von Wright: 'If humanity is lost due to her own lack of sense – she has thereby proved her incompetence for life. It is hard for me to see this as tragedy. It is maybe a tragedy to those who expect that she will be able to secure her life conditions for ages.'

My answer: 'The kind of collective reason you are looking for I would name long-range common sense. Unfortunately the world's totalitarian, one-party or democratic states are governed by incompetence, or by a short-term common sense, at most five years at the time. To survive as a ruler, politicians and leaders have to prove capable of speedy results, or become ousted from power.

As people, however, become more aware of what is happening to their deteriorating environment and vanishing resources, they awake to a new understanding and criticism. If that criticism is able to awaken a still stronger opinion in favour of measures according to a long-term common sense, affecting policy, science, production and economy, I believe that humanity may avoid to become an 'unsuccessful experiment': not to shorten her existence here prematurely by cutting off the limb she is sitting on.

Ecology and the point of no return

This is where we are now, near the point of no return, von Wright means, and if we don't use our common sense in a hurry, humanity is bound to liquidate herself, one way or the other. Either by an exterminating welfare or by poisoning ourselves to death while using up our vital resources, destroying the ecological systems we cannot live without.

Von Wright looked for a 'new Copernicus' who could cure our reckless antagonism, and stop our ruthless overexploitation of nature. Is it possible to obtain a Copernicus for the Soviet Union?

Ecology and opinion

Sweden has gained a fairly high status as a nation, really trying to take care of its waste problems. This awareness is pushed by a large, educated popular opinion, and by the Milieu Party. Compared with Poland and East Germany (with its brown coal), Sweden seems to be way ahead. But even Sweden has a long way to go. We don't have enough experts in our regions to check smaller industries with large waste problems. Our laws – and courts – are still too unwieldy to handle cases of environmental law breaches. Our 'green' party will work to better that.

I was greatly taken aback today when I read a statement by Jerzy Einhorn, our famous cancer professor. He said that every other child born in Sweden today, is bound to obtain a cancer during its lifetime due to exposure of industrial chemicals, regardless of smoking etc. What happens in worse areas than ours?

46

Ecology in the Soviet Union

Let us assume that socialist waste has the same ill effects on nature and humans as the capitalistic waste. Let us also assume that von Wright is right, or nearly so. The point of no return is near at hand, also in large areas of the SU. Suppose only a few leading persons there really are concerned, even if populations in the worst areas are wondering – and suffering. It is like an immense, slow Chernobyl spreading out over expanding areas. A good part of the airborne waste comes drifting in over the Ukraine, Byelorussia, Balticum and Leningrad by Westerly and Southwesterly winds from Poland, DDR and Czeckoslovakia. The waste goes down with the rain. Enormous amounts of pollution is spread by SU activities each year.

When I check the rain water or snow over here after a South-easterly wind there is a lot of soot and chemicals – from the Soviet Union.

In search for your environment planning

What would you do, Mr Gorbachev, and other responsible Soviet persons, to tackle this deteriorating situation in the SU?

Looking for a grand scheme, a five year plan, some practical measures or, at least, a clue, I have just checked through Perestroika again.

There is really no chapter at all, or even a sentence dealing with the largest potential threat to the SU next to an all-out war, namely its self-destruction by neglectant care of environment and premature spoiling of irreplaceable resources by wasteful technology.

Pollution control is long overdue

Pollution control has had a low priority around the world. In the industrial areas dirty, poisonous, sickening production went on for a 100 years before the new awareness emerged as a fast growing popular force in the 1960s. On the one side is the people, politically active in 'green' parties as in West Germany and Sweden, and international groups like 'Greenpeace'. On the other side are the finance people, industry and governments.

So far, popular pressure in the West has gained a fast growing opinion, awareness and knowledge, and also many practical steps and schemes of environment care have been carried out.

In Eastern Europe and the SU where popular initiatives like 'Solidarity' have been banned and prosecuted, the democratic chances to do anything for environment protection have been nil, I believe. As your trade unions have been subordinated to the industry in a corporative fashion and not independent, and when the common target has been a maximum production, the trade unions have not had any power, will or knowledge to do anything for pollution control etc.

What to do in the Soviet Union about environment protection

If you agree, Mr Gorbachev and your associates, on the whole to the description above, what would you do now and in the next few years to stave off this tremendous, large, looming threat to your people?

Would you work to wake up a common awareness, work up a popular opinion to back you up when you have to cut down on other projects in favour of large efforts in order to diminish the industrial waste – and traffic waste – in order to secure a sufficient environment? Would you favour a re-tooling of your technology in order to recycle and save scarce raw material and fuel for future generations?

I am sure this has been an irksome and growing problem to the Soviet rulers long before you came into power. Like a number of other trying problems it has been swept under the carpet.

Can Greenpeace Become a Success in the Soviet Union?

I consider you, Mr Gorbachev, as one of the bravest men in our time. If not, I would not care to put this suggestion to your attention. Would you not like to become the first powerful statesman in the world to invite Greenpeace in person to come to your country. If you agree on the details, I am sure Greenpeace could carry through an extensive survey in cooperation with your local counterparts, and together size up some of your environmental problems.

GREENPEACE, UK, *issued the album 'Rainbow Warrior' in the Soviet Union in February 1989 to great acclaim.* GREENPEACE, *Soviet Union, was established in Moscow towards the end of the same year.*

Svanvik
Norway   8 July 1988

Dear Mr Gorbachev,

The Paatsjoki river valley and the whole of the Finnmark area is naturally abundant and is at the same time a wild and beautiful land. The scenery of this region which we love is so unique that it must be preserved for future generations also.

We have followed and appreciate the negotiations between our countries to reduce environmental damage and especially industrial discharges. We hope very much that pollution of the Kola and Petsamo region can be reduced rapidly. We respectfully ask you to help advance this matter and to take the necessary measures as soon as possible.

We are pleased about the good neighbourly relations between our countries and about the development of cooperation for the protection and care of the environment. We would like to take this opportunity to wish you success in all your efforts to promote this matter.

Maisa Siirala, Architect
National Water and Environment Board
Helsinki, Finland

Tuulikki Soini, Writer
Native Region Petsamo
Naantali, Finland

Olav Beddari
Course Director
Svanvik, Norway

Moscow
Idaho, USA   2 August 1988

Dear Mr Chairman,

I am contacting you regarding a matter of grave importance; one which I have tried to contact my own President about, but to no avail.

I am sure that you are aware of the problem of global warming which is the result of unregulated burning of fossil fuels, but I am unaware as to the stand of the Soviet Union regarding this problem.

Here in the United States, society has installed the belief that each and every person must possess an automobile and that driving automobiles is a means by which an individual can express himself. I am sure that you have seen some of the advertising which romanticizes ownership of an automobile. Unfortunately the romanticized ideal of motor vehicle ownership does not bring to light the environmental disaster impending from their operation.

Apparently the position of the United States government is that unregulated operation of motor vehicles is an inalienable right of every citizen, no matter what the consequences may be. I feel that this view is both short-sighted and unrealistic.

According to a report which was aired by Radio Moscow, critical mass for CO_2 absorption in the earth's atmosphere will occur in less than twenty-five years. As you appear to be a man who is genuinely concerned about the fate of the world, I appeal to your good sense and ask that you initiate some sort of international policy which would help to curb some of the reckless disregard for the environment which has become so prevalent in Western society.

I realize that what I am suggesting is a formidable task, but I feel that procrastination in the area of environmental integrity would be

49

a globally fatal mistake, one that you, probably the greatest world leader of this century, can not afford to make.

Respectfully yours,
Lance Deverich

Benfleet
Essex, England   3 August 1988

Dear Mr Gorbachev,

We in Britain, and in parts of Europe have, since the Second World War, seen a worsening of our weather patterns, we now get far too much rain, while in India the monsoons seem to be failing, as is the rainfall in parts of America, changing wind patterns it would appear.

If all this is true then should not something be done about it now? Should we, perhaps, turn more and more to nuclear power? Surely this would be the worst of all choices? A poisoning of the whole earth, dangerous and dirty, in its effect, surely we all should have taken a lesson from Chernobyl? Nuclear power will be a constant danger to every living thing, a stockpile of wastes we cannot neutralise, etc.

So what can and should be done? So far I have mentioned cause and effect, so can we now take a look at the real, underlying cause of all causes mentioned? Will you look that cause in the face Mr Gorbachev?

Firstly, could we ask the question: could this planet, our only home, absorb harmlessly the residue of a smaller, cleaner worldwide industry, should we clean it up somewhat? Should we make the effort to clean it up and, while doing so, look to ways and means of using cleaner sources of power, the oceans, rivers, solar power etc? I believe it could if there were greater forestlands extant, which brings us to that great underlying cause of most of the world's problems, namely that there are far, far too many people in the world, overpopulation.

Mr Gorbachev, I am afraid that I view the human race, by and large, as a great swarm of locusts, all-consuming, devouring all in its path, then dying itself when it has consumed all. We are draining this planet of all its natural resources, destroying them and, should we carry on as we are, we will destroy nature, and should we do that we will destroy ourselves, it's that simple.

I write to you and ask could you not say a little regarding this most urgent of matters, a few words even from you might go a long way? May be you and Mr Reagan, and his successor, if he proves wise, could lead the world in wisdom, point out to the human race just what a mindless monster it is.

Could not political and religious ideologies of all nations be set aside, where they affect, adversely, this problem? For if you world leaders do not meet this challenge we will all reap the bitter harvest of our great racial stupidity, namely extinction.

Yours very sincerely,
R. Hubbard (Mr)

Friends of the Earth
Rome, Italy   23 August 1988

Dear General Secretary,

A common feeling is growing all over Europe, from West to East: concern about the destruction of the natural balances and the cultural heritage which up to now have permitted man to live and flourish.

The threat does not come from the military arsenals alone. If the means of production of goods and the distribution of profits have set classes and states in opposition to one another, contributing to the establishment to differing conceptions of justice and liberty, today it is the effect of production itself, the quantity and quality of the products, which create crises and conflicts, whatever the standard of living of the population or the political regime they have chosen or have to bear.

Pollution knows no national boundaries. It is the sum of human activities which is creating the greenhouse effect around the planet; there is only one ozone layer and it is under threat. The fumes from power stations kill woods thousands of kilometres away. Radioactive clouds can range for weeks over a whole continent. The wretchedness of the peoples of the Third World, international trade in tropical hardwoods, slash and burn farming are destroying the great rainforests. The environment is damaged and histories, cultures, peoples are endangered.

Public opinion is aware of all this and is beginning to seek remedies. In every country, aware citizens are organising spontaneously to defend their environment and their culture. And this is not all: they know that they must meet outside national boundaries, because only international collaboration can slow down the process of decline. This is a great movement dedicated to democratic progress and peace.

Mr General Secretary, this people's movement is an essential element in the success of a policy to defend the environment, life, civilisation. Without it the commitments of states, while necessary, will not have lasting effects, not even in the search for peace.

51

May we put forward a hypothesis? If such a movement had been able to make itself heard, perhaps Chernobyl would not have happened.

But you know all this: in your speech to the Communist Party of the Soviet Union Congress on 28 June 1988 you stated that: 'an important feature of perestroika is the rapid growth of mass associations which reflect the whole range of social interests ... Among these the various associations engaged in protecting the environment ... This is an excellent example of autonomous popular initiative which deserves the greatest support.'

We ask you to put this support into practical effect. We ask you to facilitate the spontaneous initiative and organisation of Soviet citizens in defence of the environment, encouraging and guaranteeing their complete freedom of movement, dialogue and organised cooperation with environmentalists from Europe and from all over the world.

What we would like to ask you for is prompt, active commitment. Freedom and rights do not live on abstract encouragement but need concrete support, including support on matters of detail. Our fear is that your declared desire for change will peter out in the myriad bureaucratic snares, delays and energy-sapping procedures which gravely obstruct all attempts at cooperation between Soviet and European environmentalists. Without these hidden obstacles we would probably already have built a great bridge of environmental cooperation between East and West.

Mr General Secretary, our experience has confirmed these fears. The Friends of the Earth is a great network of environmental associations which is recognised by the UN and the EEC. We are present in thirty-two countries in Europe, America, Asia, Africa and Oceania. This year has seen the establishment of the Polish Association, independent like all the other national associations, and our World Congress will be held in Poland next October.

Mario Signorini
President of Italian Friends of the Earth

Raymond Van Ermen
Director of the European
Environment Bureau

Marie Dominique Bonmariage
European Coordinator, Friends of the Earth

John Hontelez
President of the Executive
Committee of the International Federation of
Friends of the Earth

Bromma
Sweden   September 1988

Dear Mr Gorbatjov,

I have today read that your country is going to build a nuclear power plant in Llepaja only 170 kilometres from Gutland, Sweden! As I am sure you must be aware, the people of Sweden long before the Chernobyl 'accident', the 'accidents' at the nuclear plants in Sellafield and in the USA etc, decided we do not want nuclear power plants and we are closing them.

Gavle was the place that was hit the most (in our country) by the invisible poison. The poison that is so horrible just because you cannot see it and therefore not avoid it. Mutations have been found in the genes of flies in the affected areas. There are lakes not only in Gavle but in areas we love bcause of the beauty of the nature and the clean air like the mountain areas, where you should avoid the fish, mushrooms and berries. And who wants to eat the fish anyway when there is 12,000 bequerel in the fish? Just the thought of it puts you off!

If your people want nuclear power plants despite the risks, (there are always risks because humans will always make mistakes and lose their judgments), why not put the plants in for instance the area between Dikson and Tiksi where they are far away from other countries? No matter how important one job is, the longer you continue to do it the easier it is to relax and make terrible mistakes. Otherwise we would not have car accidents etc. No person can be alert at all times.

I can well understand the high suicide rate in this country. Technology is going out of control, things are going too fast, we don't know enough before we act. We are going against nature. My heart and soul cries when I think about the poisons being let out into our seas, lakes, into the air and over the land. It is a horrible thought but the right thing to do would be for us all to commit a clean joint suicide except for groups like the Indians of the Amazon jungles who live with nature.

I hope you have not found me rude, that was never my intention.

Goodbye,
Helen Angleby

TREES FOR LIFE
Wichita, Kansas, USA

19 October 1988

Dear Secretary Gorbachev,

Trees for Life would like to suggest a project befitting the greatness of our two nations: the joint planting of 100 million fruit trees in Third World countries.

These trees would be a living symbol of our commitment to stop the destruction of the environment . . . to help the world's poor . . . and to plant growing seeds of peace. This would be an action worthy of your grand vision for international cooperation.

Mr Secretary, you and President Reagan have paved the way for the US-Soviet peace initiatives. The citizens of both our nations would also like to join in your quest for peace.

The support of citizens is vital to the success of this project. Therefore, it would be advantageous if the impetus for this effort came from the people.

We propose that the people in the Soviet Union and in the United States sign a petition requesting a joint tree planting project. Then this will be a project of people all over the world joining together to promote global peace.

Sincerely,
Balbir Mathur
Executive Director

Trees for Life, Inc. has planted over 8 million fruit trees in seven countries since its inception in 1983. On April 22, 1990 the firm made a public commitment to plant 100 million trees around the world during this decade. The trees are provided to poor people in developing countries and include lemon, banana, papaya, and guava. The organizations which aid Trees for Life also educate and instruct the recipients in the care for the trees they receive. The firm claims to have undertaken an educational program concerning tree planting, and in the United States it is reported more than 826,000 students have participated.

R & D ENGINEERING
Kelso
Washington, USA

20 October 1988

Dear Mr Gorbachev,

I am an engineer in the US commercial nuclear industry, and also a recognized author of technical articles and books on issues crucial to the nuclear field.

I am writing to you because I feel it only appropriate that you are apprised of the fact that I have quoted you in my new book, 100 Grams of Uranium Equal 290 Tons of Coal (see enclosure; page 40). I feel confident, however, that you will be pleased with the context of this quotation, and in fact, the subject matter of the book as a whole.

I would also like to propose that you consider joint US-USSR research into the development of a safe and standardized nuclear power plant design. I see no reason why our two countries should have to 'reinvent the wheel' independently. Nor do I see why we should continue to independently suffer the continuing recriminations of various misguided and ignorant anti-nuclear factions. Every day that we are delayed in our pursuit of clean and safe electricity production brings us a day closer to global ecological disasters precipitated by the use of fossil fuels in electric power production. Working together, we could not only improve the global climate, we could further reduce the social climates of fear of all things nuclear and distrust of each other.

Please understand that I make this proposal not as anyone of influence in such matters, but as a mere citizen of the earth. If you, however, were to make this proposal, the persons in positions to effect such a project would listen. Perhaps both the US and the USSR should look at France and her success in the development and operation of standardized power plant designs. Couldn't our two nations do as well or better if we committed our joint resources to this end?

Sincerely,
Mark Aaron Robinson
Author & President

Cleveland
Ohio, USA   8 December 1988

Dear General Secretary Gorbachev,

In your speech to the United Nations yesterday, you proposed a halt to all underground nuclear testing. I understand that the recent detonation of a large Soviet nuclear devise was followed shortly by the earthquake in Armenia. Was there a causal connection, as well as a closeness in time?

I have attempted to generate some interest in the United States, for investigating whether underground nuclear explosions trigger seismic activity, but with little success. The subject deserves investigation, though, given the loss of life, property damage and general human misery that these earthquakes produce.

Earthquakes, however, may not be the only danger from continued nuclear testing. How can we explode nuclear devices underground without their toxins entering both the atmosphere and the aquifers? The fallacy, I think, is regarding the earth as an inert mass, when it is really quite dynamic, almost 'alive'. As a result, air and water must ultimately feel the impact of whatever poisons are being released. And, as mentioned, the force of a blast alone must be doing violence to the earth's crust – causing, intensifying or hurrying the upheavals we call earthquakes.

Evidence of the harmful effects on the environment of continued testing should certainly be gathered in support of arguments to stop such testing. If I recall correctly, environmental arguments were critical in securing the 1963 partial Test Ban Treaty.

From all I have heard and read, you appear to want the truth and do not fear it. Adequate geological investigation may well reveal the truth to be this: that underground nuclear tests cause earthquakes and poison air and water. Those, surely, are sufficient reasons for stopping the tests.

But whether testing contributed to the recent earthquake or not, my deepest sympathy goes to all of its victims. To a greater or lesser extent, these are your whole people. Every country has sufficient man-made, historical problems, without adding natural disasters to them.

Respectfully
Bruce Tyler Wick

CETACEAN SOCIETY INTERNATIONAL
Connecticut, USA

26 December 1988

Dear President Gorbachev,

The Cetacean Society International, headquartered in Wethersfield, Connecticut, USA, wishes to thank and commend you for the role which the Soviet icebreakers played in the dramatic rescue of the gray whales frozen in the ice at Point Barrow, Alaska, last October. We hope you will accept the enclosed 'CETACEAN CITATION' as a tribute to this cooperative endeavor.

We also wish to commend you for your outstanding address to the United Nations on 7 December 1988. We believe this speech represents an historic milestone in at last turning the world from war to peace. We agree with you that now 'we must put an end to an era of wars,' and that 'today, further world progress is only possible through a search for universal human consensus as we move forward to a new world order' based on international law.

We also applaud your proper reference to 'the political' legal and moral significance of the Roman maxim 'pacta sunt servanda' – treaties must be observed'.

In this connection, our whale conservation society wishes to renew our direct request to you to enhance the observance of the International Convention for the Regulation of Whaling, by officially withdrawing the USSR's objection to the current moratorium on commercial whaling.

Your country has ceased whaling. But the USSR still has not formally notified the International Whaling Commission, in Cambridge, United Kingdom, that its objection to paragraph 10(e) of the IWC Schedule has been withdrawn. Under the treaty, this means that the provision establishing zero catch limits for all whale stocks pending review by the IWC following a comprehensive assessment, is not binding upon your government. All other member nations have accepted this provision, except Norway. Only Norway and the USSR still have objections on file with the IWC.

We believe it would be beneficial for the USSR's international image, and in keeping with your UN speech, to confirm your standing with other nations by agreeing now to support this IWC treaty provision.

Best wishes for 1989!
Very sincerely,
Dr Robbins Barstow
Volunteer Executive Director

THE COUSTEAU SOCIETY
Norfolk, Virginia, USA

2 February 1989

Dear Mr General Secretary,

We believe that as the leader of your nation, you share the Cousteau Society's concerns for protecting and improving the quality of life of the people of your country.

During our many filming expeditions throughout the world, we have found people everywhere struggling with the same problems: overpopulation, waste disposal, water and air pollution, deforestation, erosion, and scarcity of food, fuel and water. Regardless of our differences in language and belief, we are connected – all members of the human family, all dependent on the earth and on each other. The world's oceans and atmosphere recognize no national boundaries or political parties. Depletion of natural resources in our part of the world affects not only a local economy but also the world's economy. The connections are often painfully clear. It is equally clear to us that all people – all nations – must act together if we hope to solve the problems that threaten the lives of all. As a leader, you know better than anyone else how severely these problems affect the life of your citizens and your prospects for development. We extend membership to you because you are in a privileged position to find solutions to such problems.

We ask you to participate in our global effort to educate people to protect and improve the quality of life for present and future generations. We ask that you set, as an example for the world, that protecting our environment goes beyond politics and national boundaries. We ask that you take steps to introduce in your country's constitution a provision for ensuring the rights of future generations to a better, healthier world. Do we not have this responsibility to our children and grand-children?

Throughout this year, as we extend our efforts to raise global consciousness, we hope you will share with us the commitment to help improve life on earth.

Sincerely,
Jacques-Yves Cousteau
Jean-Michel Cousteau

Manly
New South Wales, Australia   12 February 1989

Dear Sir,

It is my opinion that you are the greatest politician alive and the greatest humanitarian, with the exception of Mother Theresa of Calcutta.

Your contribution to 'peace in our time' gives us hope that the earth as we know it – will survive. You have made sense out of nonsense and offers you made to other world leaders could not be credibly refused, causing Reagan and Maggie to make changes too. They couldn't resist by telling you to 'get your own house in order before we concede'. Such excellent results and so quickly.

Maybe because of the state of the earth's atmosphere caused by pollution, we have had very unusual weather. A warm, wet summer instead of hot and dry. I live in Sydney (via London of Irish parents) with its once clean wonderful beaches. For the first time ever many beaches have been closed this summer due to the seas being polluted with raw sewage. It is extremely disgusting and inexcusable. We do not have proper sewage plants. The raw sewage gets dumped four kilometres out at sea via a pipe. Useless, stupid politicians.

Wishing you more success and a safe passage through life.

A grateful admirer,
Christina Scanlon

Seg Harbor
New York, USA   13 February 1989

Dear Mr Gorbachev,

I am writing you this letter because I recognize you as a man of peace. As an American Jew, I must say, it is getting harder and harder to recognize men of peace, but I do believe you to be one.

You have made partly real a lifelong dream of mine that man would grow up and finally go through what I call global puberty. This may have been thrust upon you by internal problems but you realized that your defense (offense) budget was strangling your country; just as it does to all countries with military. I can only pray that all countries make the same realization that you did. I believe they will but I also believe that it will be too late.

The ozone layer is breaking down, the oceans are dying, the rainforests are disappearing, radioactive waste is accumulating, the world is overpopulated. If we are to survive these major problems we must 1) convince the world that these problems are real and 2) come up with the trillions of dollars necessary to save us. We can no longer usurp the money from taxpayers as they are already strained beyond belief. There is only one source of money that we can tap into – that being the world's offense budgets. The money we are spending to destroy each other must be rechanneled into saving ourselves.

How?

It is time for regular global meetings – not just NATO or Warsaw but all of us. I call on you, as a man of peace, to initiate a worldwide meeting of leaders and leading scientists to discuss and prove to the world just how threatening these problems are.

It is necessary for the world to finally accept each other's differences. Nothing divides people more than our definitions of the supreme being and government. Our problems are too urgent to waste time over petty differences. We must all make the realization that we are on a sinking ship. Does it really matter who put the hole in the boat? Shall we argue about it as the boat sinks?

Sincerely,
Geoffrey L. Diner

Bologna
Italy   22 February 1989

Dear Mr Gorbaciov,
I am forty-two years old and I have been a communist all my life. I'm writing to you because I admire you for your efforts to improve the way of life of your people. I'm writing to you because I feel you are the only one who can set your people, and the world (which has such need of it) on the right path.
You are that man.
You know that humanity is at a crossroads and that it must either take that leap forward or decline.
The human race, almost without exception, wants to live in peace for those few years which Mother Nature or God has granted us, people want to live peacefully and fully so that when death comes they can say I HAVE LIVED because I have tried to improve and live fully the days that I have lived.
I see that you want to bring thousands of cars into your country; this is very good but if I may say so, cars are not as great as they seem, they bring pollution, chaos. All that glitters is not gold.
I hope I have made myself clear, and I would like to take the opportunity to invite you, if your commitments allow when you come to Italy in November, to come to my house with your wife and an interpreter, so that you can try some Bolognese specialities, and if you can't come because of lack of time, thank you anyway for what you have done and will do.

Ermanno Mengoli

Germantoron
Maryland, USA   March 1989

Dear Excellency Mikhail Gorbachev,
The problems of toxic waste disposal, deforestation, damage to the ozone layer, the greenhouse effect, ocean pollution, air pollution and overpopulation are not isolated concerns of any one nation. We must act as a global community if we hope to solve any of these problems. We must rise above the narrow political boundaries that separate us. We must forge bonds of cooperation rather than barriers of confrontation. We must encourage an ethic of sustained prosperity for all rather than immediate profit for a few.
I ask you to dedicate yourself and your nation to protecting and improving the quality of life for present and future generations. Please do this by supporting and incorporating the Bill of Rights

for Future Generations in the UN Charter and in the constitutions of all the nations. Enclosed is a copy of the Bill of Rights.

Sincerely,
Mr and Mrs Robert Colacurcio

Formal adoption of the Bill of Rights for Future Generations, which was drafted by the Society's Council of Advisors 1977.

A BILL OF RIGHTS FOR FUTURE GENERATIONS

MINDFUL of the determination proclaimed by the peoples of the world in the Charter of the United Nations to reaffirm faith in the dignity and worth of the human person and to promote social progress and better standards of life in larger freedom,

ACKNOWLEDGING that it is among the purposes of the United Nations to achieve international cooperation in solving international problems and to be a center for harmonizing the actions of nations in the attainment of these common ends,

RECOGNIZING that for the first time in history the rights of future generations to exercise options with respect to the nurture and continuity of life and the enrichment and diversity of their mental and physical environment are seriously threatened,

BELIEVING that the preservation and promotion of these rights has a claim on the conscience of all peoples and all nations,

CONVINCED that each generation has the inherent right to determine its own destiny and the corresponding responsibility to accord a similar right to future generations as an extension of the right of the living,

SOLEMNLY PROCLAIMS the necessity of securing the universal recognition of this right and this responsibility, and to this end, declares that:

Article 1
Future generations have a right to an uncontaminated and undamaged Earth and to its enjoyment as the ground of human history, of culture, and of the social bonds that make each generation and individual a member of one human family.

Article 2
Each generation, sharing in the estate and heritage of the Earth, has a duty as trustee for future generations to prevent irreversible and irreparable harm to life on Earth and to human freedom and dignity.

Article 3

It is, therefore, the paramount responsibility of each generation to maintain a constantly vigilant and prudential assessment of technological disturbances and modifications adversely affecting life on Earth, the balance of nature, and the evolution of mankind in order to protect the rights of future generations.

Article 4

All appropriate measures, including education, research, and legislation, shall be taken to guarantee these rights and to ensure that they not be sacrificed for present expediencies and conveniences.

Article 5

Governments, non-governmental organizations, and individuals are urged, therefore, imaginatively to implement these principles, as if in the very presence of those future generations whose rights we seek to establish and perpetuate.

PEACE INITIATIVES
Citizens and Soldiers

ONE OF THE TRAGEDIES of the Cold War was that it took up so much Soviet and American energy and drew almost every other conflict into it, no matter how distant. Internationally, the two superpowers and the Warsaw and North Atlantic Treaty Organisations which they had summoned to their support could think of little other than their mutual antagonism, and from Stalin and Truman through to Brezhnev and Reagan they eagerly adopted unconnected disputes arising in the Far and Middle East, in Latin America and Africa. But as they began to draw back from their Cold War positions, many leaders became increasingly aware of the folly and injustice of fuelling other people's confrontations. Perhaps because he had further to travel, Gorbachev was the first to start down the road of disengagement.

Initially it was an awareness of costs that drove him. If an East-West arms race, old or new, was too much for his ailing economy, subsidising regional conflicts around Ethiopia and Angola, or Cambodia or Nicaragua was hardly beneficial, while actually maintaining a Soviet inovation force in Afghanistan was nigh on suicidal. So from fairly early on, Gorbachev set himself the task, as he saw it, of completely reshaping Soviet foreign policy. Strong proof that he was serious came with the withdrawal from Afghanistan between April 1988 and February 1989. Following that, direct and indirect Soviet military involvement in South America and Africa was dramatically reduced.

A second factor motivating Gorbachev was his realisation that, whatever might have been the situation in the previous twenty or thirty years, not even the two superpowers acting together could any longer dominate world politics. With or without the backing of NATO, the European Community was rapidly becoming a major international actor; and almost solely on its economic strength, Japan was virtually a superpower already. Person for person, China might appear to be poor; but well started on its economic reform programme, it was obviously on course to be a superpower of the future. International relations were becoming multi-polar.

So Gorbachev took the Soviet Union's head out of the sand. He recognised the existence of the European Community, which Brezhnev had refused to do, and in 1988 he authorised direct negotiations that led to a series of Soviet and East European trade agreements with it. Beginning with his speech at Vladivostok in 1986, he started mapping out a peaceful new future for Soviet relations with the Pacific powers. In May 1989 he travelled to Beijing to bury the quarrel that had divided the two great communist countries for almost thirty years; and a year later April 1990 he received the Chinese Prime Minister in return. A visit to Japan was firmly agreed to in the Summer of 1990. One way and another, he accepted that peace depended on a community of states and not simply on two that were particularly heavily armed.

The settlement with China represented a further milestone in Gorbachev's new thinking on foreign policy. Differences might remain, but the Soviet Union finally recognised that it could not, and should not try to determine the internal politics of another country, even when avowedly communist. Gorbachev abandoned his predecessors' policy both of exporting socialism and of subsequently trying to control socialist regimes.

Gorbachev's travels took him not only directly west and east, but twice down to India which had been a friendly member of the non-aligned group of states ever since its own acquisition of independence in 1947. It was on his first visit there in November 1986 that he gave shape to his concept of a world operating on the principle of peaceful co-existence under which no state would interfere in the affairs of another and all states would work together to resolve international disputes. How genuine or practical this vision might be, it was certainly a far cry from previous Soviet doctrine and evoked a warm response from people in India and the Third World anxious for an end to what they saw as superpower domination.

Individuals in the West also responded, though their governments remained somewhat sceptical pending further progress in the arms talks. But, out of Gorbachev's reassessment of the international situation came a genuine search for new peace-keeping machinery in addition to superpower summitry. Sometimes the conferences and meetings he organised in Moscow were intended to secure propaganda advantages, while his dealing with west European leaders occasionally had a divide-and-win touch to them. But from 1986 onwards he began to regard the Conference on Security and Co-operation in Europe (CSCE), arising out of the Helsinki process that had originally been unwelcome to the Soviet Union, as an increasingly important means of promoting understanding within Europe and among its allies. Following his decision in 1990 to accept the unification of Germany and its membership of NATO, this is likely to be the main vehicle for maintaining European harmony. This particular outcome was closely associated with the completely altered position of Eastern Europe, a position that Gorbachev had not discouraged.

From the outbreak of the Korean War in 1950 the Soviet Union had mostly eyed the United Nations with grave suspicion as essentially a Western-orientated body. However, from the moment in 1987, during the Iran-Iraq war, when Gorbachev authorised payment of the Soviet Union's overdue contributions and suggested a joint naval peace-keeping force in the Gulf, he showed himself to be an increasingly active advocate of routing peace initiatives to and through the UN. As he put it in his speech to the General Assembly in New York in December 1988, the United Nations 'embodies the interests of different states' and 'is the only organization which can channel their efforts - bilateral, regional and comprehensive - in one and the same direction'.

Initially his conversion to totally international peace-keeping did not evoke a warm response in the West. Action in the Gulf remained unilaterally Western and Eastern. But the different Gulf crisis in 1990, coming soon after the removal of tension in Europe, was further proof that his policies had a permanent basis in reality. In September, Gorbachev and Bush could appear shoulder-to-shoulder in Helsinki, together upholding the right of the UN to force Iraq out of Kuwait. Their motives might be mixed, and a wholly new order might not have arrived. But Gorbachev had contributed much to achieving the unthinkable.

Bill Wallace

Warsaw
Indiana, USA   February 1987

Dear Sir,

My home town from which I am writing this letter is called
Warsaw Indiana. Although our community is named after the Polish
capital we are not Polish Americans. We are Americans and have
the same hopes, dreams, and desires as the people who populate the
small towns and villages of your country. We work hard, are resolute
in our belief of a better future and are concerned over world affairs
that touch us all.

I wanted to tell you a story taken from our history that is symbolic
of the changing nature of our two countries. The story is true and
happened at the dawning of our country. It is the story of two of
America's founding fathers, John Adams our second President and
Thomas Jefferson our third President.

Both men had a tremendous love for their country and both had
devoted their lives to serve our people. However, they had very
different visions of how this new nation should develop. Because
of this difference of philosophy they hated each other. The hatred
the two men shared for each other was so intense they that they
refused to speak to one another for years.

Long after Jefferson and Adams retired from public life this
relationship of hatred changed. Mutual friends the two former
presidents shared thought that it was a tragedy that men who
had given so much for their country would harbor such hatred
for so long. Because of the intervention of friends the two men who
were now extremely old began to write letters to each other. The
correspondence started slowly, no more than one or two letters a
year. Before long both men were writing letters to each other almost
every day. The hatred that consumed their hearts for so long was
replaced with love and respect.

In the year 1826, the fiftieth anniversary of the founding of the
United States, Thomas Jefferson, the third President of the United
States, died in his home in the state of Virginia. Jefferson's last words
were, 'My country is safe. Adams lives.' A messenger was sent to
John Adams who lived in the state of Massachusetts to inform him
that Jefferson had died. The messenger was stunned to learn that
John Adams, second President of the United States had died on the
same day. Adams last words were, 'My country is safe for Jefferson
lives.' This true story happened on the fiftieth anniversary of the
United States.

I am telling you this story with the hope that history will repeat
itself. I believe that our two nations can follow the example of
John Adams and Thomas Jefferson and change the nature of our

past relationship. Fear, hatred and mistrust must be replaced in this thermonuclear world if we are to survive. I pray that it will be achieved.

Sincerely,
Chad Curtis

THE BERTRAND RUSSELL PEACE FOUNDATION LTD
Derbyshire, England

21 May 1987

Dear Mr Gorbachev,

Since I last wrote to you, I was delighted to receive an invitation from the Soviet Peace Committee, which enabled me to participate in the International Consultation (the Fourth Information Meeting/Dialogue) last week. I found this to be a most useful event, and at the same time, I am bound to say, a profoundly moving experience. No doubt the peace movements will soon assimilate the lessons of this meeting, so that we may look forward to a great improvement in joining cooperation on questions of peace and disarmament, at any rate between activists in our societies.

Had it been possible, however, I should still have liked to have consulted with someone from your staff on a different related matter, as I began to suggest in my last letter.

During the last months, and particularly in your own speech to the International Forum on 16 February, you have taken the high ground in the world discussion on disarmament and peace. Without for one second suggesting anything that could diminish the powerful impact of your initiative on these matters, I wish to raise an associated question.

Our problem is that, to build peace, we need more than peace. As you already said, more than once, the tensions which give rise to war are reinforced by inequality, hunger, debt, and economic crisis. You have developed a splendid agenda to prevent us from blowing each other up. The next agenda appears to me to be, how, then, can we create a world that is fit to live in?

As you will know, Willy Brandt and Michael Manley have been preoccupied with the discussion of a new international economic order. They gave their support to a programme of the Socialist International entitled GLOBAL CHALLENGE. Two of the main authors of this programme are the Dutchman, Jan Pronk, and the Englishman, Stuart Holland. Holland's ideas seem to me to be particularly interesting, once one has accepted both the necessity of the difficulty of fundamental economic change within the present rickety world balance.

I was instrumental in persuading Neil Kinnock to send Stuart Holland to represent him in China last year, and I accompanied him in a series of meetings which considered this theme. As a result, the Chinese communists sent an observer to the Socialist International conference in Lima last summer. I believe they have since published the programme in question. It has also been published in Yugoslavia, where it has already aroused rather widespread discussion.

Of course, Soviet experts may well have fundamental criticisms of this document, and may well be able to develop more far-sighted and more realistic alternatives. What I believe to be necessary is that this discussion should begin, both at the political and technical levels. It is about the mechanics of such a process that I would now like to discuss with some appropriate member of your team.

The very important changes you have initiated open a perspective of still further developments. In the middle term, we could make giant strides towards overcoming the seven-decade split between socialists and communists, and create harmonious working relationships. At the same time, we could begin to address the North-South divide in a way which was far more creative than has been possible hitherto. Both these prospects would serve to improve the prospect of peace.

At the moment, those political parties which favour disarmament are doing very badly in Western elections. I am deeply convinced that we cannot explain this phenomenon by assuming that West Europeans are warlike. No – they are caught in a deep economic slump, and they are experiencing again the rule of fear. Practical proposals to remove that economic fear would change the political balance of Western Europe. They would also improve the stability of the whole continent, in which economic crisis threatens us with serious political problems. I think particularly of the case of Yugoslavia, currently undergoing traumatic problems as a result of the debt crisis.

Up to now, the efforts of Stuart Holland and his friends have only begun to open a door on alternative possibilities. But with your criticism and help, I think it may be possible to make a new start on tackling the problems of recovery and development.

With great respect and good wishes.
Ken Coates

Annandale
Virginia, USA   November, 1987

Mr & Mrs Gorbachev,
   You have won your way into the American heart. You must not
let us down. For once on the world scene there is a personality who
could easily become the Hinge of History. Dare to become what
destiny has in store for you. Move out with courage and shake the
foundations of present world systems (including your own). Shatter
the false illusions. Break through the deceptions of mere politics
and rise to the fate that is in store for you. Too many of us now
have placed our hopes in you and we wait with great expectations
to see rhetoric become deed. Again, don't let us down. You have
the unique characteristics to lead our whole world into the new
age. Don't let nationalism, yours or ours, prevent you from rising
to this manifest destiny. In you there is UNIVERSAL appeal. Don't
be confined to mediocrity by the forces around you. At last there is
hope for all of mankind and you, Michael, have been chosen to lead.
Do not be afraid. You have good news of great consequences which
shall be for all people.

   Reach out, grab hold, hang on,
   You are held by steady hands.

                                                    Dr Ted Sperduto

Westlake
Queensland, Australia   13 November 1987

Excellency,
   There is need for some statesperson to take up the challenge
put by Bertrand Russell in the New Statesman to Khrushchev
and Kennedy, replied to in that journal by Mr Khrushchev and
John Foster Dulles, Russell, Mahatma Gandhi, Einstein and others
whose political status extended beyond sovereign nationalities who
have all stressed the need for global representation of citizens – the
sovereign people from whom governments draw legitimacy – in a
world authority with global arbitration of international differences
and global policing powers to enforce its arbitral decisions: a world
federal police force able to arrest you or me without asking permission of our governments if we threaten to breach international law.
   The UN concept of law – enforceable only by sanctions
or war on whole nations through the veto-muzzled Security
Council – is limited to relations between parochial (nationally
divided) sovereignties; in a world united, as you say, in trade,
communications and other communal interdependence, and

perhaps more grimly united in its capacity to die as one if the ultimate UN enforcement of its 'law' is applied. Article 2 of the UN Charter (drafted before the Hiroshima holocaust) preserves exactly as the League of Nations did, and the prefederated US confederation did, the sovereign right of member states to be prosecutor, judge and executioner in what each sees as its own overriding, vital national interest. Exactly such law led to each world war, despite assurances our leaders gave us that war 'has become so terrible that only a madman would start it'. Kennedy assured us that such madness or miscalculation was always possible. With ever shorter warning times an error in a computer chip will suffice. Einstein said when commenting on this assurance of deterrence, 'Since Adam and Eve ate the apple, man has never refrained from any folly of which he was capable.' You yourself note that atomic weapons have been twice used and a dozen times proposed.

When Hiroshima was bombed I was elated that so many 'sub-humans' (as they had been described in our news and cartoons) had perished. There are great numbers of citizens in this country and the USA who would rejoice similarly if Moscow was so treated in some flimsy excuse today. Fortunately those trusted with bomb buttons so far seem not to be among them, but mental abnormality is no respecter of security clearances and afflicts people in charge of nuclear weapons.

It would be a major step forward if your administration could encourage, as only low-level provincial/municipal governments so far have encouraged in the West, the 'mundialization' movement. Dozens of localities and work places in Japan, Europe and I think Canada, and one over thirty years ago in Australia, have held opinion polls on a world peace authority after discussion in local publicity media. Usually three out of four people support the notion of an international authority to take over from the superpowers some of their functions of global surveillance, arbitration and enforcement of international law. How much more sane the US 'police' action in the Persian Gulf would be if a UN peacekeeping corps had authority to arrest military leaders in the Arab nations concerned instead of the US blasting sailors, perhaps all terminal workers and others who are only remotely responsible for the breaches of international law. How needless the deaths of Soviet citizens in Afghanistan if the warring parties had access to such a world community authority!

The UN Charter starts: 'We, the peoples of the United Nations, determined to save succeeding generations from the scourge of war ... ' but Article 2 and the rest ignore the peoples and speak only of member states – those structures which Khrushchev assured us were about to wither away and let the peoples have their sovereign rights.

I and millions may die happy if you decide to join the Einsteins, Russells, Gandhis and other internationalists in leading your peoples to give a lead to the world in gently insisting on their right to a sovereign voice, arbitration and enforcement of arbitral decisions – genuine law, genuine order, genuine peacekeeping by means proven by history – at the most lawless level of globicidal power.

You could make a huge impact tomorrow by reversing the resistance of your country to the General Assembly call for implementation of the 'French initiative'. Only the US, USSR and a few close supporters of each opposed the motion for an international satellite monitoring agency. Strong supporters are Austria, Sweden and Switzerland. Its costs, according to the 1982 report of the ad hoc committee to the UN, would be about one hundredth that of the arms race.

Yours for survival,
(Dr Hon) D. N. Everingham

Belefiertown
Minnesota, USA   14 November 1987

Dear Honorable Secretary Gorbachev,

I am writing to you with regard to your Afghan War, which seems to have reached a point of no return.

Why are you allowing this war to continue? Are you trying to kill all of the people there? Thousands of families have been destroyed by your hand.

Don't you have any sense of decency and compassion? Can you even imagine the tragic loss of just one family? It is a real man who admits his mistake and leaves a country unconditionally and unilaterally, without insisting on a Soviet-influenced puppet government. You will never convince the world of your credibility and good intentions as long as you perpetuate your evil in Afghanistan.

Sincerely,
C. E. Clark

Queens Village
New York, USA   4 December 1987

Dear Mr Gorbachev,

I would like to know your opinion on the Communist influence throughout the world. I was born in Angola, Africa. In 1974 my family and I were forced to leave Angola, where I was born, because of riots.

I don't approve of you supporting the MPLA with armaments. From what I know, the MPLA wanted Angola to be liberated from Portugal, and that blacks in Angola wanted independence. Well, I'm for the independence of black people, but I'm against the fact that my family and I were forced to leave Angola, because my parents were Portuguese citizens.

Since you are supporting the MPLA with armaments and making promises that would change Angola, you were spreading communist influence.

In 1974, the Portuguese Republican government was changed to a communist government.

I feel that you should remove all communist supports out of Angola. There is still some tensions in Angola. If the Soviet Union didn't get involved in the first place, maybe a compromise could have been drawn up.

Respectfully yours,
Sandra Coelho

The MPLA (Popular Movement for the Liberation of Angola) is the Marxist government of Angola. It is engaged in a long term struggle to gain territory held by pro-Western rebels of Jonas Savimbi's Union for the Total Independance of Angola. UNITA controls much of the sparsley populated southeastern part of Angola. The two organizations have been enemies since Portuguese colonial rule ended in 1975. The two parties met in mid-June 1990 to work out a cease-fire agreement.

Grantham
New Hampshire, USA   8 December 1987

Dear Mr Gorbachev,

I have absolutely no wish to adopt your socialist system. Nor do I care one bit whether or not you adopt our capitalist system. I am not afraid of losing the contest – and, if you believe in the Soviet system, you should not be afraid either.

But let's compete to see who can win at playing basketball, at raising the most wheat per acre, at writing the best symphonies, at providing the best living standards for the most people, at inventing better ways of disposing of waste, at finding cures for disease, at exploiting communications and computer technology, at educating our children, at generating power more efficiently and securely and at making peace, freedom and justice universal. Let's hear our leaders boast about these things.

Please tell Mrs Gorbachev that she is well-liked in America. She seems to be a victim of the same kind of jealousy in the Soviet Union as have our First Ladies always been in the United States. Keep smiling! As we American businessmen say, 'It comes with the territory'.

Sincerely yours,
Robert R. Weiss

GENERALS FOR PEACE AND DISARMAMENT
Ittervoort, Netherlands

9 December 1987

Your Excellencies,

A group of retired NATO generals and admirals avails itself of this opportunity to welcome the fresh meeting of the leaders of the United States and the Soviet Union which holds out the prospect of the conclusion of a very promising agreement.

A successful outcome of your meeting confirms the group in its self-imposed responsibility. We believe that this concern of ours is a continuation of the mission we were assigned during the times of our active duty, i.e. help preserve universal peace. Therefore, we chose a challenging name for our group: 'Generals for Peace and Disarmament'.

Our previous activities and responsibilities in the interest of our nations and the Atlantic Alliance have taught us to be cognizant of the threats to peace and the difficulties to reach agreements.

We realize what a courageous step it was when you, the representatives of the presently most powerful nations in the world, directed your diplomats and military leaders to seek meaningful solutions within the prescribed timeframes. Therefore, please accept our deep respect and our utmost appreciation. We believe that your meeting in Reykjavik played a key role in making the two sides recognize the principle of equal security and respect the other side's legitimate interests and leading them to initiate policies towards practical steps.

Your Excellencies, it might be of interest to you to know that our group, the 'Generals for Peace and Disarmament', has entered a dialogue on military doctrines with similar groups in the United

States, Latin America, the Pacific region, the Soviet Union as well as Eastern Europe in order to make a specific contribution to the process marked by your initiatives.

It is our profession and our experience gathered in recent years as well as our knowledge of strategic concepts that prevent us from becoming daydreamers, even in this great moment in the history of mankind. And yet we think it is possible that, in spite of all the threats still existing, the great dream of lasting peace may come true. For such are the realities in the world and the increasing readiness to keep peace.

For the group 'Generals for Peace and Disarmament',
M. H. von Meyenfeldt
Generaal-majoor b.d.
Chairman

Pontiac
Michigan, USA   15 December 1987

Dear Chairman Gorbachev,

When Ronald Reagan was elected to the office of President his election seemed to encourage the anti-Soviet rhetoric of the same old gang that has suffocated American thinking about the Soviet Union for the past forty years. For those of us willing to shed the ancient orthodoxies and see the cold war as being exhausted, an inherited ideology that has persisted long after its historical moment has passed and no longer conforms to people's daily experience and has no meaning for the young, peace is at hand. With the signing of the agreement to remove intermediate-range missiles from Europe and perestroika and glasnost taking hold within your country old attitudes are crumbling. My heart was overjoyed at the way in which Raisa and you were received by the American people and hope the Reagans will receive the same from the Soviet people when they are in Moscow come next spring.

Sincerely,
Thomas Bafile

Bindaring Parade
Claremont, Western Australia   25 December 1987

Most Honourable Sir,

I have read that you graciously listened to the plea of a little child for peace. This letter is written by one at the other end of the span of human existence – I am in my eightieth year. I beg you to show the same gracious tolerance.

An irresistible urge to play a part, although a very small part, in the quest for truth and peace impels me to write to you. Through the hazy image projected by the Western news media, there has come to me a clear picture of one of the great men of this century who could become an immortal in his dedicated quest for truth and peace.

At the outset I say: Thank our good fortune for Mikhail Gorbachev. Bless him for glasnost. Bless him for his efforts to control and abolish nuclear weapons. Bless him for his dedication to truth and peace.

Your first Herculean task, dear Mr Gorbachev, is to cleanse men's minds of the accumulated poisons of hatred and fear and mistrust. It has been told that the stables of Augeas, containing three thousand oxen, had not been cleaned for thirty years, and that Hercules performed the task of cleaning them of accumulated filth in one day by turning the waters of two rivers to pour through the stalls. You, honoured sir, must perform the modern equivalent by cleansing men's minds of hatred, fear and mistrust by a deluge of glasnost – blessed truth. Be assured, glasnost is needed as much in the United States and Western democracies as it is needed in the Soviet Union. For forty years, we in Western democracies have been drenched with hatred, half-truths and outright lies. The accumulated poisons will be hard to wash away.

For you to succeed in your quest for peace there is the Herculean task of flushing away the accumulated filth of forty years of hatred started by the Truman administration in respect of an invented danger 'to scare the hell out of the country'. Why? – in order to induce Congress to allocate preliminary funds necessary for US advisory warfare in Greece and for the taking over from Britain its role in the oil-rich Middle East. I will relate a few details.

George Kennan, the US Ambassador at Moscow in 1952, in his memoirs has credited Joseph M. Jones with describing 'in great and faithful detail the various discussions, consultations, clearances and literary struggles' that took place among the US decision-makers leading to the United States succeeding to the role of Britain in the Middle East. Both Jones and Kennan participated in those discussions, consultations and clearances. At the time Kennan was in charge of the Policy Planning Staff whilst Jones was the draftsman of the Truman Doctrine speech. It is Jones's account that is relied on for much of the following information.

In the afternoon of Friday 21 February 1947, the First Secretary of the British Embassy at Washington, a Mr Sichel, left copies of British notes at the office of the Department of State, advising that Britain could not provide the military-ecomonic aid needed for Greece and Turkey; and conveying a desire that the United States should take over the responsibility. On the following Monday morning, the British Ambassador Lord Inverchapel called and imparted the same message orally to the US Secretary of State George Marshall. A few hours later, Marshall told the Secretary of Defense James Forrestal that this 'was tantamount to British abdication from the Middle East with obvious implications as to their successor'. (The quotation is taken from Forrestal's diaries for this date.)

Since the nineteenth century Britain had considered Greece to be its sentry box to the entrance to the Middle East and to India. As late as 1946, Ernest Bevin had sent a memorandum to the British cabinet: 'The fundamental assumption of our policy has always been that . . . Greece must be retained within the British sphere.' (From Foreign Office records, cited by Lawrence S. Wittner.) And now the United States was being offered the key to the sentry box. Jones recorded that 'all [of the decision-makers] were to some degree filled with awe at the turning point that the United States had reached in its history.' Jones related the immediate reaction of all in the cabinet from the President down 'was that a historical turning point had been reached, and that the United States must stand forth as leader of the free world in place of the flagging British . . . ' The opportunity for the United States to take over from the British in the oil-rich Middle East was the sort of opportunity that comes only once in a lifetime, if at all. It was the sort of opportunity that had to be snatched whatever the cost.

This turning point occurred at an unpropitious time in history. It was at a time when Congress and the American public demanded reduced taxation and expenditure. The joint Congressional Committee had gone so far as to recommend the President's budget should be reduced by $6 billion. Although the initial money required by the Truman Administration for the take-over arrangements was euphemistically referred to as relief aid in the Truman Doctrine speech, it was in fact money required for the initial stage of what, in the Pentagon Papers, was realistically referred to as United States first post-war venture into 'advisory warfare'. And advisory warfare is costly.

Senator Vandenberg advised President Truman that it would be necessary 'to scare hell out of the country' in order to induce Congress to allocate the funds asked for. There had to be a

Greek crisis. This was accomplished by expressing feigned fear and shammed alarm that the Soviet Union was ready and able to overrun Western Europe in a matter of weeks with a blitzkrieg attack. The feigned fear generated real fear not only in the United States but in other Western democracies and in the Soviet Union.

According to Jones's account, Congressional leaders were summoned to the White House and were told that there had never been such a serious situation since Carthage and Rome. 'If Greece and the Mediterranean should fall to Soviet control', Jones paraphrased, the effects 'would be devastating and probably conclusive'. It was suggested that Western Europe was in danger of falling to Soviet aggression. If the Soviet Union succeeded in extending its control over two-thirds of the world's surface and three-fourths of its population 'there would be no security for the United States, and freedom everywhere in the world would have a poor chance of survival.' In his memoirs, Under-Secretary of State Acheson, who led the way in propagating this fear and generating the consequent hatred, proudly boasted:

> In the past eighteen months, I said, Soviet pressure on the straits, on Iran, and on northern Greece had brought the Balkans to the point where a highly possible Soviet break-through might open three continents to Soviet penetration. Like apples in a barrel infected by one rotten one, the corruption of Greece would infect Iran and all to the east. It would also carry infection to Africa through Asia Minor and Egypt, and to Europe through Italy and France, already threatened by the strongest domestic Communist parties in Western Europe.

In the meantime, evidence has been released to scholars under the Freedom of Information Act that establishes an enormous fraud was perpetrated on the public, in that the Soviet Union had neither the ability nor the intention of undertaking a war as depicted by the Truman administration to the Congressional leaders. In the words of the British Field Marshal Montgomery, in a report after a mission to the Soviet Union and dated two weeks before the fateful briefing to the Congressional leaders:

> The Soviet Union is very, very tired. Devastation in Russia is appalling and the country is in no fit state to go to war ... It will be 15 to 20 years before Russia will be able to remedy her various defects and be in a position to fight a major world war with a good chance of success.

In 1958, George Keenan, the former head of Policy Planning Staff, whose responsibilities would have included analyzing incoming intelligence reports and presumably condensing them for digestion by the Department of State. In 1958, this knowledgeable and acknowledged Soviet expert wrote:

> I have never thought that the Soviet government wanted a general world war at any time since 1945, or that it would have been inclined for any rational political reasons, to inaugurate such a war, even had the atomic weapon never been invented. I do not believe, in other words, that it was our possession of the atomic bomb which prevented the Russians from overwhelming Europe in 1948 or at any other time.

In 1965, the same George Kennan lamented that the great objectives of reunifying Germany and reintegrating Eastern Europe into a European community 'were sacrificed at a stroke to the creation of a military defence (NATO) against an attack no one was planning'.

In 1957, General Douglas MacArthur, in a shareholders' meeting said:

> Our government has kept us in a perpetual state of fear — kept us in a continuous stampede of patriotic fervour — with a cry of grave national emergency. Always there has been some terrible evil at home or some monstrous foreign power that was going to gobble us up if we did not blindly rally behind it by furnishing the exorbitant funds demanded. Yet, in retrospect, these disasters seem never to have happened, seem never to have been quite real.

The forty years of concentrated hatred have left their mark. In Australia, the general public consider the Soviet Union to be the enemy, and I am under the impression it is the same with the public of other Western democracies. It will be a Herculean task to wash away the accumulated poison.

I have decided to take the liberty of suggesting one item of truth you could well concentrate on making known to the public of Western democracies. In late 1946 and early 1947, the nations of Western Europe were on the point of collapse, and would have collapsed, were it not for the billions of American dollars that were transferred to them as gifts by the United States. It is dealt with by Jones. He referred to 'the catastrophic economic conditions of Europe'; to 'the growing feeling of hopelessness and frustration' and to 'the underfed, freezing people' who 'would accept any system that fed them and kept them warm'. (Note the implication that the Soviet system could do this.) The devastation of the Soviet Union had been even worse than that of Western Europe. The

Truman administration denied the people of its former ally, the Soviet Union, not only gifts but even loans – worse, it punished the people of its former ally for not adopting the free market system, by imposing embargoes designed to cause hunger and economic distress. Just as the Soviet Union had arisen in the 1920s from the ashes of destruction of civil war, of joint invasion (by the United Kingdom, the United States, France and other allies), and of the worst famine suffered by the human race in recorded history (according to the eyewitness historian, H. G. Wells), so also after World War II did the same miracle happen again, without assistance from the United States and despite its malignant attempts to cripple the Soviet Union.

In December 1950, but five years and a few months after World War II ended, Ambassador (Admiral) Alan Kirk reported verbally to President Truman on the general condition of the Soviet Union. The following is an extract from the minutes made by the Ambassador of his report:

> I said it was my belief that conditions for the masses of the people in the Soviet Union had been constantly improved in matters such as food, some consumer goods, electrification etc. Further, that although the use of the word 'free' in our sense of the word would not be understood in the Soviet Union, nevertheless, the Soviet people did feel that they had gained a great deal of freedom under the Soviet regime and that in general terms there was, if not contentment, at least a feeling that things were better.

For the Soviet Union to succeed, not only in feeding its people, but to become a superpower within two or three decades after such catastrophic devastation, without any help and despite the US efforts to 'rollback' and destroy the Soviet government is an astonishing achievement, bordering on the Christian miracle of feeding 5,000 people with five loaves and two fishes. This miraculous, phoenix-like power to rejuvenate so quickly from the ashes of destruction could not fail to impress the starving millions of Third World countries. I shall simply mention that it is not the arms of the Soviet Union that the United States fears – it is the example of being able to feed and care for its citizens in circumstances where capitalism would fail. The United States does not like to be reminded that on a global basis, its system had always been a failure in that two-thirds of the peoples of the world under its system have always lived in abject poverty with millions on the threshold of death. (In the attached study, I quoted from the reports of the Chairman of the World Bank on the subject.)

It is a US doctrinal tenet of top importance that for the US-dominated multilateral trading system to function properly, the system must be world-wide and must be adopted by all nations. There is no room for state-controlled economies. Truman made this clear in his Baylor University speech. According to Jones, the belief surfaced in one of the cabinet discussions thus: 'the disappearance of free enterprise in other nations would threaten our economy and our democracy.' In Latin America, the greatest threat to this system is Cuba because it is the only Latin American nation that has succeeded in eradicating malnutrition on a national basis and has installed a first-class education and health system. This is why there have been eight admitted attempts to assassinate Castro and why there have been so many sabotage attempts to destroy the Cuban economy thereby proving the Cuban experiment has failed.

In the attached study, this subject has been developed in more depth. Indeed, this letter is in the nature of an introduction to the enclosed study. I hope you have the time and inclination to read it. I have devoted many, many hours to the drafting, typing, retyping and photostatting at a public library. I do not have the assistance of a secretary or a typist, and I am in my eightieth year.

Sincerely,
N. deB. Cullen

Riihimki
Finland   December 1987

Dear Mr General Secretary,
Having just witnessed your signing of the disarmament agreement on the Finnish TV and having lit two candles at each window of our small home to celebrate the event, I feel I have to include both you and Mr Reagan in the circle of our family friends. That is why I am sending you this thank you note on our family's Christmas stationery.

I thank both of you for bringing back to life the flower of goodwill and peace, and for planting it in a soil of hope. As mother of two small children and as teacher of young people I feel proud to be part of the human race again. I can now look into the eyes of my children and my pupils and assure them – you can live in peace, there will be sincere friendship and cooperation between people and peoples of the globe.

The whole family joins me in wishing you sincerely a Christmas of Peace 1987 and a Year of Peace 1988!

Yours sincerely,
Irma Sallanniemi

МЕЖДУНАРОДНАЯ

МИНИСТЕРСТВО СВЯЗИ СССР ТЕЛЕГРАММА

ПРИЕМ: час.   мин.   ПЕРЕДАЧА:

Адрес:

Вход № V631   № связи _____

Передал: _____

TMB735 VIA ITT QIA061 4-0085195144
SUMS CO UIAX 161
FRB TDBN UG DETROIT MI 161/154 23 1013A EST

SECRETARY GENERAL MIKHAIL GORBACHEV.
KREMLIN
MOSCOW

IT HAS BEEN A PLEASURE FOR ME AND FOR ALL FELLOW CITIZENS IN THE
MIDDLE EAST THAT EVENTUALLY THE PROBLEMS OF PEACE AND SECURITY IN OUR
STRATEGIC AND COMPLEX REGION HAD BEEN ON THE SCHEDULE OF THE MOSCOW
SUMMIT DUE ON MAY 29 1988. IN THIS RESPECT AND IN MY CAPACITY AS A
CANDIDATE FOR THE PRESIDENCY IN LEBANON I SINCERELY SUPPORT YOUR
EFFORTS AND PLEDGE MY WILLINGNESS TO JOIN YOUR CONSTRUCTIVE COMMON
DECISIONS AIMING AT PROMOTING NATIONAL REGIONAL AND INTERNATIONAL
PEACE BASED ON JUSTICE FREEDOM AND HUMAN RIGHTS FOR ALL PEOPLES OF
THE REGIONS CONCERNED. NO DOUBT LEBANON DESERVES A SPECIAL ATTENTION
AFTER 14 YEARS OF BLOODSHED AND DESTRUCTION CAUSED MAINLY BY THE
ABSENCE OF CENTRAL POWER AND FOREIGN INTERFERENCES. BEST WISHES FOR
YOUR SUCCESS LEADING TO THE BENEFIT OF MANKIND.

RESPECTFULLY YOURS,
DR SALIM WAKIM CANDIDATE FOR THE PRESIDENCY OF LEBANON PO BOX
122-1226 PHONEX SWITZERLAND

London
England
                2 March 1988

To Mr Mikhail Gorbachev,

On the occasion of your 57th birthday may we work, hope and pray that by the time we will happily celebrate your 60th birthday some beginning will have been made to offset fear and suspicion through worldwide co-operation and trust. For otherwise the catastrophe threatening humanity and all life on earth, of which mankind is the most irreverent and compulsively destructive party, will overtake us and all our aims, our ambitions for power, our greed for territories and even our legitimate self-defence.

With respect and warmest greetings to you and your dear wife,

Yehudi and Diana Menuhin

Madrid
Spain   28 April 1988

Sr D Mijail Gorbachov,

I am a humble Spaniard, perhaps the most lowly of them all, but since my childhood I have been an admirer of your beloved country and people, for their good nature and gentleness, for their artistic, cultural, hardworking and humanitarian qualities.

As a citizen of this world, I wish, with all my heart, to show my gratitude and admiration for the plans and methods that you, in the name of the government and the Soviet people, are offering to all the nations who want to live in peace and harmony. When I see you on television, your face shining with justice, good nature, firmness and good intentions, I see you as a true champion of the peace that you are giving the whole world, a masterly lesson on how to eliminate the horrors of war.

All human beings love peace, although I do perhaps more strongly, because at the end of the Spanish Civil War, my father, mother and brother were sentenced to death by Military Court for having socialist ideals. My mother and brother's sentences were commuted, but my father's was not and he was shot. The passing of time has made me more conformist, but the one thing which will always remain hateful to me is war and because of this, I am asking you, with all respect and feeling, to continue along that path and struggle for peace and justice for the whole world.

With respect and kind regards,
(name withheld)

Lincoln's Inn
London, England   22 June 1988

Dear Mr General Secretary,

I take the time to write to you in order to express my appreciation for the remarkable patience and restraint you demonstrated during the course of President Reagan's visit. The manner in which you tolerated the range of insults that were visited upon your country by a guest on its soil has to be one of the finest demonstrations of public graciousness I have ever experienced.

I suggest that even the President is unlikely to be aware of the organised efforts in a small, but highly placed and effective group of seconded professional intelligence operatives to sabotage your meetings. These types have no interest in enhancing human rights. Their career work has been dedicated to violating such principles.

No, it was hoped that the programmed provocations would have the same effect upon you that their colleagues' earlier scheduling of the Powers U-2 flight (over the President's explicit prohibition) had on Mr Khrushchev's summit with President Eisenhower, who could not appear to the world that he had no control over such operations and therefore had to assume responsibility.

Only your forbearance foiled these efforts. Please believe me that the origins of the provocations are the same. Neither Mr Eisenhower not Mr Reagan, even if aware, are in a position to effectively control the group. Neither, I fear, will any other President. George Bush will not be interested and Mike Dukakis will be unaware.

I was a long-time activist in the US, ranging from successful political reform, to managing Robert Kennedy's 1964 Senatorial campaign in Westchester County, New York, and heavy involvement in both the civil rights and the anti-war movements; the former as an intimate of Dr Martin King in his last year and the latter as a published journalist in Vietnam.

I still carry considerable baggage from those years and though two members of my family have been in the Congress I abandoned that life and brought my young family to Cambridge some six years ago.

As one who has loved the United States and its Bill of Rights and early revolutionary promise I confess a certain ambivalent sadness in that it appears that the torch of individual freedom gradually being extinguished in my homeland has been ignited by you and your colleagues in the Soviet Union. How difficult it is and how strange for a child of the cold war to come to grips with the fact that your country, long considered to be an enemy of revolutionary change and all manner of freedom of expression and individual liberty has moved and is moving to gain the recognition and respect of the world, epitomising in our time a national assertion of the basic freedoms of belief, speech, association, privacy, protection from official abuse and the institution of due process of law.

Mr General Secretary, the Soviet Union has indeed become the world's largest debating society. One can only hope that you will be able to withstand those reactionary forces and pressures of vested interests in your country who have long come to identify their status and well-being with an oppressive and closed, elitist order of things.

Yours sincerely,
(Dr) W. F. Pepper

Cushing
Maine, USA   30 June 1988

Dear Mikhail Gorbachev,

On 2 June seven American walrus hunters from St Lawrence Island in the Bering Sea were lost in fog and ice floes. My son, Andrew Haviland, was one of the seven men. The other six were Yupik Eskimos; all relatives of my son's wife, Holly Slwooko.

Ships and planes from Siberia reached your waters, while the US Coast Guard and Alaska National Guard searched on our side of the International Date Line. The search continued for three very long weeks, ending with your government's unprecedented action in allowing US planes with Eskimo spotters to search Siberian shores on 23 June. That same evening the hunters miraculously reached safety on the south shore of St Lawrence Island and were picked up.

My family and the Slwooko family thank God and all our friends who prayed with us, as well as those who searched for the missing men, on both sides of the Bering Sea. We all bear witness to the hopes of Soviet and US people for peace and understanding between our nations, working together as friends and neighbors.

It is also significant that on 14 June, while the seven hunters were in their boats without food or water, people from Providenya and Nome, Chaplino and Gambell, and from other villages on Soviet and American shores were sharing together food, gifts, and photographs in a Friendship Flight that renewed bonds between Yupik families and friends who had not seen each other in thirty years. That visit and my family's near tragedy symbolizes for me, even more than your meetings with President Reagan, the new spirit in US-Soviet relations because it unites our people in friendship.

In peace,
Peter R. Haviland

San Bernardino
California, USA   3 July 1988

Dear Mr Gorbachev,

My name is Terry Jagerson. I'm an American citizen and a conservative Republican. I am forty-nine years of age and a career police officer for a local law enforcement agency in the southern part of the State of California.

I'm a patriotic citizen, one who has been consistently anti-Soviet all my adult life. I have supported any and all of my country's efforts to impede your country's government from increasing domestic and international power or influence. I have also been a strong advocate of increasing my country's military budget because of your government's behavior over the past several decades. I believe in my country, the principles upon which it is founded, our freedom and our Constitution.

I find the prospect of perestroika being successful both encouraging and frightening. Encouraging because your citizens will become recipients of freedoms I enjoy as a citizen of my country. Frightening because your country will become much more formidable in all aspects of international competition.

I hope you don't perceive this American as naive or lacking a real grasp of the geopolitical realities your and my country face. It will take much more progress towards your stated objectives before my fear of your country is reduced. Even then, unless your country gives up the belief in and commitment to world domination (by force if necessary), we can never really trust your actions.

I sincerely hope you understand how deep our feelings on this matter are. I'm sure that if the United States Constitution committed its people to world domination and/or to take over your country (by force if necessary) you would find it equally difficult to trust us, our actions or our motivations. Please, for both our countries, use your influence to resolve this issue. Until you do, how can we do anything but assure our protection against:

1. Your country's ongoing commitment to achieve world domination.

2. Your country's continual military build-up beyond an adequate level to meet your country's defensive needs.

Mr Gorbachev, I have never written a letter to any public figure, including those in my own country. I realize writing this letter to one of your stature is presumptuous, but I was moved to write and communicate with you as one honorable American to one honorable Russian. For what it's worth I've expressed what one American believes and thinks about your heroic efforts and our country's tenuous relationship.

Respectfully,
Terry D. Jagerson

Palma de Mallorca
Spain   26 July 1988

Dear Mijail Gorvachov,

My congratulations for your great work in the world. I am writing to you from Palma de Mallorca where a group of friends hold meetings in each other's homes, especially in that of our great friend Cayetano Marti. This is the Iglesai Pobre (Church of the Poor), we have no places of worship, no intermediaries and we work so as to live, as did Jesus of Nazareth, the worker carpenter, and the apostles. We try to live the true Christian life, that of the early Christians. We seek justice and equality for everyone in the world; by increasing the awareness of each person, by which I mean, that as each person changes, so will the world.

Never has a spirit such as yours emerged from the Soviet Union. All this means that the time of change has arrived, the new Age in which mankind is awakening and evolving towards Christ or the Great Universal Force that we all have within us. Because of this I say to you Mijail: continue with your example to all humanity. When you come to Spain, we invite you to come to Mallorca; you will be well received at the homes of a few poor people, a few workers.

While it is very good that you tolerate the spiritual side of every Soviet citizen, do not allow any Pope, pastor, priest, rabbi or ayatollah to live without working.

> Sincerely from a worker of the Igelsia Pobre of Mallorca,
> Maria Gilda Munoz Zuniga

Cinisello
Italy   27 July 1988

To the distinguished Soviet leader, Michail Gorbaciov.

I am an Italian woman of sixty-one, a card-carrying member of the Italian Socialist Party, and for the whole of my existence having also seen and suffered a war, I have prayed and hoped that I would see with my own eyes Total Peace in the world.

I have longed ardently for the day when I would read in the papers that at the head of nations there are men of great intellect, men of peace, disposed with all their being to make great efforts for peace, and for peace in this suffering world which has lost its way I long, at the sunset of my life, to see no more terrible pictures of unburied bodies, of children dying of hunger and thirst, inhuman slaughter, but to see some change in the world, something good, something beautiful before I close my eyes for ever. I would like Eden for all peoples.

I long one day to read in the papers that all the workers in the armaments factories from that day will be set to cleaning up the seas, the rivers, the lakes that are dying, to remove the poisons from the earth and to cultivate it with intelligence, no more arsenals full of death but silos full of grain; these are the words of our beloved ex-President Sandro Pertini, and I repeat them here so that you, the distinguished Soviet leader, may use them in your speeches to the whole world, I have such faith in you, it is the first time that this has happened to me. I feel that you are a person of good principles, a loyal, just person, you are perhaps the bud of truth and peace in the world? I believe that you are.

I would like to say so many things to you but I am not sufficiently well-educated and my eyes are no longer good, I have strained them to write to you, I hope that you will understand my thoughts and will spread them throughout the world.

Greetings to your people, greetings especially to your faithfully colleagues.

Greetings to your great country.

Signora Nunzia Martemucci Giove

USA   8 August 1988

Dear Mr General Secretary,

I wish to extend our sympathy to those Russian families whose soldier-members are missing in Afghanistan and to applaud President Reagan's statement at Moscow University that he will use his good offices to do what he can to obtain an accounting of them. I hope that many will be found and returned to their families.

As you are probably aware, we Americans have many missing in South-east Asia. Among them is my brother, Col Patrick M. Fallon, United States Air Force, missing in Laos. It is said that a number of our missing recently have been seen alive and are still held prisoner. We even have unconfirmed reports that Col Fallon was seen talking with a group of Russian officers.

This letter, then, is a plea that you and your government use your sources and your influence to help obtain an accounting of our missing and the return to us of those still alive. Believe me, we will be forever grateful for any help that you can give us. Nothing would bring greater gratitude from millions of Americans to you personally and to the Soviet people than the return of our loved ones as a result of your intercession and that of the Soviet government. It would confirm in an exceptionally vivid and dramatic way the image that has begun to form in the American mind as a result of your decision to withdraw from Afghanistan – the image of the Soviet government as a force for peace and reconciliation among peoples. It would cost your government little, but would yield extraordinary returns in goodwill and favorable publicity, all the more so for being unexpected.

Sincerely,
Eileen Fallon Coulter

Col. Patrick Fallon was commandering a fighter plane for the United States Air Force in 1968, when the plane he was flying was shot down over Laos. He has not been seen or heard from since.

Watford
Herts, England   11 November 1988

Dear Sir,

The only conflict in the future will be fought in the market place and that's what must be proposed now. Africa and South America will provide two of the largest future markets, and these areas must be helped in that direction. I'll take Africa first, with Ethiopia, the Sudan and Mozambique, the countries most in need, where, at the invitation of the leaders of each country, and only on that basis, troops that face each other now, from both sides in Europe, would be sent to the country to secure peace, maintain it and supervise the infrastructure. The troops with no nation predominant would operate under a UN flag. In the past, no major power, however strong, has been able to help another nation while acting alone. When the world's two major powers unite, military action will never be needed, just using the threat of it will suffice. The formula for South America would be the same as that of Africa. Of course, there will be obstacles, but no goal is worth winning if it's not worth fighting for, and the goal here is the very survival of mankind. I believe, Mr Gorbachev, that you're the one man who can do it and I thank God you've arrived at just the right time.

If Russia hadn't become militarily strong, and remained so, there would have been a war in Europe years ago. That has cost your country an enormous amount of money and resources in the process and you're entitled to a return on your outlay. Russia and her allies must become part of the EEC, share the benefits of its technology and surpluses – they owe you that – work together as we already play sport together, besides many other joint ventures, and show the world you mean business. I have only seen you, with your lovely wife, Raisa, on TV, but if I'm any judge of character, this is a challenge you'll make your own. Five years ago I was injured in an accident, which has affected my sight – hence the writing – and I can't afford to have this letter typed. My apologies for that.

There is one request I make of you, Mr Gorbachev, and it's a big one, one coming from a fifty-seven-year-old half blind Irish carpenter, and it's this. Go out TODAY and take down the Berlin wall, that one visible sign of a division between East and West, and then I'll know tomorrow WILL be better. I've mentioned nothing of this request in the other two letters, neither to anybody else. Thank you, Mr Gorbachev, for reading this letter, and I wish you, your family and your country all you wish for yourself.

Yours sincerely,
Jonjo Robinson

Reykjavik
Iceland   8 December 1988

Dear Mr Gorbachev,
    This is the first time I have taken the trouble of writing to a politician, let alone to a head of state. But I am so impressed by your courage and independence that I felt I had to write to you and express my admiration.
    You have made a decision that I think is quite unique in scope and proportion. This is probably the first time that any head of state makes a decision to reduce army or arsenal.
    I think you will be known in the future as the man who had the guts to opt for peace. I sincerely hope that you will keep up the good work since the Americans seem unwilling to do so.
    Your decision means that for the first time in many years the inhabitants of the globe can really hope to see their children make it to adulthood. Provided of course that other nations have the courage to follow in your footsteps.
    So let me say to you. Congratulations Mr Gorbachev. May you and your family have a happy and prosperous new year and thank you again for your magnificent gesture and contribution to world peace.

Respectfully yours,
Thorsteinn Ulfar Bjornsson

Honesdale
Pennsylvania, USA   8 December 1988

Dear Mr General Secretary,
    I am a homemaker and mother of three in a small town in northeastern Pennsylvania. I've been following your visit to New York City on the news, and was deeply saddened to hear of the terrible earthquake that devastated your country. Watching the pictures of the damage on television, I was moved to tears at the thought of what those people must be going through.

For the past couple of months, I've been setting aside a little money, trying to save up for something special. I didn't know what I wanted to use it for – "maybe Christmas", I thought – but I knew I wasn't going to spend any of it until a very special reason came along. This morning, watching the news, I know what I wanted to do with some of my money. I want you to have it, Mr Gorbachev, to help those poor people who lost so much in that earthquake. It isn't much, sir – I wish it were – but perhaps it's enough to be of some help, somehow. I wanted to send it right to you so that it could be put to what you feel to be the best use of your people in their time of tragedy.

It is my prayer that the relief efforts go smoothly and that the devastation will turn out to be less than originally feared. My sympathies to the people of Armenia in their time of sorrow and heartbreak.

God be with you, sir.

Sincerely,
Bonnie J. Reese

Belfast
Northern Ireland   8 December 1988

Dear President Gorbachev,

Warmest congratulations on your speech to the United Nations.

May you be the historical figure to bring peace to the world. I often felt that the USSR, if it changed, could bring happiness to all the world.

Please do your best to bring the paramilitaries such as the PIRA in our land, to cease by ensuring that they are not financed and armed from any source. Your strength plus that of the USA and Europe, can prevail against our terrorists.

We can make much more progress through dialogue and diplomacy and compromise than from war.

God be with you and your lovely Raisa.

I was Honorary Secretary of a Peace Movement here called PACE (Protestant and Catholic Encounter) for six years. I was checked out by Protestants, to Dublin for six years until returning to an inner-city Belfast church (Presbyterian).

Your help will be much appreciated – may God bless your efforts. If we moderate conservatives can work with others to build a good world God will bless us all.

Yours sincerely,
Reverend Desmond Mock

US bone-marrow transplant specialist Cr Robert Peter Gale visited the USSR in the spring of 1986, leading a rescue team to treat the victims of the Chernobyl nuclear plant accident. Gale's trip was expecitiously made possible through the personal help of Dr Armand Hammer who accompanied him to the Soviet Union aboard Hammer's private jet plane.

Nuremburg
West Germany   12 December 1988

Dear Mikhail Gorbachev,

I had the opportunity to visit your country in September 1987. It was there that I heard for the first time about glasnost and perestroika and I was filled with enthusiasm. Not only the incomparable impression of the vast size of the Soviet Union and the beauty of its landscape, but especially the openness and sincerity of the people I met in your country, moved me deeply. For the first time I became aware of how in the West, I had been deeply imprinted with anti-Soviet ideas, without ever really knowing anything about your country or the people who live there. When I returned from my visit, and told my friends about what I had experienced, they often merely smiled: 'Gorbi will never manage to do that' or 'the Russians have pulled the wool over your eyes', were people's opinions. But today, just as it was then, my opinion and that of so many other people all over the world, is a different one.

In June I am expecting my first child, and I thank you, Michael Gorbachev, for the fact that you have done more than all the other politicians in the world put together to ensure that this child will be born into a peaceful world. I do not know whether my child will ever see you, but I shall certainly tell him or her about the man who brought peace and hope back to the world.

Yours sincerely,
Marika Schonfeld

THE SECRETARY OF STATE
Washington, DC, USA

10 January 1989

Dear Mr Chairman,
O'Bie joins me in thanking you and Mrs Gorbachev for the lovely presents you sent us during the holidays. We appreciate your thoughtfulness and hope that you enjoyed the holiday season.

I would like to take this opportunity now as I am leaving office to express my satisfaction at the progress that has been made in US-Soviet relations in the past few years. While this progress is the result of long, hard work by many people, you have played an essential role in bringing about an increasingly productive dialogue between the Soviet Union and the United States.

I hope and trust that the efforts of our two countries in the areas of arms control, human rights, regional and bilateral issues, and people-to-people exchanges will continue to bear fruit. Please accept my best wishes for health and success in the New Year.

With warm personal regards,
Sincerely yours,
George P. Shultz

Sandy Hook
Connecticut, USA   20 January 1989

Dear Mr Gorbachev,
I would like to take this opportunity to personally thank you for allowing our team to come to the Soviet Union to help the earthquake victims.

I was part of a group of volunteers sponsored by Union Carbide Corporation that arrived in Spitak on 20 December to erect temporary shelters for the homeless.

Our team reached Spitak carrying all that we needed to live on for two weeks, including tents for shelter. We were very surprised when we arrived at our campsite to find a Soviet winter army tent that would be our home for the next week. Our Armenian hosts were so grateful to see us that they cooked us a welcome dinner on an open fire outside the tent.

The first shelter that we erected in the center of Spitak was to be used as a community center and meeting hall for about one hundred people. We had discovered that the Soviet army had supplied tents for the majority of the homeless.

My experiences amongst the people of the Soviet Union are something I will treasure for the rest of my life. We spoke about matters that have worried both peoples – especially 'war' – realizing that neither side wants that to occur. I met a man from Moscow who told me how he thought the American stereotype of a Russian was depicted: 'a tall man wearing a long fur coat, carrying four swords'. I agree that might have been my feeling at one time, but this has certainly changed.

Our team became a group of diplomats unlike any that the United States has ever sent to the Soviet Union. We were not politicians or professional diplomats, but human beings expressing our true feelings and opinions to one another. Speaking for the group, I can say that we came away with a lot more than we could have ever imagined, certainly a greater understanding of people.

The earthquake was a horrible tragedy, but as our hosts said in a farewell toast, 'From out of the rubble the seeds will grow for a new beginning.' May these seeds be harvested into a closer relationship between the Soviet Union and the new American administration. My dream is to be able to return to the Soviet Union someday, to renew old friendships at a happier time, and make new acquaintances in other parts of the country.

Sincerely,
Kenneth Graff

Shelton
Connecticut, USA   24 January 1989

Dear Mr Secretary,

We are an Amercian couple who have always wanted children of our own, but unfortunately cannot. We have tried unsuccessfully so far to adopt a child/children in our own country and through the United Nations, but have run into several stumbling blocks.

When we heard about the devastating natural disasters that have struck your country over the past several months, our hearts went out to your people and the thousands who were killed, maimed, left homeless; and we especially grieved for the children left homeless without parents and/or families.

It has been said, Mr Secretary, that 'Our Children Are Our Future', but these children's future seems less than bright without the parental guidance so needed for their total growth.

We realize that we could never replace these children's natural parents, but we could offer them a home full of love, security, and growth.

We ask your help, Mr Secretary, to adopt one of these homeless children. We pledge on our honor that this child would be raised with love, and would also be taught of its homeland and all it has to offer.

We would hope that this child would be a symbol of the new understanding between our two nations; that are so different and yet so similar.

We would appreciate any help you could give us in this matter or perhaps a direction you could point us to where we would gain a family and a child gain love.

We look forward to hearing from you, Mr Secretary, and we wish for both our nations in this New Year, greater understanding and mutual friendship that will benefit all of mankind!

Sincerely,
Robert H. Bostock
Helen R. Bostock

cc: The President of the United States, George H. Bush

Neuenkirchen
West Germany   1 March 1989

Dear Mr Gorbachev,

I have read your book, Perestroika, with growing interest and would like to write to you today about what you say there. I was surprised about what I read in this book. I certainly do not belong to that group of people who see the Soviet Union as the 'enemy', but nevertheless, the premises and perspectives of the Soviet state and its politics were unfamiliar to me. This is certainly in part because here in the German Federal Republic, we find very little written about the Soviet Union, its politics and the people living in that country.

I had never understood why your army marched into Afghanistan; it was certainly not made clear in the Federal Republic that you were brought in to provide help. Nevertheless I cannot approve of military intervention by one country in the politics of another.

For that reason, I particularly welcome your stated intention of allowing every country to determine itself. This is the only real way to guarantee a country's healthy development and especially its subsequent advancement. The fact that the USA does not take this view does not, in fact, surprise me. In my opinion, the USA is a 'power-crazed monster' whose government consists of puppets controlled by industry, especially the armaments industry. All the interventions by the USA into the many countries of the Third World are, in my view, the perverse products of a lust for power. I was already aware that the USA has always want to be the one and only real World Power, but it is alarming to learn of the measures it used in the past, and is still using now, in order to achieve this position. Today I can very well understand why you, why the USSR, has always felt itself threatened by the USA. In your eyes, and in the eyes of your fellow-countrymen, the USA must have appeared as a fearsome aggressor. The fact that you, nevertheless, are prepared to negotiate with such a country and have even achieved and are continuing to achieve far-reaching preliminary concessions, arouses my deep admiration.

Only by going along the path that you have chosen can world peace be achieved. But I doubt whether the USA appreciates the pressing necessity of the situation. Therefore I would like to thank you for having been prepared to take such steps, in spite of the stationing of Cruise missiles and Pershing 2 on FRG territory, and for having made a start on unilateral disarmament. The stationing of that particular weapons-system on the territory of the Federal Republic represents a permanent threat to you, and therefore I am going to write to Oskar Lafontaine and ask that if he wins election to the Bundestag in 1990, he will work toward the removal of these weapons, and indeed of all atomic weapons, from the FRG.

It is necessary for the Federal Republic to leave NATO. You speak of the dissolution of both military blocs. What we can do if we are to meet your suggestions is 1. to withdraw from NATO, 2. to convert the German Federal Armed Forces into a defence force, and 3. to expand economic links with your country. I will therefore call upon Mr Lafontaine to initiate our withdrawal from NATO. In his book Angst vor den Freuden (Fear of Friends), written in 1983, he too says that this withdrawal from NATO is necessary.

If we want to create peace, it can only be done without weapons. An end must be put to the escalating armament spiral, and the money thus saved, invested in social policy. Continued armament means the holocaust. Our present government is blind and deaf to such views. It prefers to negotiate with the British over rearmament or over the development of a new fighter-bomber. Mr Kohl and company, slavishly dependent as they are, prefer to assent to each

96

and every American development and suggestion. Sadly, the FRG often seems to me today to be more American than the USA.

Yours sincerely,
Johannes Lammers

Wellman (Hindustan) Private Ltd
Bombay, India

8 March 1989

Dear Mr Gorbachev,

This is a personal letter to one of the greatest leaders of our time from a widely travelled technocrat of India who feels deeply concerned for the future of mankind.

Since the days of Mahatma Gandhi, the world has not seen a political leader of your calibre destined to usher in a new ray of hope for the future of human society. Not only have you forced the hand of the Americans and made effective disarmament a distinct possibility, you have also embarked on the formidable task of restructuring the system (perestroika) in your own country with a refreshing air of openness (glasnost). As an ardent admirer of your mission, I would like to draw your personal attention to some basic fundamentals necessary for providing the essential foundation for lasting peace and prosperity of mankind.

It is a fact of life that in this whole wide world, there is only one place where each one of us finds peace and happiness; and that is our own home. East or West, home is the best; but why? Home is where each of us is woven into a fabric of love and understanding and has a relationship, a sense of belonging to one another. Unless this relationship of love and brotherhood at the micro level of a family is extended to the macro level of human society at large, man across the globe will continue to suffer the crippling disease of selfishness and greed, jealousy and exploitation, crime and violence, none of which have a place in any family worth the name.

This is no longer an abstract concept, confined to the books of philosophy or religion. It has already been put into practice by millions of different castes and creeds in India and overseas. I am one of them and we call ourselves 'swadhyayees' (students of the self). Inculcating this fundamental understanding and building a bond of love with fellow human beings practising different religions and belonging to different economic strata of the society, we have truly built a brotherhood of man under the fatherhood of the Creator, transcending all barriers of caste, creed and colour.

Using feelings of devotion and gratefulness to our Creator as a social force, a silent revolution is taking shape in India and overseas under the inspiring leadership of Rev Pandurang Shastri Athavale, the founder of this unprecedented selfless work. He has successfully launched a number of socio-economic experiments to show to the world how the gulf between the 'haves' and the 'have-nots' can be bridged, how the hatred and selfishness can be replaced by brotherly love and understanding and how we can forge unity in the diversity which is a fact of life on this planet.

The selfless work that Rev Athavale has silently done over the past forty years, without any publicity or fanfare, has now created a working model for the world to see how man can be brought closer to man, transcending all barriers, and how he can be selflessly motivated to work for his own good as well as the good of society at large.

The centre for the Study of Developing Societies, affiliated to the United Nations, is already studying our work and its far-reaching consequences for the future health of mankind. We will be only too glad to show you or your representatives personally the positive transformation our work has brought to the life of the individuals and their communities in thousands of villages in our countryside.

Some of us can, if you like, come over to Moscow to make an audio-visual presentation to you of various aspects of our work and answer all questions that you may have with respect to it. The utmost relevance that our work has to what you have set as the goal of your leadership has, in fact, motivated me to write this personal letter to you.

Looking forward to hearing from you, I am, with brotherly feelings,

Sincerely yours,
Baldev K. Mehra

Costa Mesa
California, USA   15 March 1989

Dear Mr Gorbachev,

What I want to say briefly is this: I hope that in your pursuit of more freedoms for your people, you will not experience the excesses of freedom that we in the United States are experiencing at the present time.

The crime rate in this country is incredible. Criminals are very hard to convict or are released on technicalities. Very serious crimes are punished, if at all, by short sentences. The prisons are overcrowded, so criminals are released early.

In one case, everybody awaiting death on 'Death Row' was released, allowed to go free after killing. We give criminals 'furloughs' from prison, and some of them commit serious crimes while on furlough. Even murder.

Drugs have destroyed a basic tenet of our ethical values; responsibility for your own actions. Drugs have become an extenuating circumstance. Thousands of our people have died as a result of drug use, and there is no serious attempt to stop this deadly traffic. Too much money involved. We are a greedy people. I suppose everyone would be, given the opportunity.

We are struggling at the present moment over the issue of owning guns. The National Rifle Association insists we should have the right to own any kind of weapon we want, even automatic weapons. This approaches national insanity. However, the public is against NRA policies, and we will win this fight.

So, freedom is a two-edged sword. Right now we have too much freedom in this country, but I believe in twenty to thirty years we will get these excesses back under control. Freedom has the ability to right itself.

I wish you all the luck and good fortune.

Bob Bowser

Pasadena
California, USA   12 April 1989

Dear President Gorbachev,

I am involved in our own space program, a member of the navigation team for the Voyager spacecraft on its way to an encounter with Neptune this August. I am very proud of the accomplishments of Voyager, but I see my country pulling back from other endeavors in space. The United States is no longer the leader in manned space activities. You are!

Our peaceful competition in space is good for both of us. Many people say, 'Let us cooperate, and do something together.' That might be desirable, but either cooperation or friendly competition in space are in the interest of both our peoples, and everyone else in the world as well. We are mutually at the edge of a vast frontier which beckons to the spirit of adventure and exploration in all of us.

Sincerely,
Tony Taylor

ICEWALK
Yorkshire
England

2 August 1989

Esteemed Sir,

This Spring we, representatives of seven nations, USSR, United Kingdom, USA, West Germany, Japan, Canada and Australia, united our efforts to win victory on the cold ice of the Arctic Ocean under the most dangerous and hostile conditions. We, of so many nations, were able to overcome not only the conditions, but the barriers of disconfidence and misunderstanding. National and individual problems were overcome for the sake of our scientific, environmental and historical objectives. We cannot help being proud of our achievements.

On 14 May 1989 the state flags of our countries and the United Nation's Flag, which we had received from The Secretary General in person, were set upon the North Pole. Once again, the North Pole has become the Pole of Peace. The participants of the expedition have been greeted by Mr George Bush, President of the USA, Margaret Thatcher, Prime Minister of Great Britain, Chancellor of West Germany, Mr Ryzhkov, Prime Minister of the USSR.

Following our example, young people from fifteen countries formed an International Youth Expedition in the Northern part of Canada, showing the whole world their support of tight cooperation and environmental concern.

Mankind is living through a time when many of our problems can be solved by pulling together. Our expedition is proof of that. Not only leaders, but all people over our world, should work together and understand each other for the sake of peace.

One of us has won the South and North Poles on foot for the first time in history, the other has reached the North Pole twice on foot. We are determined people.

In 1992, we are planning to succeed in the project 'Tomorrow'. The representatives of many countries will make up the team of two airships which will start their journey at the Olympic Games in Barcelona under the Flag of the United Nations and will visit all continents with the purpose of involving young people of all nations in their future. We hope to show the world that the people of our planet have differences of minor importance when they are united by the common cause.

We hope it will become our modest contribution in the development of international cooperation and understanding.

Respectfully yours,
Robert Swan

Utrecht
Holland
20 September 1989

Dear Sir President M Gorbatjiov,

Please don't be afraid! I am a simple Catholic priest from Holland.
I send you my congratulations and hearty greetings.

I think you have chosen the best way for your own people and for
the whole world.

May all the leaders of peoples follow your example, for justice,
freedom and cooperation and bring peace and prosperity and
happiness.

I wish you wisdom, courage and perseverance in your function,
and happiness in your family.

I think a lot (a big lot!) of countries have certain great hopes of you
and your people.

My four sisters and I (four nuns and one priest) pray for you
all many times! I hope this letter will be reached to you and
encourage you.

Yours,
Father Christian Houbin

London
England
8 October 1989

Dear Mr Gorbachev,

Having just read your book Perestroika I wish to take up one
point you made in dealing with the process of disarmament. In
the chapter on 'Problems of Disarmament and USSR-USA Relations'
section: The US – 'Shining City Atop a Hill' you mention the
existence of 'millions of working people ... who are generally
peacefully disposed' alongside whom are 'reactionary groups who
have links with the military-industrial complex and who profit from
arms manufacturing'.

This of course is the case in all developed capitalist countries
and in a large number of Third World countries. Hence it
is worth studying as a global phenomenon to ascertain basic
common features. The concept of 'millions of working people'
needs further elaboration. There are within the working people
millions of armed services personnel and millions employed in arms
manufacture or provision of goods and services to the armed forces
and arms manufacturers.

Many of these people are doubtless very scared or confused by the
arms race. Certainly some of them are positively disposed toward

101

disarmament. The principal problem is that for these millions their livelihood depends on continued employment and they may fear that mass scale disarmament would lead to massive job losses and their subsequent impoverishment, the destruction of their dignity and family lives. This makes them easy prey for the political representatives of the military-industrial complex. Many labour disputes have arisen in Britain as a result of defence contracts being awarded to foreign firms leading to job losses in Britain. This fact will influence many when they are faced with the consequences of reduced military expenditure for themselves as individuals.

It seems to me that before these millions of working people will fully side with the forces of peace against the political representatives of the military-industrial complex they will need to be deeply convinced of the viability of transferring resources from military to civilian production. They must be confident that as their turn comes for 'demobilisation' that they have a bright and WELL DEFINED future. This is of the utmost importance in relation to armed services personnel since they are in a position to threaten or even start shooting at governments which have come to power on the basis of peaceful, progressive policies. The barbaric murder of President Salvador Allende and many of his fellow citizens in 1973 is but one grim example of how the political will of the masses can be frustrated through lack of support from armed services personnel.

It is a great political battle to build the understanding and confidence needed for the employees of the military-industrial complex to actively support the process of disarmament, and the winning of this battle is not aided by any fear of losing one's place in society. I put the question this way because although I am an ordinary office worker I am sure that armed services personnel have a genuine, albeit misplaced, sense of pride in their work along with traditions of their own which are needed in addition to a living wage. It is no use telling an army engineer that he could get a job selling hamburgers when his unit is disbanded even if his pay were to remain the same. I do not intend any insult to those who already sell hamburgers for a living, it just has to be recognised that persons who have achieved high levels of skill and a certain social prestige will not happily give this up for something that they regard as a step backwards in life. Respect for people's dignity, self-image and place in society cannot be disregarded without endangering social progress.

I have seen that the Soviet Union and other socialist countries are leading by example in converting arms factories to civilian production. More needs to be made of this in terms of publicity. This aspect of disarmament needs an extra verification or auditing process. Finance experts, perhaps from neutral countries, could be invited to look at governmental accounts both to certify that funds and capital resources had indeed been transferred to civilian production and to show that this is a profitable process in all senses of the word. Western television crews could be invited to make documentaries showing the physical replacement of weapons manufacture by consumer goods manufacture and perhaps the building of hospitals and schools using monies released by closure of military facilities. Such auditing or verification would assist confidence-building by showing that the disarmament process can be carried out in a deeply humanistic way reflecting in material and social terms its goal of saving humanity and creating a prosperous, non-violent world.

An acute problem will arise in capitalist countries where the benefits of planning and social control in the economy are minimal or even non-existent. Here is the greatest danger and I speak particularly of the USA and Britain where deregulation mania and slavish worship of uncontrolled market forces are rampant. There needs to be an international attempt at some specific linkage between each act of disarmament and the constructive use of the resources thus released. The USSR obviously cannot interfere in the internal affairs of other countries but it could press for agreements that would ensure the constructive development of at least some workers released from the military sphere. These people could be employed in a variety of roles by international agencies, consortia of countries or large enterprises contracted to work for them. UN peace-keeping, international disaster task forces, conservation and relief work along with many other forms of work are needed in an expanded form. Finance for this expansion could be directly related to funds saved through disarmament.

Not all Western workers released from military work could be employed in this way but some could and their actual experience of this process at work – together with the highly publicised domestic achievements of the socialist countries could defuse the potential for violent resistance to disarmament in capitalist countries.

Whatever the actual solutions they have to make soldiers and armaments workers feel that they are truly progressing to a better life and not being callously dumped on the social scrap heap to become cheap labour or part of the reserve army of labour so beloved of private entrepreneurs looking for high returns on investment.

I have no doubt personally that disarmament could release vast wealth-creating potential in a deeply humanistic way but the people who need convincing are not ordinary civilians like myself. It is the foot soldiers, tank drivers, back-up personnel and workers in military industries who need convincing. More than just slogans and indeed more than just abstract moral arguments are required here.

There has to be a convincing programme of action to re-employ people in a constructive way.

Yours sincerely,
Simon Sheffield

Guarapari
Espirito Santo, Brazil   10 October 1989

Most excellent Senhor,

My wish is to praise you as you have succeeded in giving lasting peace and understanding to humanity.

As every day goes by, we are even more amazed and admire you with respect, knowing that you are someone who devotes himself to the cause of the oppressed, giving life meaning and dignity, such as is impossible to achieve by any other means. I feel that I can confidently call you The Knight of Good. It seems to me, that from the wisdom of St Thomas Aquinas, you have learned the supreme value of praising reason; with dismay, we see that love and respect for one's neighbour are on the wane, giving way to individualism, materialism and scepticism. And should this continue, we will certainly end up by destroying man's confidence in himself as a rational being. There are moments when we might think that God is being taken away from the throne of the universe. Without understanding why, we feel that mankind is moving towards discord with himself, and, restless and exasperated, is attempting to conquer the world, albeit at the cost of his own propriety.

Even though your admirers have moments of anxiety, we confidently expect that the greatest gift, that of love and respect for one's neighbour, will never leave you and that the light which brightens all your deeds will never perish, giving you a life of wisdom, so that you can bestow the dignity of human nature and meaning of life on to your fellow creatures. This, together with hopes for those who are living in despair, so inexorably beset by evil, that in the near future, this period of torment and misery in which humanity is living, will soon end and become the dawning of a new era of harmony among all human beings.

Here, from the other side of the world, I keep hoping that you will be the next one chosen for the Nobel Peace Prize and that your perestroika will meet the receptiveness needed in your politicians and people to bring about this enormous task successfully. When the economy and well-being of this great nation have been brought about and we are able to share in the success of your aspirations, the good of serving the people of your country, why not say so to all the people of the earth.

I hope, one day, that many Mikhail Gorbachevs will appear, especially in the developing countries such as my own Brazil, where, in spite of our having immense natural resources, fifty per cent of our population live in absolute poverty and unparalleled inequality, for which our politicians, so lacking in ideals, are completely responsible. And so, distressed, we await the dawning of a new day, which will bring reforms, pointing men towards new laws and obligations and when this era has truly arrived, we will see men of wealth on all sides, with no distinction of creed or ideology, forming a chain, whose unbreakable links will form the security of peace and prosperity among all peoples.

I hope that you will visit my country soon, I send my kind regards to you, your distinguished wife Raisa and all the citizens of your revered country.

Americo Rodor Filho

Bad Essen
West Germany   16 November 1989

Query:

Why do we in Germany still not have a peace treaty? What conditions still have to be fulfilled for us to get one?

I address myself to you, and also to your colleagues in the USA, France and Great Britain, because our politicians are incapable of giving me clear information. Please be assured that my question is meant entirely seriously. I have no interest in a large German Empire (1937 borders) and reunification.

Thanking you in anticipation.

Yours sincerely,
M. Herrmann

Zephyr Cove
Nevada, USA   December 1989

Uvazchaemij Mikhail Gorbachev,

Kak vashe zdorovje?

This letter is intended to clarify a misconception that I have heard recently. It was said at an informal gathering of people who want to understand our relationship with your people better, that one of the main differences between Russia and America is that Americans have never fought a war on their own soil. This statement is accurate but not true. There are American men and women who are walking on our soil every day who are inhabited by war. They served in World

105

War I, World War II, Korea and Vietnam and came back to America with the mind-set of war still invading them. War can explode at any time like a hidden mine within them. Their hidden wars affect their wives, husbands and children every day. Some walk our streets homeless but none are warless.

I have written a poem about a returned soldier after the 'end' of World War II.

THE BARKING MAN

We celebrated with relief the end
Of World War Two when I was only twelve.
Wars end for those who never truly delve
Into the lives of men who cannot mend.
We heard he'd been a prisoner over there.
So damaged were his nerves they couldn't send
The message to his vocal cords to bend
And so he barked and made civilians stare.
He couldn't help himself any more.
At lunch, his presence spoiled a pleasant meal.
At night, his presence kept us all awake.
We couldn't stop his barking at the war.
It hounded him without the slightest break,
Nor let him heal, nor ever let him heal.

My point is that it doesn't matter what soil wars are fought on if they are internalized. Wars are with you as much as your own shadow and that war-shadow darkens everyone's soil.

Sposibo,
Rosamond Larson

Oberstdorf
West Germany
4 December 1989

Dear Mr General Secretary,

I was going to write this letter after your new year address of the American people four years ago, after you had taken over the leadership of the USSR, but fear of ridicule stopped me.

At the time I immediately recognized that you are made of a different stamp than your predecessors, especially Stalin, who was the same for his country that Hitler was for Germany, maybe even worse, because he had millions of people murdered even before the war, just to increase his power.

Born in 1899, it was a miracle that I returned from both world wars, I hate war and all violence like nobody else.

When the war was over and Germany had been destroyed it was the wish of the three Western allies to ban war for all time – at least from Europe, and they began to disarm. Not so Stalin! His motto was 'in this world power counts for more than rights'. I had to live in East Germany until 1954 and I had first-hand experience of the conditions there at the time. Intoxicated with victory he really began to produce arms, to become the strongest in the world. It was only this fact that started the vicious circle of the arms race. Only when you came to power in the Soviet Union you realized that the world couldn't live like that much longer. You learnt from the mistakes of your predecessors, and immediately after taking over as General Secretary I recognized you as the Prince of Peace in our world.

On 4 May 1945 I was for two hours a prisoner of war of the Russians in Pritzwalk, Province of Brandenburg, but I managed to escape. I promised my Lord, if ever I should become retired, that I would read the Bible every single day. Up to the present I have kept that promise. The Bible is the only book which speaks only the truth. For me it is a never-ending source of inspiration, comfort and hope at the same time. I know it by heart. Unfortunately, none of the politicians ever use it.

Even Helmut Schmidt, a religious man, said when he was Chancellor that unfortunately the Sermon on the Mount could not be applied to politics. But only because no politician has ever tried it. Jesus said in the Sermon on the Mount, 'Blessed are the meek, for they shall inherit the earth' – Matthew chapter five, verse five.

As a disabled person it has been natural to me to ask our Lord for peace for all politicians, especially for you, Mr Gorbachev, because otherwise the human race is heading for the end of the world. So my request is, don't waver on the path you have started to walk down. Only the day before yesterday I had to realize that God will always be stronger, when he squashed your plan to meet President Bush on your navy ships and you had to meet on the *Maxim Gorki* instead.

Yours sincerely,
Friedrich Ruff

OCCIDENTAL PETROLEUM CORPORATION
Los Angeles, California, USA

4 January 1990

Dear Mr President,

Congratulations on your being named 'Man of the Decade' by TIME Magazine!

Your understanding and vision for the need of economic and governmental transformations are virtually helping to reshape our world. Your incomparable statesmanship, I am convinced, will help you meet the challenges of the extraordinary undertakings you face to improve the lot of the peoples of the Soviet Union as well as of the undeveloped countries of the world.

As 'the force behind the momentous events of the 80's' you have inspired and helped effect the road to disarmament and peace. Although mankind may never turn all its swords into ploughshares, I believe nuclear war is no longer thinkable due to the development of mutual trust between you and President Bush.

With best personal wishes for the new year,

Respectfully,
Armand Hammer

Herborn-Schönbach
West Germany   23 February 1990

Dear Mr President of State Gorbachev,

For many years now I have been an interested reader of the Soviet Union Today, and I have read your books Glasnost and Perestroika, as well as your biography (TIME-book). In short, I respect you greatly and have confidence in you. As former Woijna Plenni who did assembly work in Welikije-Luki and came away from there with permanently damaged health, I follow your politics with great interest, because I love the people of your home country. We got on very well with the simple people on the building sites or on the kolchose, and they would often share with us what little they had. For example, Tonja, our post-girl, often brought her dinner ration with her to give to me when I got weak and ill. She would say, 'Paul, you not die, you *damoi*!' I have not forgotten that to this day, and it was like 'flowers in the snow'.

I enclose a little prayer of blessing which I have written out myself, and I hope it will give you pleasure.

Yours,
Paul Klein

BENEDICTION

The Lord be before you
to show the right way.
The Lord be beside you
to enfold you in His arms
and to protect you.
The Lord be behind you

to keep you safe
from the treachery of wicked men.
The Lord be beneath you
to catch you when you fall
and to free you from all snares.
The Lord be within you
to comfort you
when you despair.
The Lord be round you
as your defense
when others attack you.
The Lord be above you
to bless you.
May the God of kindliness bless you.

Fourth century

Los Angeles
USA

12 March 1990

Dear Mr Gorbachev,

Permit me to 'thank you' for your historical removal of the infamous 'Iron Curtain' between East and West. This wise action has allowed me to go back to the USSR after eight years of absence and reenter it as an American citizen. As an independent business woman I'm glad that I'm able to contribute to the economy of the country of my birth, which I still consider my homeland – 'rodina'. The incredible changes that are taking place at the moment have become even more special when I was able to visit, in the southern part of the country, the grave of my beloved mother who died shortly after I left the USSR in 1981.

It gave me an incredible joy and nostalgia to see the place of my youth and all my relatives who I still love very much, and who all remained in my old home town.

You can be rest assured that we, the Native Russians, will be forever grateful to you for your wisdom and goodwill in opening up the communications between East and West, and that we will work very hard toward our common dream of a peaceful and prosperous homeland.

Sincerely,
Rosa Gireyev

Mikhail Gorbachev and Ronald Reagan before the Soviet-American Summit in Geneva, November 1985. *Photograph: Yu. Abramochkin*

Gorbachev and President Mitterand during their joint Press Conference in Paris, October 1985. *Photograph: Yu. Abramochkin*

At the Soviet-American Summit in Geneva, November 1985. Mr Shevardnadze, Soviet Minister of Foreign Affairs, and George Shultz, US Secretary of State, sign an Agreement on relations in the fields of science, education and culture. *Photograph: Yu. Abramochkin*

Gorbachev with his grand-daughter in Moscow, February 1985 during the ballot for the elections to the Supreme Soviet. *Photograph: V. Romoy/V. Rodionov*

Prime Minister Rajiv Gandhi receives Mikhail Gorbachev and his wife Raisa at the airport on an official friendly visit to India in November 1986. *Photograph: Yu. Abramochkin*

On his Indian visit Gorbachev lays a wreath on the site of the cremation of Mahatma Gandhi. *Photograph: Yu. Abramochkin*

Gorbachev on a walkabout in Budapest on a friendly visit to Hungary in June 1986. *Photograph: Yu. Somov*

Presentation of Camilla Taylor's petition (one of the letter writers) on Capitol steps in Washington with Senator Howard Metzenbaum and Louis Stokes kissing her. Photograph: *Ackron Beacon Journal*

A living chain of people stretches for many kilometres along the Baltic Coast in a demonstration to protect the Baltic Sea. *Photograph: A. Zemlyanichenko*

Soviet and American rescuers attempt to save the Californian grey whales that were trapped in the ice in Alaska after a sudden freeze in November 1988. The story caught the imagination of the world due to the unprecedented cooperation between these two countries and the lengths they were prepared to go to save two members of this endangered species.

Some of the letter writers from the USA. Top left: Samantha Smith, the one who started it all; top right: John Crystal; centre left: Balbir Mathur; centre right: Carol Rosin; below left: Ray Waterman; below right: Martin Allin.

A member of a brigade of construction workers from France help in rescue operations in Leninakan after the Armenian earthquake. *Photograph: A. Makarov*

Those suffering from the effects of the Chernobyl disaster come out onto the streets of Minsk in September 1989.

Bystanders at a meeting in Minsk on the Chernobyl disaster and its effects on the health of the Byelorussian nation. *Photograph: Ye Koktysh*

A protest rally at the Dynamo Station, Kiev, calling for more awareness of the consequences of Chernobyl. *Photograph: V. Maruschenko*

Gorbachev during an audience with Pope John Paul II at the Vatican on a state visit to Italy in November/December 1989. *Photograph: D. Donsky*

Twenty minutes to detonation: American observers at the Sanjozek testing ground during the blowing up of the last intermediate missiles in October 1989. *Photograph: V. Borisyenko*

Mr and Mrs Gorbachev on a walkabout with Fidel Castro in Cuba, April 1989.

Gorbachev talks with Deng Xiao Ping, Chairman of the Military Council of the Chinese Communist Party on an official visit to China in May 1989. *Photograph: V. Runov*

A large crowd gathers around Gorbachev as he walks on the Great Wall of China, May 1989.

Gorbachev talks with the U.S.S.R. People's Deputy, Sergei Stankevich, at the Congress of People's Deputies in the Kremlin, May/June 1989. *Photograph: O. Ivanov*

Gorbachev in the Presidium at the Congress of People's Deputies of the U.S.S.R. *Photograph: Yu. Abramochkin*

Gorbachev lays forth to the Congress of People's Deputies of the U.S.S.R. in the Kremlin in May/June 1989. *Photograph: L. Palladin*

During a break between meetings of the first session of the Supreme Soviet, Gorbachev talks to V.I. Matveenko, A Deputy from Leningrad.

President Gorbachev and President Bush meet aboard ship in Malta, December 1989.

Gorbachev is welcomed by Margaret Thatcher at the airport on his official visit to Great Britain in April 1989.

HUMAN RIGHTS

Justice, Dignity and Freedom

FOR A VERY LONG TIME the most divisive issue in relations between the Soviet Union and the West was human rights. There were several reasons for this: the deplorable Soviet record; Soviet secretiveness in the face of Western challenges; and generally rising international concern.

It was only towards the end of the Tsarist period in Russia that human rights received some attention. The peasants were not finally liberated from their feudal bonds until 1905; and right down to 1917 the Tsars maintained a secret police and steadily persecuted their most consistent opponents. It was a tragedy that in the name of Socialism the Bolsheviks adopted some of the worst practices of their predecessors and then, in Stalin's time, improved on them. On paper the Soviet Union was a democracy; in practice it degenerated into the dictatorship of a small clique or, at times, of one man. In theory, Soviet citizens had the protection of the law as administered by the courts; but the law was biased against the individual and the courts were either abused or disregarded.

Stalin had millions killed in his collectivisation and industrialisation drive, and he sent millions more to their deaths in labour camps. He had many thousands of those who even just appeared to challenge him tortured, forced to sign false confessions, and executed. After the war he repeated the process on a more limited but still grotesquely inhuman scale. What the West deduced or alleged is now openly admitted in Soviet writings. Krushchev removed some of the worst abuses, but was selective in his rehabilitation of those who had been falsely accused. At least, after his famous attack on Stalin at the 20th Party Congress in 1956, it was easier for non-conformists in literature and the arts to express their individual views without fear of retribution.

Brezhnev reacted against what seemed to him Khrushchev's dangerous liberalism and from 1968 onwards, the year of his suppression of the Prague 'Spring', acquired an increasingly repressive reputation. The camps began to fill up again and psychiatry was abused to confine the innocent to mental hospitals for questioning the communist elite. Jews who wished to emigrate were refused permission, whereas writers, such as Solzhenitsyn, who wished to stay at home, were forced abroad. Andrei Sakharov, the physicist who had been mainly responsible for producing the Soviet hydrogen bomb, moved steadily from concern about nuclear testing to disillusionment with a society that imprisoned and silenced its own

112

best thinkers. For publishing abroad, campaigning for human rights at home, and speaking out against the invasion of Afghanistan, he was banished to Gorky in 1979, far removed from other than secret contact with Moscow dissidents and foreign sympathisers. Gorbachev's inheritance was not just a decelerating economy, but an imprisoned society.

As a student, Gorbachev had a reputation for being outspoken though still communist. But going through university in the fifties and growing to maturity in the midst of the Cold War, he could not help but be susceptible to the argument for restricting civil liberties, that those who challenged communism were secretly serving the American cause. A society that was fed on Marxism and its more vituperative offshoot, Leninism, could hardly fail to suspect that capitalism would try to undermine socialism as socialism was bent on undermining capitalism. So when President Carter praised Andrei Sakharov in 1979, it was proof of Sakharov's disloyalty, not of his improper treatment by the Soviet authorities. And when Reagan appealed to Gorbachev in 1985 and 1986, imploring him to free his dissidents, it was proof at the very least of an American desire to embarrass the Soviet Union and Gorbachev personally.

The war that ended in 1945 was supposed to put a stop to aggression and oppression. By and large, open aggression was swept out of Europe, but oppression intensified in Eastern Europe and open aggression became very much more conspicious in the Third World. So when Gorbachev took command in the Soviet Union 40 years later, the world as a whole was much more concerned with human rights. Without necessarily being anti-socialist, outside observers were therefore inclined to be much more critical of Soviet attitudes and behaviour than they had been before, even if with slightest reason. And Gorbachev's initial insistence that such matters were purely internal concerns and not theirs simply had the effect of making those comments more stringent still.

Gorbachev was soon under considerable pressure from abroad. To begin with there was not much he could do. To secure his own position and ease the way to reform in general he first had to get rid of top-level Party opponents, which took time. He also had to avoid provoking resistance throughout the Party by avoiding highly contentious issues. But the external message gradually got through to him as the West began to make an improvement in human rights in the Soviet Union a condition of progress in the arms talks. In any case, to facilitate economic reform he gradually stimulated a domestic political debate, and there was simply no way in which that could avoid the subject of human rights as incriminating evidence poured out about past Soviet malpractice. The dissidents took new heart and found growing support at home for their pleas for a fundamental change; and Gorbachev was soon faced with a combination of demands from outside and inside the country.

Appeals on behalf of Soviet Jews touched a particularly new nerve. Anti-semitism, widespread in Tsarist times, did not vanish with the Revolution; so Gorbachev was anxious to exhibit his impartiality. Jews had contributed to the revolutionary movement, but many were subsequently victimized by Stalin. So this was another reason for Gorbachev wishing to make clear his own unprejudiced position. On the other hand, unceasing pressure came from the Jewish lobby in the United States and from Israel, which made it internally uncomfortable and internationally embarrassing. There were also so many talented Jewish families waiting to emigrate that the economy could lose valuable skills at the very time it needed them.

But realism prevailed. Anatoly Sharansky, one of the leading 'refuseniks' Jews denied permission to leave the country was dispatched to Israel in February 1986 as part of an East-West prisoner exchange. In January 1987 the law on emigration was relaxed; and whereas the number of Jews emigrating in 1986 was only 1000, it had risen by 1988 to 22,000. The flood was to cause difficulties abroad and even to produce fresh anti-semitism at home. But at least Gorbachev had reinstated one cherished human right, the right to travel freely.

He also moved on other fronts, and more conspicuously on humanitarian grounds. Aware of growing world interest, he established a commission on Human Rights in July 1986. In December, the month in which the prominent dissident Anatoly Marchenko died in jail, he freed Sakharov with his wife to return from Gorky to Moscow. The following February he started a broad review of the penal code. And by October 1989 Amnesty International could report that Gorbachev's amnesties had reduced the number of prisoners of conscience from about 600 in 1986 to under 100.

Although it took a good deal of pressure to force Gorbachev to take action on human rights, there is really no reason to doubt his humanitarianism. It was simply that, like Sakharov himself in an earlier period, his senses had been dulled to what was happening around him and that he had other priorities. Speaking to the Party in the middle of 1988 Gorbachev could claim that 'the ultimate goal of the reform of the political system, and the main yardstick of how efficiently we manage to carry it out, is the all-round enrichment of human rights'. But it was October 1989 before psychiatric abuse was finally thought to be at an end, and November before Gorbachev's visit to the Vatican signalled the end of Soviet restrictions on religious observance.

Gorbachev finally put himself in a position where people like Sakharov gave him respect and co-operated with him for what he was attempting to do and achieve. When Sakharov died suddenly in December 1989 he paid him a warm tribute; and many of the political changes Gorbachev introduced during 1990 were precisely those that Sakharov had urged him on. Whatever the position he started from, it was no wonder that in due course he was felt to be a champion of human rights.

Bill Wallace

To: General Secretary Mikhail Gorbachev

Dear Mikhail Sergeyevich:

First of all, let me express my deep gratitude that my wife, Elena Bonner, received permission to travel abroad to visit her mother, children and grandchildren, and to obtain medical treatment. I assume that this permission, so important to us, was made possible by your personal intervention.

I hope that your intervention may help to resolve another problem which deeply concerns me. It is also humanitarian in nature, but it is more complicated, and it has broader, national significance.

I am referring to the fate of prisoners of conscience, the term adopted by Amnesty International to describe persons detained for their beliefs or for actions motivated by their beliefs, provided that they have not used or advocated violence. The term 'prisoner of conscience' is thus more narrowly defined than the term 'political prisoner.'

In your interview published in *L'Humanite* on February 8, 1986, you asserted:

> 'Now, about political prisoners, we don't have any. Likewise, our citizens are not prosecuted for their beliefs. We don't try people for their beliefs.'

Mikhail Sergeyevich, it is true that the Criminal Codes of the Russian and other republics do not use the term 'political prisoner.' Articles 190-1, 70 and 142 of the RSFSR Criminal Code and the corresponding articles in the Codes of the other Soviet republics are not called political. (2) This may provide formal justification for saying that we don't have political prisoners, and that no one is prosecuted for his beliefs, but your advisors have misled you as to the real state of affairs. They may have done so unintentionally, influenced by their preconceptions. It is for you to decide whether this makes things any better.

Article 190-1 makes it an offense to circulate fabrications *known* to be false which defame the Soviet state or social system. A commentary on the Criminal Code published by *Yuridicheskaya literatura* states that 'the circulation of fabrications ... is not a crime under Article 190-1 if the person circulating them does not know them to be false.' In all the cases with which I am familiar, however, the courts have completely ignored this issue posed by illegal experts and common sense; they have avoided any discussion as to whether the defendant had knowingly circulated lies or had been expressing his or her sincere beliefs. In fact, the latter has been true. The absence of any proof of conscious intent is crucial under the law. *It means that people have in reality been convicted in court for their beliefs.*

My wife Elena Bonner is one victim of this illegitimate practice; I have written you in detail about her case.

The interpretation by the courts of Article 70 of the RSFSR Criminal Code is equally unjust. (This article is taken almost word-for-word from Stalin's Criminal Code. It was one of the points in the notorious Article 58. . .)

In all the cases known to me, honest, selfless people have been convicted under Articles 70 and 190-1 for the circulation of information which they firmly believed to be true and which in most instances was in fact true. (The information included objective news about: unjust trials, psychiatric abuse and other repressions; the important right to choose freely one's place and country of residence, to leave any country and to return to one's own country; the persecution of religious believers; and – of particular importance – conditions in places of detention, which are often incompatible with human dignity.) Despite the diatribes in our press, their motives in the overwhelming majority of cases were honorable – they were striving for justice, for openness and for the rule of law. People do not sacrifice themselves because of greed or vanity, for base or insignificant aims!

Article 70 speaks of 'agitation or propaganda carried on for the purpose of subverting or weakening the Soviet regime or of committing particular, especially dangerous crimes against the state, or the circulation for the same purpose of slanderous fabrications. . . ' In the cases known to me no one convicted under Article 70 had or could have had the purpose of subverting or weakening the Soviet regime or of committing a crime against the state. The courts have never attempted to prove that Article 70 defendants had such intentions. In both Article 70 and 190-1 cases, the courts substitute the endless repetition of empty, ritualistic formulas for a discussion of real issues, and sometimes, as in my wife's case, they resort to outright forgery. That may be the reason that the defendant's right to an open trial has been violated in every single case known to me of prosecutions under these articles. The courts have been packed with specially selected audiences; friends and sometimes relatives of the defendants were kept out by police cordons, even when the judge pronounced the verdict. Wrongdoing shuns the light of day.

Trials under Articles 70 and 190-1 clearly constitute prosecution because of the defendants' beliefs.

That is also true of many prosecutions under Article 142. It is formally concerned with the separation of church and state, but it is often used to punish nonviolent religious activity.

I am greatly disturbed by the revival of the cruel and unjust practice of trying prisoners again and again while they are serving their sentences. Prisoners of conscience 'resisting reeducation' – which means those who remain unbroken and defend their beliefs – can be tried using summary procedures and sentenced to new terms of imprisonment on the basis of inspired denunciations by their fellow convicts or charges directly initiated by the camp authorities.

I shall name a few of the prisoners of conscience known to me.

My friend, *Anatoly Marchenko*, has been sentenced under Article 70 to 10 years imprisonment and 5 years internal exile. (He was the victim of several prior unjust trials.) The main charge of his most recent trail involved his letter to the late Academician Petr Kapitsa asking him to protest my illegal exile to Gorky. (3)

(In regard to myself, let me simply repeat here that I consider the measures taken against me to be unjust and unlawful. I am ready to answer for my actions, like other prisoners of conscience, but I alone should bear the responsibility. It must not be shifted onto my wife or anyone else.)

Ivan Kovalev and his wife *Tatiana Osipova*, were convicted under Article 70 for public statements they made as members of the Moscow Helsinki Watch Group and as private individuals. The plight of this young couple, separated for many years, illustrates the illegality and cruelty of the persecution of prisoners of conscience. An affidavit about Kovalev issued by the camp authorities states that he was repeatedly confined in a punishment cell and subjected to other penalties *because he did not change his beliefs*. What idiots the camp overseers are! During Tanya Osipova's pre-trial investigation, her interrogator threatened that she would not receive needed medical care and thus would never be able to bear children unless she cooperated and altered her beliefs. A year ago, Osipova was sentenced to an additional two-year term after a camp trial.

Yuri Orlov, a corresponding member of the Armenian Academy of Sciences, *Victor Nekipelov*, a poet, and *Anatoly Shcharansky*, are other convicted Helsinki Group members. Nekipelov had been previously sentenced for his poetry; a court ruled that it contained slanderous philosophical ideas. Nekipelov is an exceptionally decent, intelligent and compassionate person. Now he is seriously ill.

I want to make a particular point about the Shcharansky case. No one should object to the exposure and prosecution of spies – that is the job of the state security organs. However, the charge against Shcharansky that he gathered information about refuseniks for publication (1) in an American newspaper has nothing in common with espionage.

Tatiana Velikanova, *Alexei Smirnov*, and *Yuri Shikhanovich* were convicted for editing *A Chronicle of Current Events*. (My friend Sergei Kovalev, a distinguished biologist and the father of Ivan Kovalev, served a ten year sentence on the same charge.) Tatiana Velikanova exemplifies the best traits of prisoners of conscience: absolute integrity, a desire to act openly and devotion to justice. From 1968 until 1982 *A Chronicle of Current Events* published objective information on the human rights situation in the USSR without editorial comment. Its history is the embodiment of the ideals of many self-sacrificing individuals.

Sergei Khodorovich was tried for administering a fund which assists political prisoners and their families. The fund is supported by contributions of Soviet citizens and by royalties from Alexander Solzhentisyn's books.

Smirnov and Khodorovich were severely battered during pre-trial detention by prisoners who were assigned to their cells for that purpose. The beating continued for many days. I do not know if other prisoners of conscience have suffered similar torture.

Mustafa Dzhemilev has repeatedly been tried for his defense of the Crimean Tatars' right to return to their homeland.

Mart Niklus was sentenced to ten years labor camp and five years internal exile for Helsinki Watch Group activity in Estonia and for signing a collective letter demanding the repudiation of the secret articles of the Molotov-Ribbentrop Pact. (Juri Kukk, who also signed the letter, died in a labor camp.) One has to meet Niklus, an ornithologist and a true scientist, an absolutely honest and sensitive person, to appreciate the full cruelty and injustice of his sentence.

Merab Kostava was sentenced to exile in 1978 for his attempts to preserve the cultural and historical heritage of the Georgian people. In contrast to his codefendant, Kostava refused to repent and was tried again on trumped up charges. I sent a telegram about this to Eduard Shevardnadze at the time. I do not want to condemn Kostava's codefendant; Shevardnadze disparaged him in a speech by saying that he was 'not a chevalier.' Every individual has his own problems and code of behaviour in extreme situations. But Kostava, to borrow Shevardnadze's phrase, is certainly a chevalier and a true son of Georgia.

I know everyone on this list except for two individuals, and absolutely trustworthy friends know those two well. Even if there is no general amnesty for prisoners of conscience, *I ask you to release all those named above*. I vouch for the good character, civic responsibility, integrity and altruism of every one of them.

I do not have recent information on these cases. One or two may have been released by now, but I rather doubt it.

Unquestionably, prosecution for one's beliefs or for actions motivated by them is a relatively rare occurrence now. There is no comparison with the deplorable Stalin era. I believe that the existence of prisoners of conscience in our country is a legacy of the intolerant, dogmatic ideas of those years, ideas that still affect the thinking and actions of some government officials.

I know personally some thirty prisoners of conscience. The figure of 200 prisoners, which you cited in another connection, probably is a significant portion of the total number. Additional prisoners of conscience are confined in prison psychiatric hospitals. Others have been convicted on fabricated criminal charges, such as hooliganism, resisting arrest, parasitism, and attempted rape. I suppose, however, that even with these additions, the number of prisoners of conscience is not very great, although I cannot supply exact figures.

There should not be any prisoners of conscience at all in a just society.

We can do little to affect the fate of prisoners of conscience in other countries, except through the example we set. We can, however, free our own prisoners of conscience. (Amnesty International works with some success on this problem in all countries.)

Release them and get rid of this painful issue. There are so few prisoners of conscience in relation to our population, but their release would have real humanitarian, moral, political and, I dare say, historical significance. It would substantially increase our country's prestige. It would make all international contacts easier. It would advance the openness of our society, international confidence and the cause of peace. It would gain the support of a significant part of the Soviet intelligentsia. It could change the psychological atmosphere in our country, and thereby open the way for a solution of the problems facing us. It would bring happiness at last to the prisoners' families after many years of underserved suffering. And this wise, humanitarian act would certainly evoke a positive response throughout the world.

I ask you to take steps to secure the release from prisons, labor camps, and exile of all prisoners of conscience convicted under Articles 190-1, 70 and 142 of the RSFSR Criminal Code and the corresponding articles of other republics, as well as those confined in special psychiatric hospitals (their release should not depend on the complete absence of mental illness) and those convicted on trumped up criminal charges.

Mikhail Sergeyevich! I hope you will ask your assistants to acknowledge receipt of this letter and, if possible, let me know your reaction to my request. I assign exceptional importance to the fate of prisoners of conscience.

with respect and hope,
Andrei Sakharov

In a letter to Gorbachev written on June 29, 1985, Sakharov stated his 'wish to cease public activities (apart, of course, from exceptional cases) and to concentrate on scientific work.' Sakharov was then on an extended hunger strike seeking permission for his wife to go abroad for medical treatment.

Article 190-1: The circulation of fabrications known to be false which defame the Soviet state or social system. Article 70: Anti-Soviet agitation and propaganda. Article 142: Violation of laws on separation of church and state and church and school. Articles 190-1 and 70 were abolished by the First Congress of Peoples' Deputies, in June 1989.

Marchenko is the author of My Testimony, *an account of the post-Stalin labor camps. On August 4, 1986, in a letter smuggled out of Chistopol Prison to the Vienna Conference, Marchenko announced a hunger strike demanding an end to the abuse of prisoners, punishment of the guards who banged his head on the cement floor of his cell, a visit with his wife, and an amnesty for all political prisoners. His 'Open Letter to Academician P.L. Kapitsa' was printed in* On Sakharov, *Knopf, New York, 1982, pp. 31-37. Marchenko died in prison presumably as the result of his hunger strike.*

In a telephone conversation with his relatives in Newton on September 1, Dr. Sakharov stated that he had not received a reply to his letter. He asked that Viktoras Petkus, *who was sentenced in July 1978 to ten years imprisonment and five years exile for his participation in the Lithuanian Helsinki Group, be added to his list of Article 70 prisoners of conscience.*

All of those mentioned in the letter, expect Marchenko who died, have been released; some because their terms expired.

Floral Park
New York, USA   31 March 1987

Dear General Secretary Gorbachev,

I read this morning of the visit of British Prime Minister Margaret Thatcher to the USSR. She had the hypocrisy to be critical of the Soviet Union's record on human rights. She also asked that the human rights issue be linked to the arms talk. You did rebuke her on that and for that I thank you so much. I only wish that you have been critical of Britain's record on human rights in Northern Ireland. I only wish that you had mentioned Northern Ireland in particular.

The British occupy the north-east corner of Ireland with military force and imprison and murder the Irish who oppose them. The British maintain a concentration camp at Long Kesh and a women's prison at Armagh. They have some one thousand political prisoners.

It seems that only the USSR is there to speak out in defense of those who are oppressed by Britain. You must do so with courage.

Please speak out and condemn British colonialism and oppression in Ireland.

I also ask that you speak out and condemn the United States for the continued imprisonment of Joseph Doherty. He has been held in a US Federal prison for over four years on no charge.

Thank you for anything that you and the USSR do to bring attention to the continued oppression of the Irish people by Britain.

Sincerely,
Patrick McVeigh

In 1981, Joseph Doherty escaped from the Crumlin Road Jail in Belfast and fled to New York where he was arrested by federal authorities under a warrant of extradition from the British Government. Three US courts have refused to turn Doherty over to the British Government, citing the political nature of his offences. However, he is being held without bail.

Tamarac
Florida, USA   29 September 1987

Dear Secretary Gorbachev,

Public opinion has taken over and recently when the US press mentioned you might be ill, there were expressions of genuine concern for your well-being and hopes that your leadership would continue for a long time to come because at last the world is breathing easier.

Something that may not have specifically been reported to you took place at a Human Rights Panel. Attention was called to the booklet entitled 'Criminal Alliance Between Zionism and Nazism'. The audience was shocked that such a vicious booklet filled with lies was still being printed and distributed by the Soviet Union in an era of glasnost.

Mr Samuel Zivis said it probably would not be reprinted, but he was too vague in his reply to win friends for the Soviet Union on this issue. This booklet is a source of deep pain to Jews all over the world because of its exaggerations. It even infers that Jews were responsible for the onset of World War II. Such nonsense does a terrible disservice to your country and counteracts much of the wonderful developments taking place under your leadership that people outside of the Soviet can identify with.

A statement from you that defamatary anti-semetic literature will no longer be published or tolerated would do more to create the kind of trust Minister Petrofsky spoke of in his magnificent speech than mention of mere technical matters.

Yours sincerely,
Florence & Michael Ross

COMMISSION ON SECURITY AND COOPERATION
IN EUROPE
Washington, DC, USA

29 September 1987

Dear General Secretary Gorbachev,

In April, I had the honor of visiting your country and meeting with you as a member of the Congressional Delegation led by Speaker of the House Jim Wright. Since then, I have followed events in your country with heightened interest.

As Chairman of the US Commission on Security and Cooperation in Europe, I am especially interested in human rights developments in light of commitments under the Helsinki Final Act. It seems to me that as your policy of glasnost grows, the human rights situation in your country will continue to develop in a positive direction. In this way, I hope the Soviet Union will move still closer to fulfilment of its human rights commitments under the Helsinki Final Act.

During my visit to the Soviet Union, members of the Wright Delegation also met with Soviet Foreign Minister Eduard Shevardnadze on 17 April. At that time, I presented Minister Shevardnadze with a list of cases of great concern to the eighteen Congressional Members of the Commission on Security and Cooperation in Europe. This list contained the names of 484 men and women imprisoned in the Soviet Union for their peaceful human rights activity.

When Minister Shevardnadze accepted these lists, he indicated that I would receive a response to them. I was gratified to learn from other sources that some of these cases have been solved. Nevertheless, I would appreciate receiving specific information from your government about the resolution of the human rights concerns which I have raised with you and other government officials.

It seems to me that more open communication between our government should be one of the benefits of glasnost. Certainly, I and other Members of Congress want to continue and deepen the process of dialogue. I look forward to hearing from you on this important matter.

With kind regards, I am

Sincerely,
Steny H. Hoyer
Chairman

The 484 persons referred to was based on Cronid Lubarksky's List of Political Prisoners in the USSR, published annually in Munich, FRG. Lubarsky was

123

a Soviet political prisoner who is now based in Munich. As a result of amnesties promulgated in February and June 1987, that list has been reduced and the majority of those not on the list are serving their term at Perm Labor Camp 35 in Russia. A few disputed cases are being held in psychiatric institutions. In early 1988, a Soviet spokesman claimed that a total of 356 prisoners confined on political charges had been released.

Genoa
Italy   30 November 1987

Dear Comrade Gorbaciov,

I learn with pleasure that you are examining the opportunity of renewing some aspects of your political-economic structure. In the West your initiative has been received with respect, but I must also say with some amazement, by those who are not irredeemably prejudiced. Bearing in mind that you are now gathering the fruit of past experience and showing the world and your own people that seventy years of Soviet communist learning have not been spent in vain, it becomes clear that this progress is a logical one and therefore nothing to be amazed about. This is confirmed by, among other things, the fact that you are the second greatest power in the world, and this not only for military reasons. The seventy years may seem to have been long, but they are in fact very short if one thinks of ancient Egypt, ancient Greece, or the Italy of the Caesars or of Leonardo. If man had made good use of his time, we would not still today be taking up arms, or discussing whether or not to take them up.

In the light of these facts, it must be agreed that modern man remains a poor creature, and this is true of all, regardless of classes or conditions, or still less of castes. You have reached a maturity which today provides you with certain guarantees which you are comparing in a very intelligent way with the results obtained by the Western democracies. It must be said that in these democracies, all that glitters is not gold.

Dear Gorbachiov, Italy is a free, democratic country thanks in part to you and the Resistance. But those sacred conquests have not always shown themselves to be worthy of those who created them. In fact, the trust of the Italian people diminishes constantly, and the need to look again at this type of democracy becomes ever more urgent; since people realise that probably, just as this democracy was born through the efforts of sincerely honest and democratic men, so it gives too much space to individual initiative which does not always contribute to collective well-being.

In fact, governments have shown themselves to be weak in the face of this phenomenon, incapable of putting a stop to the rising

124

tide of immoral behaviour which threatens to engulf our democratic institutions, leading the country once more into the chaos of a new dictatorship. We are weak and in this weakness many evils flourish: Mafia, Camorra, terrorism, criminality, vandalism, drug abuse, tax evasion, kidnappings, robbery, fraud, corruption particularly among politicians and public officials; the failings of transport and the postal system, rampant absenteeism in the public sector, poor health and hospital care, the dubious functioning of the judicial system and many other things which make the functioning of the democratic institutions ever more dubious. In addition retirement is too easy and we have an army of fake invalids. This phenomenon has been caused by politicians for their own electoral purposes, and also partly by the trades unions which in Italy number seventy and which have reduced the world of work to tatters, and the strange thing is that the workers agree to it. Finally, we have about twenty political parties which, according to them, exist to put Italy straight but, as you can imagine, it's not quite like that.

This is our democracy, which I believe is not very different from other Western democracies, and I should like to ask you this: do you have all these problems? If you have them, you are already a democracy and therefore do not need to make changes. If on the other hand you do not have all these evils which unfortunately afflict the democracies, I should like to give you a piece of advice, speaking as an honest socialist of long standing: go carefully, very carefully, because unfortunately man is more inclined to misunderstand than to value and to understand that the progress which is made towards a better society is a sign not of weakness but of maturity.

My dear Comrade, disarmament is not enough to ensure a finally real and sincere peace in the world. You can't talk about peace or disarmament if there isn't bread for everyone, love and brotherhood, honesty and trust, education and good sense. Sit round a table to help the world be better, more peaceful and more secure. Help the weak and the feckless, because you are not immune from the dangers which can arise everywhere and anywhere, at any moment. History, recent history, teaches us that.

Yours fraternally,
Libero Fontanini

Flushing
New York, USA   1 December 1987

Dear Mr Gorbachev,

I am very glad I have this opportunity to write to you. After watching and listening to you on American television, I am now better able to understand your ideas on many subjects that have been on my mind. Unfortunately I do not agree with many of your plans.

It is your opinion that if Nicaragua was taken over by the communists it will not represent a threat to the United States. I do not agree with your conclusion. How can American citizens feel safe from communism knowing that this threat is growing so close to their borders? How can we feel safe knowing that nuclear weapons might be aimed at the United States from strategic bases so close to us in Central America? You should be sensitive to our concerns and not let Nicaragua be influenced by the Sandinistas and a Marxist system of government.

I feel very strongly that your provisions for allowing Jews to emigrate are inhumane. The slow, complicated, and discouraging process for Soviet Jews to receive an exit visa is unfair. I am sure you understand how the Jewish people in your country are being treated. Soviet Jews have special reasons for wanting to leave the Soviet Union. In the land of their birth, they are not permitted religious and cultural freedoms. They cannot worship freely, publish Jewish books or newspapers, learn the Hebrew language, train rabbis, or teach their children. Soviet Jews are sick of reading anti-semitic articles in the Soviet press. They are tired of seeing Jews being portrayed as 'Zionist traitors' and 'Nazi criminals' on television.

That is why so many of them want to emigrate to Israel, the homeland of the Jewish people, or to other free countries. Many Soviet Jews have relatives in Israel and the United States with whom they hope to be reunited. Those Soviet Jews who have applied for exit visas have lost everything they have lived and worked for – their money, their belongings, and their professions. Soviet Jews who want to leave are branded as traitors and double-crossers. They have neither past nor future. They cannot plan anything, they cannot strive for anything, and they cannot dream of anything – except leaving the USSR for freedom.

Please Mr Gorbachev, free the Soviet Jews who want exit visas, and give them the chance they want.

Mr Gorbachev, you can change history. I am watching you. The world is watching you. Look to your heart and do what you know is right. You will be a better person for it, and your country will win more friends with this action than with all the missiles in the world.

Respectfully yours,
Marc Strongin

Düsseldorf
West Germany   14 January 1988

Dear Comrade Gorbachev,

I have read your book *Perestroika* with enthusiasm and it has provided me with a good deal of interesting information and arguments for my political work. I am very much in agreement with your new policy as it is set forth in the book, and hope that the good intentions you express will be put into effect as soon as possible.

I am not in agreement with the Chapter 'Women and the Family'. Here it seems to me that, by and large, you are satisfied with the present situation and you do not develop any suggestions of how true equality for women can be achieved.

In the theories and suggestions you put forward, you are still far behind what is being discussed in the progressive women's movement in the FRG or in other capitalist countries, and which is very much more difficult to put into effect in these countries than in a socialist society.

I agree with you that the Soviet Union has an exemplary record in achieving equal rights for women. I find it excellent that many women – as you describe in your book – are engaged in industry, science and politics. And it only remains for me to hope that still more women will move on up to more responsible positions, perhaps even one day make their way into the Politbureau.

But there is one thing I cannot understand: why do you give these committed women a bad conscience by attributing to them alone the blame for problems that arise within the family and among our young people?

In my opinion one can arrive at such a reproach only if one believes, as you do, that it is the task uniquely of the woman to be the housewife and educator and in addition to ensure that there is a good family atmosphere. I just ask myself: have men and fathers no responsibility at all for family and children?

Is it not time, at last, to bring about a change in men's awareness? Sadly there is not a word about that in your book.

A discussion of that subject would, it seems to me, be more relevant than a consideration of how women are to be enabled to return 'to their true womanly task in life'.

Is the intention to relegate women once again to the home, perhaps with them even taking on paid work that they carry out at home? It was a suggestion of this kind that I read recently with horror in the *Soviet Union Today*. This would mean going two steps backwards.

I think that in Women's politics as well, it is necessary to look forwards, and for me that means the following:

Men and women have equal responsibility for household, family and education of children. The working hours for both must be reduced. Working life must be so arranged that women and men can combine both paid work and the task of bringing up their children.

Now I know very well all these changes cannot be accomplished overnight. But in my opinion they ought to be formulated as one of the goals of a socialist society. Moreover, I am quite sure that in this way, you could gain the support of the majority of women for your new policy. I hope, however, that a policy that perpetuates the old assignment of gender roles will not be accepted by Soviet women.

Yours sincerely,
Gertrud Siemantel

Navrangpura
Ahmedabad, India   9 February 1988

Dear Mr Mikhail Gorbachev,

I have read with great interest your book *Perestroika*. It is a policy statement that elaborates what action has been taken during the last three years in the sphere of perestroika and glasnost and what further measures are sought to be taken.

Before I write in detail, I would like to introduce myself. From the age of seventeen, in 1920, I joined Gandhi's independence movement and had been in jails for a number of years fighting against the British rule. I have been a social and political worker and also industrialist having started many industries and have also done some governmental industrial and business assignments in the 50s and 60s.

I have studied Gandhian and other philosophies and written a book on Gandhian Trusteeship theory. Marx, Lenin and Gandhi wanted to establish equality as the ultimate goal though through different methods. In the present situation, yours is the only right way towards the goal they had in mind.

I feel your thinking and the method of execution is correct and the time for the same is ripe.

GANDHI'S SIX POINT FORMULA

1. Trusteeship provides a means of transforming the present capitalist order of society into an egalitarian one. It gives no quarter to capitalism, but gives the present owning class a chance of reforming itself. It is based on the faith that human nature is never beyond redemption;

2. It does not recognise any right of private ownership of property, except insofar as it may be permitted by society for its own welfare;

3. It does not exclude legislative regulation of ownership and use of wealth;

4. Under State-regulated Trusteeship, an individual will not be free to hold or use his wealth for selfish satisfaction or in disregard of the interests of society;

5. Just as it is proposed to fix a decent minimum living wage, a limit should also be fixed for the maximum income that would be allowed to any person in society. The difference between such minimum and maximum incomes should be reasonable and equitable and variable from time to time, so much so that the tendency would be towards obliteration of the difference eventually and

6. Under the Gandhian economic order, the character of production will be determined by social necessity and not by personal whim or greed.

Vadilal Lallubhai Mehta

ICFTU INTERNATIONAL CONFEDERATION OF FREE TRADE UNIONS
Brussels, Belgium

11 February 1988

Dear Mr Gorbachev,

INF Treaty, Human Rights

I am pleased to inform you that at its last meeting (Brussels, 14–18 December 1987), the ICFTU Executive Board received the report of the meeting between yourself and the ICFTU delegation on Peace, Security and Disarmament held in Moscow on 9 October, welcomed the signing of the INF Treaty, and urged the Supreme Soviet and the United States Senate to ratify the Treaty at an early date. May I thus take this opportunity to personally congratulate you for this important success on the path to total elimination of nuclear arms, and express the hope that the examination of the Treaty recently initiated by the Commissions for Foreign Affairs of the Union's and the Nationalities' Soviets will lead to its rapid ratification by the USSR Supreme Soviet. May I also add that the Executive Board very much appreciated your receiving the ICFTU delegation in October and the comprehensive discussion which took place.

Turning to other matters, let me express the ICFTU's satisfaction at the recent release from psychiatric hospitals of Vladimir Khlebanov and Vladimir Gershuni, two independent trade unionists about whom the ICFTU had been making representations to Soviet authorities for many years, including at the time of our recent visit to Moscow. In our view, this is a positive measure and will be appreciated as such by the affiliates of the ICFTU.

However, we have received information concerning a number of other individual cases where it appears that basic human rights of Soviet citizens are still violated. In this connection we refer to the continuing detention or exile of a number of persons who, according to our information, were imprisoned or interned on the basis of their personal convictions, or to other persons who appear to have been otherwise victimised, including by discriminatory measures at their place of work. A memorandum of some of the cases about which we have recently received information is enclosed.

The considerable amount of reports reaching us on these subjects leads me to request, on behalf of the ICFTU, your personal intervention with the appropriate Soviet legislative authorities in order that they take positive steps with regard to the adoption and immediate implementation of amendments to a number of provisions of the RSFSR Criminal Code and corresponding legislation in the other Republics, which have been the basis for judicial action against independent trade unionists and other advocates of human rights in the Soviet Union over a number of decades. For instance, the obtaining by Mrs Dalia Tamutyte, from Klaipeda (mentioned in our memorandum), of practical guarantees against arbitrary psychiatric internment, appear essential to the ICFTU, particularly since the USSR Supreme Soviet has approved revised rules concerning the legal basis to admissions in a psychiatric hospital, as reported by the Novosti Press Agency on 14 January 1988.

Furthermore, I would appreciate learning whether the Supreme Soviet of the USSR is indeed considering abolishing internal exile as a form of criminal punishment, as suggested by the USSR Minister of Justice, Mr D. V. Kravtsov on 9 November 1987 in Moscow and, if so, when the adoption of such a positive measure may be expected.

Another measure which would be highly appreciated by the ICFTU's membership would be the withdrawal or revision of articles 70 and 190 para. 1 of the RSFSR Criminal Code, which are the legal basis for sentences imposed on a considerable number of prisoners of conscience, including several on behalf of whom the ICFTU has intervened over the years with the Soviet authorities. While we have noted several press reports indicating that such a legislative process was presently being considered we have no information of any practical steps taken in this respect. If this revision is indeed to take place, the ICFTU would hope that any new legislation would fully take into account the need to protect the universally recognised right to freedom of opinion and expression, and that the new rules would not be applied so as to impair the free exercise of this right.

May I thus request you to let me know whether and, if so, when art. 70 and 190 para 1 may cease to exist in their present form. I would also be grateful if you could inform the relevant Soviet legislative bodies of the ICFTU's concerns regarding these two laws as they are currently formulated and applied.

Yours sincerely,
John Vanderveken
General Secretary

ICFTU request to CPSU General Secretary M. Gorbachev for intervention on specific cases of human and worker's rights violations (February 1988)

Ms Dalia Tamutyte, from Klaipda (Lithuanian SSR), has, according to our information, received an official reprimand at her workplace, the Klaipda Committee of Trade, on 10 September 1987, for having attended a peaceful rally on 23 August 1987 in Vilius, was fired from her job on 18 November, on the same grounds, and had earlier been barred from working in her own profession (as music teacher) on the basis of her religious convictions. Furthermore, we have been informed of a failed attempt to remove her from her home against her will in order to commit her to a psychiatric institution after her dismissal. An agent of the militia by the name of Kazlov, accompanied by an officer of the local branch of KGB, is also reported to have inquired subsequently from her mother why Ms Tamutyte refused psychiatric care. Ms Tamutyte's mother was reportedly also told by local militia authorities that her daughter was a psychiatric patient, a fact which the Klaipeda psychiatric institution was unable to confirm. The ICFTU thus requests you to intervene with respect to Ms Tamutyte's employment (which could constitute an infringement of her rights under Convention 111 (Discrimination in Employment) of the International Labour Organisation, ratified by the USSR) be immediately repealed, that she be fully compensated for any losses incurred and that all necessary measures be taken in order to fully guarantee her safety from arbitrary psychiatric internment.

According to our information, **Mr Valentin Pavlovich Yelchaninov**, from Krasnoyarsk, was dismissed form his post in a local school on 22 December 1987, while **Ms Natalya Grigoryevna Voronina** was reprimanded at her job and threatened with dismissal, after a radio broadcast on 18 December of a resolution by the local Workers' Deputies Soviet concerning informal associations. The resolution specifically criticised the 'Club for the Assistance of Perestroika' and the 'Fatherland' Club, founded by V Yelchaninov, N Voronina and Andrei Zaitsev, in order to promote the democratisation process in the USSR and defend human rights. The 'Fatherland' Club, which had been forced by the authorities to cease its activities soon after its foundation, had been reconstituted on 20 October. The ICFTU thus requests you to intervene with the competent authorities in Krasnoyarsk with a view to reinstating Mr Yelchaninov in his previous post and protect both him and Ms Voronina from any further discrimination in employment, which is contrary to the provisions of ILO Convention 111.

Mr Balys Gajauskas, sentenced in April 1978 under art. 68 of the Lithuanian SSR criminal code (art. 70 of the RSFSR criminal code) to ten years of hard labour (special regime) and five years exile, for circulating samizdat literature, and previously detained from 1948 to 1973, is now reported to be in internal exile in Chumikan, in the Chabarovsk Territory (Far East). The ICFTU has reasons to believe that Mr Gajauskas has been sentenced for the peaceful expression of his convictions, despite the publication on 26 December 1987 by the New York Times of a letter from the Soviet Prosecutor Rakhmanin, presenting Mr Gajauskas as a common criminal. The ICFTU thus requests you to intervene with the competent judicial authorities in order that Mr Gajauskas, whose state of health is reported as serious, be immediately released from exile and authorised to reside at the place of his choice, including abroad if he so wishes.

Mr Levko Hrygorovich Lukyanenko, from Chernigov (Ukrainian SSR), sentenced in August 1978 to ten years forced labour (special regime) and 5 years of exile, under art. 62 paragraph 2 of the Ukrainian SSR criminal code, for his participation in independent human rights activities, recently released from uchr. VS-389/36-1 (Permskaya obl.), is presently, according to our information, in internal exile in the Tomsk region. We have been informed that he suffers from several ailments, including myocardial ischaemia. The ICFTU thus requests you to intervene with the competent judicial authority in order that Mr Lukyanenko be immediately exempted from serving his full term of exile, and that in the meantime, he be allowed to benefit from adequate medical care, including outside his zone of exile if needed, as provided by relevant Soviet legislation. The ICFTU would also appreciate receiving full information as to the exact location of his place of exile.

Mr Mikhail Ignatievich Kukobaka, a metal worker from Bobruisk (Byelorussian SSR), re-arrested in labour camp in 1984 while nearing the end of an accumulated term of six years hard labour, and sentenced under art. 70 (RSFSR criminal code) to an additional term of seven years hard labour (strict regime) and five years of exile, has also been reported as suffering from several ailments. The ICFTU has furthermore been informed that Mr Kukobaka has already spent over seventeen years in detention because of his personal convictions, and would therefore urge you to intervene with the competent judicial authorities with a view to obtain the immediate and unconditional release of Mr Kukobaka, for humanitarian reasons.

All of the people mentioned in the ICFTU Request as exiled or in labour camps have subsequently been released.

Langeskov
Denmark

8 March 1988

Dear Michael Gorbachev,

... The reason why I, as the representative of the Danish pacifist movement, Beyond War, write to you is to draw attention to a particular point at which so far very little, or indeed nothing at all, has been done. As a movement, our work has always been devoted to the dissemination of peace. As we see it, the objection to military service on the grounds of conscience has always been an indispensable means to this end. Therefore we have fought for the recognition of this right all over the world – a fight which in Denmark as early as 1917 resulted in the establishment of the right to conscientious objection. Recently both the United Nations and the European Community recognise conscientious objection as one of the human rights.

For reasons of conscience, a conscientious objector cannot bear arms against his fellow men – he or she does not recognise the existence of human beings as enemies and therefore cannot direct weapons against people. Organisations, ideologies and structures can be enemies. Trained in non-violent methods, the conscientious objector will be able to take effective action against, for example, organisers of coups working internally or foreign forces of occupation. Inspired by, among other things, Gandhi's struggle for India's independence, we believe that we can set up a significantly more effective and more acceptable defence against war than the army, which itself makes use of the methods of war.

This means that conscientious objectors can actually be of use to their country. Experience with conscientious objectors has shown that their loyalty and the contribution they make to the country's cultural, social, economic and moral development and defence, is second to none, provided their pacifist principles are respected and they get the opportunity to use their initiative where they feel that it can be of benefit.

In Denmark, conscientious objectors are stationed in social institutions, museums, in relief organisations, and peace institutes,

133

in research institutes, in theatres, colleges and many other useful places. The same thing could well be done elsewhere, including in the Soviet Union. Whether the work carried out is social or cultural work, development projects in outlying areas of the Soviet Union, or voluntary help in countries of the Third World, can be determined in accordance with the individual's capacities and wishes. The most important thing is that the person concerned feels that he or she is doing useful work, and is respected - in other words: that conscientious objectors also have the experience of contributing to their country's well being.

Unfortunately, there are indications that openness in the Soviet Union has not extended that far. On the contrary, conscientious objectors are still sent to jail. Among other groups, members of the religious sect, the Pentecostalists, refuse, out of deeply felt religious principles, to carry out military service. For this, they are imprisoned and according to Amnesty International, are often subjected to demeaning treatment in Soviet prisons or camps.

Developments may gradually have progressed so far that even the right to refuse military service can at least be contemplated.

In conclusion, I would not want to omit drawing attention to the fact that in his day, Lenin himself signed a decree concerning conscientious objection which, since that time, has been completely pushed aside. On 4 January 1919, Lenin signed the decree 'concerning exemption from carrying out compulsory military service on the ground of religious convictions'. In its first paragraph, it states:

'1. Persons who, because of religious convictions, are unable to take part in military service are, in accordance with the decision of the people's court of justice, granted the right to carry out that duty in the form of service in the medical sphere, preferably in hospitals that deal with epidemic diseases, or in other corresponding work that is of benefit to society, selected according to the conscript's own choice. The period of service will be the same as that of the military service.'

This is an excellent precedent on which you can take your stand in this case. In the middle of a civil war, in 1919, Lenin himself was able to accept the principle of conscientious objection for those who found the use of weapons contrary to the promptings of their conscience. If he was able to do so at that time when the very existence of the young Soviet Union was threatened, how much more easily can it be accepted when the existence of the Soviet Union and its borders are firmly established, and we are moving into a period of detente.

Yours in peace,
Peter Kragh Hansen

National Rainbow Coalition
Washington DC, USA

April 1988

Dear Mr President,

I am addressing this communication to Your Excellency to express our full support for the recently concluded agreement, signed at the United Nations, providing for an end to South Africa's illegal military occupation of Namibia and a process for the exercise of independence by the Namibian people. Yet it is also important to express our deep apprehension and concern regarding certain recent developments that threaten to undermine that significant achievement.

The thaw in the 'Cold War' in which your government continues to play such a vital and decisive role, is the most hopeful development in recent times. It is my fervent hope this process will continue to rapidly expand aided by more people-to-people contacts, and a diplomacy of peace between the US and the USSR.

The signing of the agreement last December represented an important breakthrough in the long-standing problem of Namibian independence. Undoubtedly this breakthrough was assisted by the favorable political climate, resulting from a relaxation of East-West tension and the growing international recognition of the United Nations as an instrument for the settling of regional conflicts.

In recent discussions I have held on the continent with a number of African Heads of State, my lasting impression is of the high hopes they have that the road to peace in Southern Africa has finally been opened up by this agreement. Yet, side by side, with this cautious optimism there are some harsh realities that serve as a warning and must be heeded.

1. The apartheid regime, through the forced conscription of Namibian youth has created an indigenous military force under South African command. There is evidence this military force build-up will be used to terrorize the local population, especially during the months prior to the upcoming elections. 'Death Squads' are already an organized component of their everyday operations.

2. Futhermore the apartheid regime's paid mercenaries, UNITA, under Jonas Savimbi are currently being granted 'citizenship' in Namibia and provided with ID cards enabling them to operate as a fifth column, carrying out South Africa's orders and further destabilizing the situation.

3. South Africa is accelerating the system of plundering Namibia's mineral resources in violation of the inalienable rights of the Namibian people to exercise sovereign control over their resources.

These and other developments are obviously designed to torpedo the agreement reached in December. They prove, once again, the apartheid regime cannot be trusted to abide by the rule of law that governs international relations between countries. The role that your government played in helping to formulate the original resolution #435 which has served as a cornerstone of the independence agreement was most significant.

Since your government is a permanent member of the UN Security Council I appeal to you, Your Excellency, to use the full weight of your good office in this present emergency, to strengthen the role of UNTAG as the guardian of the agreement and the best hope for peace in the region. A strong presence by the UN in Namibia is an indispensable prerequisite for the protection of the peace process and the right of the Namibian people to gain their independence in free elections this year. It will be most unfortunate if budget constraints were used as an excuse to undermine this goal. To weaken our resolve in this matter or abandon the Namibian people at this critical moment would be an unconscionable act.

I am sure we are in one accord in our firm commitment to the principle of international cooperation designed to bring an end to apartheid in South Africa and Namibia. Today this commitment has its most visible and concrete manifestation in the kind of resolute support our country gives to a strong UN presence in Namibia, guaranteeing free elections this year.

Beyond the elections, the permanent member states of the Security Council should set the example by extending to a free Namibia the kind of long-term development assistance that will help secure their economic and cultural requirements. This will enable them to intensify their efforts to overcome the deprivation imposed by a century of colonialism.

Such a UN presence will help bring to victorious conclusion the long arduous struggle of the Namibian people for their national sovereignty. This will mark a victory for all humanity and it is within our grasp. With all best wishes for your good health and with kindest personal regards to Your Excellency.

Sincerely,
Jesse L. Jackson
President

cc: Secretary General, Dr Javier Perez de Cuellar

As of March 1990, the South African government began a judicial inquiry into political killings. A military unit called the Civil Cooperation Bureau established in 1985 under Viljoen, is connected to a covert war against 'enemies of the state.'

Resolution 435 adopted in 1978, established the process for 'free and fair elections' in Namibia. It was implemented on April 1, 1989 after the US and the Soviet Union brokered an agreement calling for South African and Cuban troop pull-outs from Angola.

After 75 years of South African rule, Namibia held its first elections on November 7, 1989. Ten parties were represented, including SWAPO and DTA. 701,483 voters chose a 72- member constituent assembly to draft a constitution. SWAPO won the election and independance was granted from South Africa on March 20,1990. Sam Nujoma was sworn in as president after serving three decades in exile.

On March 21, 1989 the flag was lowered and replaced with a new one.
SWAPO (South West Africa Peoples Organization) has led the Namibian people in an unrelenting struggle to rid the country of South African occupation. It has been recognized by the United Nations as the sole authentic representative of the country.

Wiesbaden
West Germany

20 May 1988

Dear General Secretary Gorbachev,

In the photographs I am sending, you can also see a small Russian boy. My father wrote at the time that this was a boy of my age, and every time my father saw him, he thought of me. At that time, Adolf Hitler had given permission for sons to visit their fathers in the area close to the Front Line and my father invited me in his letter to come and visit him. But my mother would not allow me to go. Sadly my father has since died and I am unable to find his letter. My mother, now almost eighty-three, is able to confirm all this.

Because my mother's refusal to let me travel to the USSR at that time probably prevented the development of a close friendship between me and the boy, I have decided to try to make up for lost time now, within the framework of my Peace and Aid programme. For that reason, I would like to ask Pravda in Moscow to publish the picture of my father with the boy, so that the man, who must now be about fifty-four years of age, can be traced and we can catch up on that friendship. At the same time I shall get the picture published in a German newspaper, so that perhaps some wartime companion of my father who has survived may be able to provide some information on the place where they were stationed in the USSR. On one of the pictures, the registration number of the tracked vehicle can be seen very clearly, so it will be possible to establish the operational area.

Yours sincerely,
Werner König

WORLD COMMITTEE FOR THE
UN DECADE OF DISABLED PERSONS
Washington, DC, USA

25 May 1988

Dear Mr General Secretary,

The United Nations Decade of Disabled Persons has entered its final half. I am writing again, in my capacity as Chairman of the World Committee for the UN Decade of Disabled Persons, to request your leadership and cooperation.

We ask that you speak out at the 1988 UN General Assembly on the imperative for action to realize the potential of the Decade of Disabled Persons.

As you know, UN Secretary General Javier Perez de Cuellar was charged in a General Assembly resolution again last year to generate greater worldwide visibility for the UN Decade and its goals. But he needs the help of all of us – and especially of yourself and other world leaders.

Let us help the Secretary General fulfill his mandate and bring this significant commitment adopted unanimously by all nations to full realization! Five hundred million disabled men, women, and children, and all nations of the world, stand to gain.

Respectfully yours,
Alan A. Reich
Chairman

cc: His Excellency Javier Perez de Cuellar

A TEN-POINT WORLD AGENDA
FOR THE DECADE OF DISABLED PERSONS

The following ten points are based on the UN World Programme of Action:

1. Increase participation of disabled persons in social, cultural, religious, recreational and community life, and in decision-making at all levels.

2. Expand education, training and job opportunities.

3. Remove all barriers – architectural, transportation, communications and legal – to full participation and equalization of opportunity.

4. Increase acceptance of disabled persons through communication and education programs.

5. Prevent disabling diseases and conditions through expanded immunization and improved environmental, occupational and other health programs.

6. Prevent disabling accidents at home, at work, on the road. Everywhere.

7. Restore sight, hearing, movement, and communications to disabled perons through increased access to known, appropriate measures.

8. Expand community-based rehabilitation services and self-help programs involving disabled persons and their family members.

9. Conquer or cure major disabling conditions through greater and more purposeful application of biomedical research.

10. Involve everyone – disabled and non-disabled, young and old, rich and poor, men and women, from every country, culture and creed – in cooperative efforts at local, national, regional and international levels to conquer or prevent disability and release human potential for the benefit of all.

THE SENATE OF THE STATE OF TEXAS
Austin, Texas, USA

6 June 1988

Dear Mr Secretary,

My name is Carl A. Parker. I am a State Senator from the state of Texas, in the southern part of the United States. I have been an elected official for more than twenty-five years and currently represent more than 500,000 constituents.

I write to you today to express my great admiration and respect for your leadership role in bringing about glasnost in your country. You have truly improved the well-being of all Soviet people and made the Soviet Union a greater nation in the eyes of the world.

Of particular merit is the marked increase of Jewish emigration allowed in 1987. As I understand, more than 5,400 Jews were allowed to emigrate in 1987 as compared to only 914 in 1986. However, with more than 380,000 Jews applying for emigration from your country, it would seem that more might be done to allow the freedom of movement recognized by your policy of openness.

I call on you with the backing of a large number of Americans to continue to increase the number of Jews allowed to emigrate and to surpass the 1979 level of more than 51,000.

Your entire term of office has been marked by great strides forward for the Soviet people. The entire world community watches your administration with fascination.

Should you make another trip to the United States, I extend my hospitality and that of my fellow Texans.

Sincerely,
Carl A. Parker

Winchburgh
West Lothian, Scotland   13 June 1988

Dear Mr Gorbachev,

I write as an individual within my country of Scotland but my belief is that my views represent those of many of my countrymen.

My specific reason for writing to your arises out of remarks made by President Reagan both while he was in Russia and also his speech at the Guildhall in London.

Firstly, his quite insensitive remarks about human rights in the Soviet Union. While I agree there is a need for even greater freedom within your country – and I pray for the release of 'prisoners of conscience' – I am fully convinced that you are doing all that you possibly can to improve the situation. I am sure you must feel you are walking a tightrope as you decide how far and how fast you can take each step. It seems to me this is fairly self-evident to most of us – albeit from outside your country. I was appalled that President Reagan should make such a statement while a guest within your country. More importantly I feel that it was the height of hypocrisy for the leader of a nation which profited so greatly from the slave trade and took so long to bring about reform (as indeed was true for the United Kingdom). More recently his nation, in full world view, took an endless time to respond to the Civil Rights Movement inspired by Dr Luther King and others. I feel a sense of shame at being part of the so-called 'West' when such blatant hypocrisy is displayed by one of our leaders. We all long for improved 'human rights' in every part of our world but I pray that leaders such as President Reagan can deal with you and others with a great deal more humility than has so far been shown. My belief in the character and nature of God leads me to believe that this hypocrisy and lack of humility will be called to account one day. In the meantime I can only hope you can forgive the 'West' for these things.

Secondly, as you will probably know, Mr Reagan claimed at the Guildhall that the progress made at the Summit was due to the 'strength' of the United States and Britain over the past decade. Once again I felt ashamed at the audacity and self-deception which allows both he and Mrs Thatcher to make this claim. It seems clear to me, and again to many of my countrymen, that the only reason there has been progress has been your policy of 'glasnost'. Indeed,

140

the path seems to have been strewn with such horrendous obstacles (such as the so-called Strategic Defence Initiative) that it is a miracle that you kept going with the process at all. I cannot repent on behalf of these 'leaders'. No doubt they would claim that they have nothing for which they need repent. It is however a clear biblical principle that those who would be true to God should repent, at least before God, for the sins of the leaders of their own nation.

Yours respectfully,
Ian M. Reed

Baylor College of Medicine
Houston, Texas, USA

16 June 1988

Dear Mr Gorbachev,

I would like to express my appreciation for your efforts to promote peace and understanding between our two countries. As a token of that appreciation I am enclosing a copy of my book, *The Human Rights Movement*, which seeks to promote dialogue between the US and the USSR on human rights.

Like many Americans, I was embarrassed by President Reagan's behaviour at the Moscow summit. His failure to understand that we have our own human rights problems (American Indians, homeless) and his inappropriate sermonizing on human rights did little to enhance dialogue on this important subject and demeaned human rights by turning it into a polemical weapon.

I agree with you that each country needs to learn more about the other's concept of human rights – that we need a lot more listening and a lot less confrontation. This is the basic argument of my book.

I agree with Reagan that, as an American, I would like for the USSR to show more respect for political and religious freedoms. But I also believe that we Americans have just as much, if not more, to learn from the socialistic countries regarding the right to jobs, housing, and basic medical care. In the book I argue that the US should not try to foist its own concept of human rights upon the rest of the world but that we should work toward a rapprochement between Western and non-Western points of view.

With great admiration,
Warren Holleman PhD

141

Mahanoy City
Philadelphia, USA   30 June 1988

Dear Mr Gorbachev,

First may I introduce myself. My name is Victor Sherkness,
Mahanoy City, Philadelphia, USA.

Second the reason I'm writing this letter is to ask your help in
finding someone, if possible, because I know you are very busy with
many important matters.

Many years ago my grandparents came to America, from Russia.
I'm sending some information that I have from my grandmother's
family when she used to write to her sister Dorothy in Russia. I
only have an address. She also had a sister Fredia. I do not have
her address. My grandmother Christine's maiden name was Tahill.
I'm not sure but I'm also sending you a copy of her passport, or what
is left of it. I hope it can help out. My grandmother was born in 1895
– died in 1978.

As for my grandfather I only have his name – Prockup Hruniuk
1888–1935.

If you can help me in any way to find out if I still have family in
Russia and give them my address and send me theirs so we can write
to each other.

You see Mr Gorbachev, I loved my grandmother very much, and
in my heart I would like to know about my family in Russia and
maybe someday visit with them if possible in your Great Country.

Caachoo.
Thank you,
Victor Sherkness

Rosyln
New York, USA   4 July 1988

Dear Sir,

Before I offer you my suggestions, I want to tell you who the writer
of this letter is. My grandparents came to the United States in the
early 1900s. They came because the village of Miedseritz which was
part of the Ukraine prior to 1918 was an unsafe place to live. Jews
lived in Miedseritz, or Meseritz, since the 1600s. They were invited
to the region from the city of Frankfurt-on-the-Main in Germany
because they were given religious freedom. The Ukrainians, and the
Czars massacred the Jews because their religious training included
hate and murder of the Jews. I therefore trust that your plea for
world cooperation with the new policies, laws, aspirations of the

Soviet Union is not a propoganda ploy that is not the initial phase of another plan for world conquest.

May I suggest that if you are going to restructure the Soviet system, justice dictates that all political prisoners be freed from your prisons and gulags. Usually the brains, the leaders with leadership ability are often found in the prisons. A different road for the Soviet Union dictates that the political opposition be freed from their shackles so they may contribute to the growth of your free society. If the society is to be free the political prisoners may be of great assistance in the new plan. Your approach appears to be a departure from the old system. It was said that, 'The Russian has three principles: perhaps, somehow, and never mind.' Your plan is a departure from these principles, only if changes are made soon.

Restore the principles laid down in the Soviet constitution. 'Officials eat hot food, the people eat cold.' People must be given the opportunity to go to the market and buy new products, styles change and the people cannot buy 'fresh food' if all they see and can afford is 'stale'. The Soviet Union does not send its products all over the world. I cannot buy a Soviet computer in New York. I am unable to find any products from the Soviet Union in the marketplace. May I offer my suggestions to you for consideration:

A. Restore private ownership of essential goods and services. Greater productivity will result from a planned transition to this free marketplace economy.

B. Organize a banking system that encourages the investment of foreign funds in your country. 'Counting other people's money will never make you rich.' The ruble should float free in the free currencies of the world.

C. Restore your stock exchange. Encourage national and international acceptance and faith in your country by hard currency. A planned movement in this direction would encourage greater planning in an open market and encourage greater economic, political, and social progress. The leadership of your tremendous country did not carve their words in stone, changes have to be made with the changing conditions of the times and events. I urge you to consider this idea, and plan for this change in an orderly manner acceptable to your principles and philosophy.

D. Re-evaluate the Marxist-Leninist philosophy of international revolution as the method of making the world a socialist state. You will have no problem of finding converts to socialism if socialism creates political, economic, and social freedom. If a government of the people does not create happiness for the general population that government becomes evil and the country becomes a prison.

E. Maintain a strong line of defense for your country, but recall all your soldiers from their positions in foreign countries. Call on all peace-loving countries of the world to do the same in a planned systematic manner that maintains a strong defense capability without being hostile or aggressive.

F. Your country is a land of beauty, culture, diversity, and enormous wealth. The USSR should establish both an immigration as well as an emmigration policy. This system should be carefully planned so that the USSR truly takes on the mantle of a free country. True freedom means that a country becomes a home not a tolerable prison.

Sincerely yours,
Aaron Stein

Kew Gardens
New York, USA · 20 July 1988

Mr Secretary General,

I am writing to you, without any illusion that you will read or respond. Nevertheless I have to write because today I am a very disappointed Armenian. I am disappointed with the decision of the Supreme Soviet concerning the Autonomous Region of Artsakh (Nagorno-Karabakh). But especially I am disturbed by the unkind, untrue, and inflammatory attitude and remarks of the members of the Presidium about the Armenians. The proceedings of the Presidium have forced us, millions of Armenians, to reassess our cherished fond sentiments about the Russian people, and reassess our longstanding and firm support for Armenia's perpetual membership within the Soviet family. The Presidium has penalized the Armenians for making a constitutional, rightful, and peaceful request. But it has rewarded the Azerbaijanis for the Massacre of Sumgait and their oppression of the Armenians. What is the moral lesson to be drawn from this?

As the resolution of the Supreme Soviet recognizes, the constitutional rights of the Armenians in Artsakh have been systematically violated by the Azerbaijani authorities. The Armenians have known this for decades and in vain tried to bring it to Moscow's attention. Now then, Mr Secretary General, who are the true anti-Soviet and nationalist agitators? The oppressed Armenians who are asking to assure their constitutional rights? Or the Azerbaijani authorities who have oppressed them, disenfranchised them from the ideals and goals of Lenin and the Soviet system?

144

We, Armenians of the Diaspora with close ties to our ancestral Homeland, are willing to participate in any dialogue. Our sole purpose and desire would be simply to facilitate your task and assist in the subsequent development of the region. We can bring our resources and a different perspective to the problem which would contribute to a speedy and satisfactory resolution. We could also contribute towards the realization of your broader plans of glasnost and perestroika.

Sir, I would have liked to say all the above, and much more, looking at you directly in the eyes. Maybe one day. In the meanwhile I earnestly hope that through your words and deeds you will rebuild our shattered confidence and restore our fond sentiments. With my best wishes to you and Mrs Gorbachev.

Respectfully yours,
Simon Yeznig Balian

Angers
France   September 1988

Dear Secretary General,

The 'Monastery of the Caves' in Kiev (Kievo-Petcherskaia Lavra), the birthplace of Russian monasticism, was one of the foremost Christian spiritual centres. The names of Anthony and Theodosius, its founders, are the first in a long list of saints venerated throughout Russia and the Christian world. The relics of many of them are still in place, intact.

It is thus particularly regrettable that this monastery was closed for worship and community life in 1961 and was transformed at that time and still serves today as a museum of atheism. This use for such a place deeply shocks the consciences not only of Christians but also of men of good-will who cling to respect for basic human rights.

We beseech you to put an end to this intolerable situation by giving back to the Church, 1,000 years after it came into existence, the possibility of using as it sees fit the Monastery of the Caves in Kiev, that monument of Christian art and architecture. At a time when you claim that you wish to re-establish the principles of democratisation and when the thousandth anniversary of the baptism of the great prince Vladimir is being solomnly celebrated, you would in this way be making a concrete gesture which would allow believers in the Soviet Union to hope for the reintegration into the national community as full citizens rather than remain 'second zone' citizens, to use the expression employed by the Metropolitan Alexis of Leningrad.

Yours faithfully,
Renée Levesque

145

Delaware
Ohio, USA

October 1988

Very respectable Michail Sergeevich,

Fifty-two years ago, almost to the day, as a sixteen-year-old living in Kiev, I wrote a three-page letter to Pavel Petrovich Postyshev. It was a passionate appeal for justice.

My father, Josif Severinovitch Trachevski, director of a very large state farm belonging to the Kiev-based 64th Moto-mechanized Corp of the Red Army, was arrested on charges of being a White Army colonel. For three months after his arrest we did not hear from him.

My father was practically illiterate. He was the son of a Polish deportee following the 1863 Revolution where his grandfather was a leading revolutionary deported to the Siberian city of UFA where he died in Katorga.

My father was very handsome. He had the immaculate fingers of a horseman, had a mustache and was always dressed in the paramilitary clothes which were popular at that time. For that appearance, he was arrested seven times in his life in the USSR and was once sentenced to death by shooting. Only the relentless energy and efforts of my mother helped him to get out of prison all of these times.

However, in 1936, in Kiev, it was different. This time the officials at NKVD did not even let my mother speak to them.

I decided to write a letter to Comrade Postyshev. At the time of Postyshev's service in the party apparatus of Ukraine in 1934, 1935 and 1936, all of us lived good. There was enthusiasm, there was spirit of joy, there was mass rehabilitation of parks, schools, apartment houses, and a lot of new construction. The stores were full of good (excellent!) food and clothes and other goods were readily available. There was a feeling of freedom in the air of our streets.

In my letter to Postyshev, I wrote (among other things), 'my father was never in any army except in the 1st Cavalry where he was in charge of mustering horses for the Army. He is not educated sufficiently enough to be a sergeant, let alone a colonel in the White Army. His entire education was four years of parochial school in the village church.'

I wrote about my excellent grades in school. I wrote about my mother sitting up long nights sewing clothes to make a living so that we could buy my father good food which I brought in a small basket to the prison every morning before going to school. Every time I did that, I was afraid that the guard would not accept my basket because that would mean that, the night before, my father had been shot in the head by a small caliber Nagant revolver.

I mailed the letter.

Three days later, in the evening, I was riding in a blue Cadillac convertible driven by an NKVD sergeant to the building of the Central Committee of the Communist Party of the Ukraine, about five short blocks from my home. A young captain of NKVD was sitting next to me. He was very polite. I was very scared.

In the building of CK, I was led to the office of Comrade Postyshev. In real life he looked much older than on the posters which were carried by people on May Day and October Revolution parades. He was stern and quiet. He had my letter in front of him. He called me 'Yura', just as if he were my uncle. He told me that I must study for straight A grades, and that the 'mistake' with my father would be corrected. He held out his hand to me, I shook it and left.

Two days later, my father came home.

Two months later, in September, supported in my decision by my parents, I joined Comsomol.

The following January 1937, Pavel Petrovitch Postyshev was arrested by a special commission of the Communist Party, headed by N.S. Khryschev and the Moscow NKVD, and shot. So was his wife and two teenage sons, one of whom was my age. Then the whole government of the Ukraine Republic was shot ... Lubchenko, Kosier, Balitzkiy, Yakir, and later thousands and thousands of others. Kiev University President Kocherga, former Division Commander of the Red Army of Civil War time, was shot along with his family. A secretary of the Kiev District of the Committee, my father's boss, Civil War hero, Andrey Osadchuk, was shot. So were Comandarm Gamarnik, Comandarm Dubovoy and many others. Finally the shooting wave reached our family. In November, my uncle Anton, a leading self-taught engineer who was a cripple, and his wife Lina, were shot. My ninety-two-year-old grandfather, a machinist by trade, was killed with a pistol whip to his head by an NKVD guard. My aunt Maria was exiled into the Medvezhia Gora concentration camp for eleven years. It came to the point that my family – father, mother, my father's younger maiden sister and myself – did not know a single person whose family did not have at least one person who had been executed or exiled.

Little ten and twelve-year-old children were forced by the Comsomol leaders of their schools to publicly vote, demanding the death penalty of their arrested fathers; several times I was a witness to this macabre procedure in our school.

In 1938, I graduated with straight 'excellent' grades for all my ten years of study and was sent by the Committee of Kiev District of Comsomol to the Highest Navy Engineering School – Dzerzhinskiy in Leningrad. Three months later, I was thrown out of the school as 'politically unreliable'. The commissar of the school told me that the Soviet navy did not have room for people of Polish descent. I was also thrown out of Comsomol without explanation. A year and a half later, I was dismissed from the Leningrad Shipbuilding Institute, in spite of the fact that, during the shameful Finnish War, I had volunteered for front duty in a special skiing battalion consisting of Leningrad athletes.

At the beginning of World War II, in June 1941, in Kiev, I listened to the false propaganda on German radio that promised us a free and democratic Russia and I used all legal means to secure a deferment that allowed me to stay at the Kiev Polytechnic Institute until February 1942. On 19 September 1941 the German Army took the city.

. I resisted the Germans in Kiev from 1941 to 1943 by organizing student groups fighting for a free Russia. I was arrested by the Gestapo twice, tortured but escaped death.

Along with my wife, father and mother, we ran from the German occupation traveling with a Hungarian echelon. After reaching Hungary, we fled the approaching Red Army and arrived in Austria, then moved on to Bavaria which was under American occupation. We declared ourselves old stateless immigrants who had never lived in the USSR. That saved me from being delivered to the Soviet powers in 1945, which would have meant twenty-five years in a concentration camp for me and death to my family.

In 1948, I came to the USA.

Very respected and dear Michail Sergeevich! I don't have any crimes on my conscience. I never cooperated with the enemies of my homeland, even though the people in power treated me and my family as enemies and shot us like wild beasts. I love my homeland. I was raised on the achievements of the colossal Russian culture from past centuries, especially the nineteenth century – the Silver Age of Russia.

Last May (1987), I was in Leningrad. For several years, my wife and I saved our money for a vacation in the Soviet Union. I had told her so much about it. I had lived in Leningrad from 1938 to 1940 and I remembered it well. We had wonderful accommodations at the Leningrad Hotel. My wife loved the magnificent panorama of Neva and all of the imperial beauty of the city. We walked along the Petrogradskaya Storona, one of the best districts in the city. I wanted to show my wife the Kshesinskiy Palace and the balcony from which Lenin made his famous speech. The palace was partially destroyed. The mosque next to my dormitory was covered with scaffolding for restoration. The scaffolding was partially deteriorated from age and no work was being done. The surrounding streets were dilapidated.

Buildings had rotted window frames, downspouts and doors, yards were junky and there was an overall feeling of despair and poverty. The few stores we passed had practically no goods for sale, only several tin cans of beef stew sat in the windows. A horrible quality of workmanship was everywhere. If Leningrad looks like that, how does the Soviet countryside look? I dread to think about it.

What happened to cause the colossal downfall from the glory of the nineteen hundreds? Where are the writers? Sculptors? Artists? Poets? Philosophers? Actors? Artisans, the famed Russian craftsmen? What happened to the breadbasket of Europe? Immaculate railroads? What happened to the fabulous riches that overflowed the wealthy men's villas, churches, monasteries? Where did the butter disappear? Plump geese? Sturgeon? Caviar, meat, pork, chicken, lamb, furs, clothes, shoes, and all the glitter of the preceding years?

As a boy, and later as a youth, I lived in a small town in Poltava Oblast' where the agricultural technology and agronomy froze on the 1905–12 level. And yet, during my time, people had boots, woolen skirts and pants, every woman had gold earrings and fur coats, and horses and other livestock were all pedigree. Where and how did all of that disappear?

Let me make a list. A list of tragedies which befell our homeland. At the peak of the blossom of Russian culture and civilization, on 31 August 1914 the First World War started. In three days, the colossal Russian army was mobilized very efficiently and engaged the German and Austro-Hungarian armies on its borders. Compared to that feat of efficiency and management skill, the general mobilization declared at the end of June 1941 was a miserable flop. After superior German troops had already deeply penetrated into Soviet territory, the mobilization had to be called off and substituted with the partial alphabet mobilization of the individual military precincts. During World War I, there were defeats and there were victories. More victories than defeats. In the first four months of the Second World War with the Germans, the Soviet Union lost almost three million soldiers to German POW camps. Soldiers who in most instances dropped their weapons and went over to the German side voluntarily, only to die later from exposure and starvation.

Within the first four months of the war, the German flag was placed on Elbrus Mountain, two thousand kilometers east of the border, and German soldiers rode on Moscow tramways within the city's suburb limits. World War I, as it was fought, was a gigantic meat grinder, and armies of all countries engaged in it carried heavy losses. The history written by professional falcificators presented the losses on the Russian side to be excessively high. In reality, chances

149

were great that, if Russia had kept on fighting for one more year, it would have marched victoriously into Berlin some time in 1918. But that is for future historians to determine.

Be as it may, the losses of the Russian army during World War I counted millions of dead and crippled men.

Then came the February Revolution and the collapse of the Empire. The following October Revolution sent the fifteen million army home to 'rob the robbers'. 'Peace to huts and war to palaces' was declared and Red Terror began to reign the nation, putting to death the ablest managers and administrators of the country. 1918 was the beginning of the bloody and destructive Civil War. Horrible atrocities were committed on both sides. Millions of able-bodied, strong, healthy, young people died.

Hungarian communist Bela Kuhn, personal friend of V. I. Lenin, put to death 72,000 Russian White officers in Crimea, throwing their bodies into the canyon of Simeiz after Leon Trotzkiy gave them his word that they would not be prosecuted for taking part in the Civil War on the White side. The exodus of the White Armies from Russia to Europe was approximately two million, counting the families. Meanwhile, the derailed, schizophrenic and personal enemy of the Russian people, rabid Polish nationalist, and mixed-up 'Marxist' Felix Dzerszinskiy, did his macabre work in Russian cities, butchering the upper administrative layer of previous government and industry.

Millions of Russia's ablest people were put to death. The economic and political structure of the country disintegrated. A slogan was released that 'every kitchen maid should know how to govern'. Widespread, severe famine started around the country. Some relief came from far away America when President Hoover enacted the famous American Relief Association and sent ships full of wonderful American flour to feed the desperate Russian population who never saw that quality flour for years. The cotton bags in which the flour came served Russian women as handy material for dresses, blouses and skirts.

Let's add several million people who died from hunger to the list above. Most were educated, professional people who were least adept to withstand the hardship.

By 1922, some drastic, principle measures had to be taken to prevent wholesale cannibalism and dehumanization of the nation. The NEP (New Economic Policy) was declared and concessions were given to foreign capitalists to revitalize the outdated and pilfered industries.

Meanwhile, all kinds of sadists, criminals, drug addicts and adventurers, who were so plentiful within the Soviet secret police (now called the GPU), were selling Russian treasures, confiscated from the homes and villas of exterminated or immigrated aristocrats and wealthy citizens, on the world market to supply the country's treasury with the needed hard currency, some of which went world over to finance the defunct foreign revolutions, or was stolen or got drunk away.

NEP revitalized the country as if by miracle. In a year, food became plentiful, items of basic necessity reappeared on the open market, stores were open and full of goods.

A simple explanation can be offered to that miracle. At that time, the job at hand was proportional to the means available to do it. The majority of the population were peasants. Their land parcels were small and manageable by the family. The tools to do the job were available – primitive small agricultural equipment such as simple plows, harrows, horses and oxen. People were still there to do the work using hands-on methods. Whenever over one hundred million people worked, the results showed. Food became plentiful, exports were partially restored and the gold standard was reestablished giving people trust in the system they lived in.

But it did not last long. By 1926, NEP was dying. The draconian measures of Stalin and his henchmen destroyed NEP.

Meanwhile, the shooting of people in the small of the brain continued. This time it was Henrik Yagoda, who was the boss of the GPU or OGPU, I really don't remember which, who kept on arresting former Imperial Army officers, members of nobility class, cossaks, lawyers, medical doctors, and businessmen. They were either shot or sent to the camps of Kotlas, Novosibirsk, Norilsk, Medvezhia Gora, Solovki, and others.

In 1928, hell broke loose. Stalin started to collectivize the Russian, Belorussian and Ukrainian villages. People from cities, wearing black leather jackets with a red stripe on their left sleeve and Nagant revolvers strapped to their hip, came to the USSR villages. At night, they conferred in Selsovets (village counsels) with GPU agents and local militiamen. In the morning, they spread across the villages visiting better-off farmers, shooting their barking dogs, arresting men and women and putting them into unheated cattle wagons to be transported to different camps in Siberia. Children were separated from each other. Their names were changed and they were placed in foster homes established in former convents.

Horror reigned in the Russian countryside. This was the 'extermination of the Kulaks [better-off peasants] as a class'. Their clothing and possessions were stolen or dispensed among the poorer peasants. Horses were not fed. Cattle were not fed. Buildings were destroyed. In some instances, Kulaks and their wives were shot and buried in ditches half a kilometer long. Remember Vinnitsa?

Those who were awaiting their fate slaughtered the livestock, made homemade vodka and ate and drank their possessions away.

Lines of peasants stood with sacks full of meager possessions on their backs in the front of the railroad station's ticket office windows. They would stick a handful of paper rubles at the ticket officer and request tickets 'for all the money', no matter where, as long as it was far away. As far away as possible. Millions were exterminated and others were placed in Siberian camps.

Another wave of terror came in 1931.

Now, it was in the cities where the new upper layers of the Russian nation were arrested, trumped-up charges were pressed and the people were either killed or deported.

Next was the horrible famine in the richest portions of the nation, including the Ukraine, Don Oblast', Northern Caucasus, and Novorussia. Whatever little grain was left was taken from the collective farms by force. Nothing was left to eat and mass starvation began. Those who tried to eat the collective farms' livestock or seed material were shot (remember the law of 7 August 1931?). People ate dogs, cats, crows, bark from trees and, when those were gone, they died. In the spring of 1933, as a boy of thirteen, I remember dead bodies laying along the roads and around the churches in the mud of the richest country of the world. Men, women, and children, an estimated six million people died.

Then came the bloodbath of 1937 and 1938 when nearly 160,000 people a month were killed in the USSR.

Then came the shameful war when, clattering his teeth on a glass of mineral water, Stalin appealed on the radio to 'brothers and sisters' to save the nation.

Then came the butchery of the war when inept officers sent hundreds of thousands of people in mass attacks to die in battles they did not know how to win.

Three million Russian POWs died in the German camps.

Several million died from German atrocities.

Twenty million additional people, soldiers and civilians, died in the war. One-third of the country was devastated beyond comparison to anything that ever happened before.

About two million people, mostly Soviet intelligentsia and their families, left the USSR by the end of the war, using any means of transportation including German trains, just to get out from underneath Stalin's revenge. Their crime? Presence on the territory occupied by Germans. Their probable punishment? From hanging to concentration camps or, at the very least, being branded for life as second-class citizens.

After the victory, Stalin sent all Russian soldiers who had been captured by Germans to Siberian concentration camps for punishment. That does not happen in any civilized nation. Why does it happen to us?

Let me start concluding my letter.

By very conservative estimates, Russia lost about sixty million of its inhabitants to violent deaths between 1914 and 1953. Half of them by extermination, famines and deaths in concentration camps. Words are not sufficiently strong to describe the sufferings of the people of Russia. Why? Why did it happen?

Michail Sergeevich, you declared glasnost, you started perestroika. There is a tremendous improvement in the quality of life in the Soviet Union since you came into leadership. However, there are hundreds of questions in my mind on this subject. Same questions that are on the minds of my countrymen back home. We should be patient. It is hard to improve and reconstruct all that was destroyed during almost seventy years of horror and mismanagement. During these seventy years, we did not live – we suffered.

What is in the future? What is the future for the children of our children? Same lies? Same Nagant bullets to the accompanying slogan: 'Life is better now, comrades, life is more joyful now!' (Stalin, 1937).

The eyes of the whole world are upon you and your deeds, Michail Sergeevich!

Will you be too hasty with perestroika? If so, chaos will result. Will you be too slow? If so, nothing will happen.

'100% freedom of glasnost' does not exist in any country. One may not scream 'Fire!' in an overfilled movie house. It is not glasnost – it is murder. Not enough freedom of speech would be a hollow mockery.

In conclusion, I would like to express that it would be nice if I could write this letter directly to you and receive a telephone call from you in return. I don't believe in that happening. It would be nice if I could publish this letter in any Moscow newspaper and start discussions on this subject. I don't believe in that possibility either.

It would be nice to have Stalin's skeleton removed from the vicinity of the walls of the ancient Kremlin, the historic symbol of our nation. I don't believe in that possibility.

It would be nice to remove the monument to the madman Dzerzhinski from the square of Lubianka and convert the blood-soaked building to a national shrine. The French destroyed the Bastille stone by stone!

Wouldn't it be nice to disband the KGB (Che-ka, GPU, OGPU, NKVD, MVD) whose crimes are undescribable. All together, there was already so much innocent bloodshed, so many people killed and so many crimes committed against humanity.

I don't believe it will happen very soon.

It would be only just if you would telephone Solzhenitzyn and invite him to come back home where he belongs. Why don't you? Michail Sergeevich, do it!

A horrible thought creeps into my mind. Could it be possible that, with all these colossal human losses, Russia has depleted its genetic stock? Just like France in the Napoleonian wars, just like Sweden in the middle of the seventeenth century, just like Greece, Turkey, Rome, Egypt, and now Germany?

Michail Sergeevich, out of all the people in the world who can affect the destiny of mankind the most, you are one. The other is John-Paul II. Invite him to Moscow. Meet with him, or better yet, go to the Vatican. The eyes and hopes of the world are upon you. Humanity is looking to you for leadership. Now is the time for the spiritual Russian messianism, which was the basis of our culture, to prove itself once again. Or is it that the seventy years of tragedy was all Russia was capable of withstanding and the future is up to others?

The hasty perestroika is dangerous - it might explode the nation by giving impetus to the centrifugal force and disintegrate our land. You obviously know that, but so does the rest of the world. To slow it – who knows what that will bring. Remember the ancient Chinese proverb (You are so good at proverbs), 'He who rides the tiger cannot get off'?

The future of mankind is pregnant with super colossal problems.

Will they be solved?

That depends upon the definition of what the meaning of the word solution is or will be.

I firmly believe that YOU will be one of the leaders of mankind who will work for these solutions.

With feelings of deepest respect,
George (Yuriy Iosifovich) Trachevski

AMNESTY INTERNATIONAL
International Secretariat
London, United Kingdom

27 October 1988

Dear President Gorbachev,

Forty years ago the Universal Declaration of Human Rights was adopted by the United Nations (UN) General Assembly as a 'common standard of achievement for all peoples of all nations'. The goal of this historic document was to promote respect for the human rights and fundamental freedoms set forth in the Universal Declaration and to secure their universal and effective recognition and observance.

In his Human Rights Day message last year, UN Secretary-General Javier Perez de Cuellar reaffirmed the universal character of these rights and freedoms. As he said then, the Universal Declaration 'has equal relevance and validity for every political or social system and also every cultural tradition. It can be truly said to belong to the peoples of the world.'

We also urge all states, when ratifying or acceding to these international instruments, to do so without reservations and, in particular, to recognize fully the various recourse provisions contained in them and the competence of the different monitoring bodies set up pursuant to them, all of which are crucial to their effective implementation. Such provisions include the recognition of the rights of individual and interstate petition and, in some cases, recognition of the jurisdiction of a special court. These mechanisms not only provide a forum where human rights problems can be constructively addressed but also where incompatible or ill-founded allegations may be dispelled.

Adherence by all states to these important instruments would be a major step forward in the further development and strengthening of the emerging international human rights order for the benefit of all people. Again in the words of the Un Secretary-General: 'The common standard of achievement embodied in the [Universal] Declaration is the birthright of all peoples. It is our joint responsibility to make it a living, universal reality.'

Amnesty International has expressed its appreciation of the proposal you made in 1987, before your election to the Chairmanship of the Presidium of the USSR Supreme Soviet, to promote and strengthen the role of the United Nations in protecting human rights. We believe that such a public commitment by the USSR is a powerful example to other governments.

Amnesty International welcomes the fact that the USSR has ratified the International Covenant on Civil and Political Rights and the International Covenant on Economic and Social Rights, and also that it was among the first countries to ratify the Convention Against Torture and Other Cruel, Inhuman or Degrading Treatment or Punishment. However, we regret that the USSR has not yet ratified the Optional Protocol to the International Covenant on Civil and Political Rights.

Yours sincerely,
Ian Martin
Secretary General

In September 1990, Amnesty International gave us the following statement which brings up to date the developments that have taken place in the last four years.

155

The Soviet perspective on human rights has shifted dramatically since 1986. At international gatherings the USSR has supported new mechanisms for countries to monitor each other's respect for human rights, and it has acknowledged that individuals need their civil, political, social, economic and cultural rights equally protected. The Soviet press has also begun to refer to 'universal human values' which transcend the interests of social class. Previously the USSR gave priority to social and economic rights and rejected international human rights monitoring as interference in its internal affairs.

Two major statements by the General Secretary of the Soviet Communist Party, Mikhail Gorbachev, have signalled this new perspective. In October 1987 *Pravda* published an article in which he advocated a stronger role for the United Nations in promoting and protecting human rights. He also urged states to ensure that their own laws conform with international standards and said that they had not only a right but an obligation to monitor each other's behaviour in the field of human rights. In December 1988 President Gorbachev told the United Nations General Assembly that the USSR was planning to 'increase its participation in human rights monitoring agreements'. Two months later the USSR accepted the jurisdiction of the International Court of Justice in six international treaties, among them the UN Convention against Torture and Other Cruel, Inhuman or Degrading Treatment or Punishment. It had never before recognised the competence of international bodies to have a role in disputes between states.

To some degree this new outlook has been reflected in the treatment of individual prisoners of conscience. At the beginning of July 1989 Amnesty International has details of over 90 individuals whom it knew or suspected were imprisoned for trying to exercise their human rights. At the end of 1986 it had known of nearly 600. Around one third of these people were freed after they had served their sentences in full, but 340 were released early from prisons, corrective labour colonies or internal exile. Another 54 were let out of psychiatric hospitals, where some had spent 15 years or longer confined against their will. They make up the largest single group of prisoners of conscience to have been freed since the 1950s. Political arrests have also fallen noticeably since 1986.

The most promising prospect for long-term reform is a major review of law, which was announced in early 1987 and still continues. It is apparently aimed at bringing Soviet law into line with international standards and creating a 'society based on the rule of law'. In the course of the review the use of the death penalty has been re-examined, and lawyers involved in the process have suggested that laws restricting freedom of expression, religion, assembly and movement may be repealed or radically changed. The review means that some human rights issues have been discussed in public for the first time, and that some legislative changes are now being made.

Despite this clear trend towards reform, however, the human rights picture in the USSR is deeply confusing. While plans to protect human rights are being discussed at length, the Presidium of the previous USSR Supreme Soviet has adopted decrees that further curb them. The rights of unofficial groups to hold meetings, for instance, were restricted by a decree of July 1988 and electioneering for radical change was effectively banned by a decree of April 1989. New armed police units, set up in July 1988 to combat 'public disorders' have been used against peaceful crowds in a way that has alarmed official commentators and human rights advocates.

Old Windsor
Berkshire, England   20 November 1988

Dear Mr Gorbachev,
    In the USSR, I have been told everyone is guaranteed reasonable accommodation at a modest rent and no one goes hungry.

Unfortunately in the UK, this is not the case, under her government, the profits of landowners, landlords and property speculators are considered more important than providing affordable housing for decent, young, hard-working people, on a modest wage. In the south of England the price of the land a house stands on, is often more than the cost of building the house on it. This I believe to be one of the great faults of the capitalist, free market economy.

Margaret Thatcher's government is making virtual slaves out of decent young hard-working people to afford a house in order to line the pockets of the idle rich. Hence, many young people cannot afford a small house of their own. Families are having to live in cramped bedsits, often only one small room, paying exorbitant rents, to private landlords, having very little money left to live on, or prospects for the future. Single people or couples without children are often homeless, sleeping rough in the streets of our cities.

The government just does not care; if market forces do not provide accommodation, at a price someone can afford, too bad, let them sleep on the streets in a cardboard box, that's Margaret Thatcher's record on human rights.

I believe, as in the USSR, the government should guarantee to offer everyone a reasonable minimum standard of accommodation, at a modest rent they can afford, or, if they are unemployed, for doing some work for the state, within their capabilities. I do not agree with someone being able to laze about all day at the expense of the taxpayer.

I have made a scathing criticism of Margaret Thatcher, which I believe she deserves in every way. However I feel it only fair to give her every credit for the many other good things she has done for this country.

1. Making us realise there is not an endless pot of money to spend on social causes. Having cost benefit analyses before making decisions. Thus the government's financial position is now one of the strongest in the world. (Not its economic policies through.)

2. Excessive union power has been moderated and brought under democratic voting. Unfortunately an equal effort has not been put into stopping the exploitation of workers by some employers.

3. Tax rates on the rich have been reduced, yielding both more revenues to spend on socially worthwhile causes and keeping businesses, highly knowledgeable and skilled people in this country, rather than emigrating, the jobs of millions of ordinary working people depending on them staying here.

I believe the problems of people throughout the countries of the world are not the fault, nor can be solved, by capitalism or communism. While there are many fair and caring people in every country, any political or economic system is open to abuse, by those in a position of power, to exploit their fellow man. It is only by trying to change human nature the problems of the world will be solved, not by one political or economic system or another.

It is with great sadness I see in the UK, one of my nationalities (I am equally a Canadian) Margaret Thatcher's government believes because she's been elected, with a minority of voters in this country, she has a mandate to dictate to the nation what policies it should follow, largely disregarding the other political parties' ideas, opinion polls on policies and charities. I believe she should make far more effort to accommodate the wishes of other MPs, not in her party, rather than push through many divisive policies that are polarising the nation without effective consultation, by which I mean a national debate, and only when it is shown that she has the backing of the people of this country behind her, should she go ahead and implement said policies.

Yours truly,
Russell Shapcott

Chico
California, USA   8 December 1988

Dear President Gorbachev,

From published reports it appears that the Soviet Union has over 300 soldiers missing in action. As you know, the United States has about 2,400 MIAs from the Vietnam War (missing in Vietnam, Cambodia and Laos).

We all know that the war does terrible things to people and that most of the MIAs will never be accounted for. In fact, the United States has 8,000 MIAs from the Korean War and 75,000 MIAs from World War II. I'm sure the number is much higher for the Soviet Union.

There is, however, much accounting to be done for MIAs in Vietnam (US) and Afghanistan (Soviet). This is where our interests lie.

I ask you to do everything possible to urge the Vietnamese to continue to cooperate and expand their efforts with regard to the US MIAs in South-east Asia.

I urge that you discuss with the Chinese the US MIA problem, since they are a strong ally of the Khmer Rouge, who may possess critical information.

The Cambodian government announced a year ago they have the remains of about ninety Americans. I urge you to ask them to turn those remains over to the Red Cross. In return, ask the American government to intervene regarding Soviet MIAs in Afghanistan.

There is no need for American families to continue to wait for information about sons or husbands who disappeared twenty years ago. Enough is enough.

The same is true for the Soviet families. The time is ripe to move on the MIA issues.

I hope you will give considerable effort to this remaining issue.

Sincerely,
Bob Mulholland

According to Soviet sources, the number of MIA's have been placed at 311 and at 313 men. The Soviets maintained a deployment of 115-120,000 soldiers in the country, with approximately 30,000 across the border in the USSR who frequently participated in operations directly from Soviet territory. Over the course of the entire occupation, the Soviets cycled through at least 500,000 men according to one source and as many as 1,000,000 according to another. The true figure is probably closer to the larger one. Soviet soldiers normally spent from 12-18 months in the country once assigned there. The Soviets invaded on Christmas Eve, 1979, and withdrew their last combat unit on February 15, 1989. However, there still remain several thousand military advisors in the country and Soviet pilots are suspected of flying combat missions in support of the regime they helped install.

CONGRESS OF THE UNITED STATES
House of Representatives
Washington, DC, USA

8 December 1988

Excellency,

Please accept my deepest sympathy over the tragic loss of life in the Transcaucasian republics resulting from the recent earthquake.

It is my most sincere desire that you had both an enjoyable and productive stay in the United States. I found your speech to the United Nations to be most encouraging in regard to promoting human rights the world over.

I am writing to you to express my desire to see an end to the recent conflagrations in the Transcaucasian Soviet Republics of Azerbaijan and Armenia. This ethnic strife is the result of longstanding animosity amongst the Christian Armenians and the Moslem Azerbaijanis over the annexation of the Nagorno-Karabakh region, populated mainly by Armenians, into the Republic of Azerbaijan in 1923.

Clearly, this crisis represents a fundamental challenge to, and opportunity for, your policies of glasnost and perestroika. The challenge lies in the opportunity to put these new policies to work to solve the crisis in a manner that will be acceptable to both parties by reinforcing the rule of law and protecting fundamental human rights in the two republics.

I urge you to carefully consider the recent four point proposal of Dr Andrei Sakharov in this regard:

1. Complete and objective information about the situation. Free access for Soviet and foreign journalists to Armenia and Azerbaijan;

2. The Soviet authorities must take the necessary measures to ensure the safety of the Armenian population, including the introduction of sufficient troops into Azerbaijan for this purpose;

3. The Armenians in Azerbaijan and Nagorno-Karabakh should be allowed to organize self-defense units;

4. Nagorno-Karabakh should be removed from the administrative control of the Azerbaijan republic and placed temporarily under control of the All-Union Administration.

It is my premise that only with such bold and open action can disaster be avoided. In allowing the country and the world to report on the progress of events in the Transcaucasian region you stand to increase the chance of world support and a greater unity among the other Soviet Republics for actions that are designed to address the current abuses against the

Armenian population of Azerbaijan. Failure to resort to the practices of glasnost and perestroika in this crisis is to risk casting a pall of uncertainty over future invocation of such policies.

As you return home from your visits to the United States and other countries I urge you to put your platform into practice in helping to rectify the wrong done to the Armenians of the Nagorno-Karabakh region in 1923. I implore you to act on their behalf before more bloodshed occurs to Armenians, Azerbaijanis and Soviet forces stationed there.

Sincerely,
Barbara Boxer
Member of Congress

A massive earthquake, 6.9 on the Richter scale, hit Soviet Armenia on Wednesday, December 7, 1988 at 11:41 am, leaving as many as 400,000 homeless and more than 45,000 dead. In the midst of the relief effort, the Kremlin issued a formal request for American aid. Washington responded immediately with offers of medicine and medical equipment, doctors and trained rescue teams, the first time that large-scale US assistance had been given to the Soviet Union since the end of World War II.

Traneberg Ålsten Social Democratic Women's Club
Sweden

December 1988

You state in your book that you receive huge quantities of letters from various parts of the world and that you try to find time to answer them and the questions they contain. We, too, should like to ask you some questions and hope that you can find the time to answer.

Our first request, Mr Party Secretary, is that you should explain further your views on the question of women. On the one hand, you say in your book that women must be encouraged to take a more active part in economic life, cultural development and social affairs. To achieve that, women's committees have been set up across the whole country. The Plenary Session of January 1987 considered the question of promoting women to leading positions within a range of fields. And you say that women have been given all the chances of education and career in order to be able to take part in social and political work. But on the other hand you state that, during the great struggles the

161

Soviet Union has undergone, it has not been possible to pay attention to

'those special rights and needs which women have as a result of their role in the family and in the home and because of the invaluable part they play in the upbringing of children. Those women who work in scientific research, in the construction industry, in the production and in the service sector or cultural spheres quite simply no longer have time to carry out their domestic tasks in the home: doing the housekeeping, bringing up the children and making a pleasant home for the family. We have to come to understand that many of the problems that involve the moral, cultural and working behaviour of children and young people are partly caused by a weakening of family bonds and by a weak attitude [weak on whose part, is what we ask] to responsibility for the family. It is a paradoxical result of a genuine and politically motivated desire to give women equality with men in all respects. But now we have started to get to grips with these difficulties. That is why there are lively debates in our newspapers and in public organisations, at work and in the home, about how we shall make it possible for women to return to their purely womanly role'.

You also consider that there are certain functions that purely are physically too demanding for women and which can put their health at risk.

Now, however, we wonder how one is to provide enhanced study possibilities for women and enable them to occupy positions of leadership while at the same time getting them 'to return to the womanly role'? Within the women's movement we believe – and it is an idea which has wide acceptance and to a certain extent legisative recognition too – that the man also has a responsibility for the care of the home and the upbringing of the children, and he should accept this responsibility to a greater degree than he has done so far. Unless the husband takes his share of this work, it will be quite impossible for the wife to take the promised chances of further education and more senior management posts. Also, as to your statement that certain types of work can put a woman's health at risk: it is an argument we have often heard from men who selfishly wish to keep women away from their spheres of work. When women have to be allowed access to such areas, they have been quite able to hold their own. We believe that it is for the woman herself to judge whether a particular type of work is unsuitable for her. It is, in fact, a question for the particular individual and relevant to both men and women. If a job is risky for a woman's health, it is probably also risky for a man's.

162

We also wonder how many women there are in the Supreme Soviet, and we have looked in vain for female faces among the people who represent the leadership in Red Square during the 1 May parade, for example. And do all women in the Soviet Union enjoy equality and an equal right to enter all possible professions, even Mohammedan women, for instance?

You also take up the question of the fight against alcohol and say that you expect a great deal in this matter from the work and initiatives of the women's councils. But this cannot be an exclusively female task. Men, too, must cooperate.

With our greatest respect,
Ulla Larsson
Chairperson

Gunhild Höglund
Vice-Chairperson

National Committee against the *Berufsverbot*
Copenhagen, Denmark

January 1989

Dear Michael Gorbachev,

Taking as a starting point the visit by Helmut Kohl to Moscow in November 1988, and the Chancellor's declared interest in human rights, we would like to draw your attention to the fact that human rights are being violated in Helmut Kohl's own country.

The committee which sends this letter has followed developments in the Federal Republic of Germany for almost fifteen years. We have been able to establish that teachers, and employees in postal administration and the railways, have been deprived of the right to work and therefore of the ability to provide for their families. The reason is not that these people have carried out their work badly. Their dismissal is always motivated by the fact that the persons concerned have stood at an election as candidate for the DKP (German Communist Party), or that they have been active in the Peace Movement.

This practice, known as the *Berufsverbot*, has been described and criticised at the United Nations' International Labour Organisation (ILO), most recently in May 1988.

Among other things, ILO showed that the German practice is a clear violation of the organisation's convention No 111, as the government in Bonn has itself accepted. But the Federal Government did not wish to draw any conclusion from this criticism.

Therefore we request, as a matter of urgency, that you take the initiative of placing the question of the *Berufsverbot* in the German Federal Republic on the agenda of the coming conference on human rights, the third stage of which it seems the USSR will be hosting.

Yours sincerely,
Bernhard Baunsgaard

Cerrillos
New Mexico, USA   15 February 1989

Dear Mr Mikhail Gorbachev,

I am writing this letter in concern for the Soviet soldier returning from the war in Afghanistan. I hope that your government will start treating the soldiers right away for post-traumatic stress disorder. Don't wait eleven years like the US government did to soldiers coming back from the Vietnam War.

I was nineteen years old in 1967 when I went to Vietnam, with the United States Marine Corps. I served near Dong Ha on the DMZ for twenty-two months (two tours). I came home in July of 1969. My life has been in total turmoil for the past eighteen years, as a result of my war experiences. Our government did not recognize PTSD as a problem until 1980 and I did not get treatment for it until 1988. In 1976 I went to a VA hospital. They said that the war in Vietnam had nothing to do with my problems. How can a person go on forty-three combat missions and it not affect him?

Now after being out of the war for twenty years, the United States government has awarded me ten per cent disability for my war-related mental wounds. I feel that if I were treated early for the PTSD that I would not have had to waste twenty years of my life going around in circles.

Post-traumatic stress disorder in the US has affected the entire population in one way or another. Right now forty-five per cent of the homeless and thirty per cent of the prison population are Vietnam combat veterans that were never treated for their PTSD problems because our government denied it existed.

When we came home from the war we were treated as second-class citizens. I hope that none of your war veterans has to go through the treatment that the US government has put the Vietnam War veterans through.

164

Thank you very much for your time and please help your war veterans with their mental wounds. Don't make your war veterans end up like the Vietnam veterans of America. Early treatment of post-traumatic stress disorder is very important.

Thank you,
Frank Spillman

Humboldt
Tennessee, USA   27 March 1989

Dear General Secretary Gorbachev,

While we in the West have been encouraged by some of the political reforms we see begun by your government we are not naive enough to believe you are ushering in a new birth of freedom. Do not be deceived by the plaudits you receive from some of the most liberal elements of our country. In a true democracy, anyone can speak and be heard without fear of retaliation. However, you must be made aware they represent only a small segment of our population. Most of my countrymen firmly believe your country engages in very repressive measures to quiet the voice of protest.

We know that certain words and phrases such as 'peace' and 'freedom of expression' have very different meanings in your vocabulary than in ours. We also know you desire something from the West that can only be achieved if you exhibit, at least outwardly, evidence of political and economic freedom for your people at all levels of the socio-political system.

If glasnost and perestroika are to be successful, at least in our eyes, it will need to be very real and very pervasive. I suppose real evidence of that success will be when peoples of the world are as anxious to get into your country as they are to get out.

We are watching you and your efforts at reform with a certain renewed hope and expectation, but I must confess with a degree of wariness as well.

Yours very truly,
James T. Buford

МЕЖДУНАРОДНАЯ

МИНИСТЕРСТВО СВЯЗИ СССР   **ТЕЛЕГРАММА**

ПЕРЕДАЧА:

Адрес: _____

№ связи _____

Передал: _____

```
KSA757 FCA647 RP034
SUMX CO CATO 079
TDTN DON MILLS ON 79/72 19 1138 PAGE 1 54/50


GENERAL SECRETARY MIKHAIL GORBACHEV
STARAYA PLOSHCHAD, 4
103132 MOSKVA SSSR, RSFSR


ON MAY-22ND OF-THIS YEAR, PEACEFUL COMMEMORATIONS WILL-BE HELD-IN
LITHUANIA ON-THE 40TH ANNIVERSARY OF STALLIN'S DEPORTATIONS OF
200,000 LITHUANIANS TO SIBERIA.
MR. GORBACHEV - YOU YOURSELF HAVE CRITICIZED AND CONDEMNED THE
ATROCITIES CREATED BY STALLIN.  IN-THE SPIRIT OF GLASNOST AND
PERESTROIKA WE-ASK YOU TO-ALLOW THE PEOPLE OF LITHUANIA TO
COMMEMORATE IN PEACE.
        ALVYDAS SAPLYS, PRESIDENT EXECUTIVE COMMITTEE
        WORLD LITHUANIAN YOUTH ASSOCIATION INC.
```

Padua
Italy   April 1989

Dear Mr Gorbaciov,

I am an Italian citizen, unemployed all my life and an ex-drug-addict (I came off drugs five years ago). To complete this unworthy introduction I'll tell you my name – Sandro Sassu. If this letter should ever reach you, I'd like to wish you every success with perestroika.

I would like to make a few comments on your book, if I may, on the basis of my negative experiences with drugs and with full awareness of my limitations. It is my humble opinion that your book, allowing for its basic ideology, displays limitations which are nothing more or less than feeble silences (whether deliberate or not I can't tell). I hope you will forgive my directness in stating my opinions without frills and formalities. On the other hand, I'm sure that your book has been sufficiently praised, and by people who are in no way comparable to my humble self.

I don't know to what extent you have to face the problem of drugs;

166

I can only say that if there are even only tiny fringes which use drugs, if I may offer my advice, rip this illness out at birth without pity; don't find yourselves in the situation we are in, I beg you.

I'd like to ask you one last thing, which you may find a little strange. I'm fatherless, I never knew my father; I'd be happy if you would take his place, and so I have taken the liberty of imagining you as my adoptive father. If I had had a person like you beside me in my childhood, I would certainly not know the meaning of the word heroin. Keep on the road you have taken, because it is the right one.

Best wishes,
Sandro Sassu

UNITED STATES SENATE
Washington, DC, USA

18 May 1989

Dear Mr Chairman,

I am writing to solicit your views regarding the establishment of an international criminal court.

During the course of my service in the United States Senate, I have become convinced that an international court with jurisdiction to try terrorists, trans-national drug traffickers and other international criminals would be an important component of any comprehensive strategy to combat these global ills. At my urging, the US Congress has twice called for the commencement of negotiations on this subject.

I believe an international court would be a useful mechanism for addressing complex jurisdictional issues in international criminal law. In several highly visible cases in recent years, political considerations have made the extradition of criminal suspects from one nation to another difficult or impossible. In such cases, extradition to an international forum would be a viable option for bringing these individuals to justice. Moreover, negotiators working to create the court would necessarily explore the contours of international criminal law. The development of this jurisprudence is a vital step toward the abatement of international crime.

My discussions with a variety of foreign leaders persuades me that our interdependent global community is now prepared to speak with one voice to condemn terrorism and other international crimes. Creation of an international criminal court would be an eloquent expression of that condemnation.

Sincerely,
Arlen Specter
Pennsylvania

CONGRESS OF THE UNITED STATES
House of Representatives
Washington, DC, USA

28 August 1989

Dear Mr Gorbachev,

The spirit of glasnost which you have promoted has done a great deal to encourage a rapprochement between our two nations and to encourage the citizens of the United States to view relations between the Soviet Union and its people in a more optimistic light.

Nonetheless, I and many other Americans continue to be troubled by your government's apparent interference in religious practice. Freedom of worship, without government intervention, is a fundamental human right of every individual. As a signatory of the Helsinki Accords, your government has secured that right for its people. Yet, in numerous cases you have not permitted expression of this basic right.

I respectfully ask that you introduce judicial and institutional safeguards for government non-interference in religious worship, including the right to perform missionary work, to build schools and centers of religious study, to manage and solicit funds for such purposes, and to perform other functions related to the practice of religion.

Best regards,
Ronald K. Machtley
Member of Congress

House of Lords
London, England

22 January 1990

Your Excellency, Esteemed President Gorbachev,

As a participant in the Global Forum on Environment and Development, I was privileged to hear your wise and challenging address in the Kremlin on Friday evening.

Personally, I was particularly touched by your reference to Immanuel Kant and his 'ecological imperative'. I was born in Konigsberg (now Kaliningrad) and my late father, a great admirer of Kant, named me Immanuel after him.

I missed an earlier opportunity to meet you in London. Our Prime Minister, Mrs Margaret Thatcher, had invited me to be among her guests at the Downing Street dinner in your honour last March. Unfortunately I was ill with a heart by-pass operation.

In my dual capacity as Chief Rabbi of Great Britain and the Commonwealth, and as President of the Conference of European Rabbis, I wished to greet you as one of history's great liberators. As Jews we particularly hail the religious, educational, cultural and emigration rights now enjoyed, with few exceptions, by our two million (or more) co-religionists in the Soviet Union, and we hope that these rights will soon be formalised in constitutional reforms already promised.

No-one prays with greater fervour for your welfare and your success than the Jewish people. For no-one suffers more from instability, religious discrimination and racist oppression. The six million Jews (perhaps two million of them Soviet citizens) butchered by the Nazi fascists constantly remind us of this. For the same reason we also salute your opposition to the reunification of Germany – at least so long as there are not absolute international guarantees that the ordeals inflicted on both the Soviet poeple and the Jewish people – the worst victims of German aggression – can never be repeated. I am confident that representatives of the Jewish people will be consulted alongside all other nations affected in any agreement on German reunification.

May you for long continue your courageous, wise and inspired leadership in good health as the epoch-making architect of a better world, in which the ideals of peace, tolerance and respect for human values will prevail.

Most sincerely yours,
Immanuel Jakobovits
Chief Rabbi of Great Britain and the Commonwealth
President, Conference of European Rabbis

PERESTROIKA AND GLASNOST
Hand in Hand

SITUATIONS ARE INCLINED to change and politicians to evolve with them. It must already be obvious that, whatever Gorbachev's views before he came to power, he tended to alter them with events, sometimes as a result of internal, sometimes of external pressure. This does not mean that he was the plaything of circumstances, still less that he was devoid of objectives. It was partly that he was prepared to learn and partly that he saw leadership as the art of the possible. This is why he not only survived but acquired authority at home and reputation abroad. But from time to time it led to unexpected consequences.

Outsiders watching developments in Moscow early in 1985 wondered who would succeed Chernenko, how quickly he would establish himself, and whether the new leader would make an impact on Soviet foreign policy. There were both specialists and ordinary people critical of the economic system and the political culture, but few expected major internal changes. To Gorbachev, however, domestic policy was paramount. Easing international tension had a mainly economic value. Eventually it acquired an importance of its own, as did issues of the environment and of human rights. But at the start Gorbachev's real aim was to make communism work.

For some time, therefore, commentators tended to concentrate on his arms proposals and to miss what was happening within the Soviet Union - except every so often when he removed celebrated political rivals or encumbrances such as Andrei Gromyko, long foreign minister and briefly president. Yet it was not altogether their fault since it took Gorbachev some time to bring his reform proposals into play, and rather more time to develop them to accord with new situations.

The first effective announcement that restructuring, or *perestroika*, was under way came during the 27th Party Congress in March 1986; and it was a bit later that the policy of openness, or *glasnost*, emerged. For a long time, too, *perestroika* remained ill-defined, and *glasnost* when introduced, was not an end in itself, but an instrument of reform. However, as the effects of internal change began to manifest themselves to outsiders, hostile as well as friendly, the two words became shorthand for the kind of turnaround that had never been expected of a very static society. The concepts could hardly be credited to a leader who emerged by a non-democratic process, so the ideas took on the atmosphere of a fairytale for many people.

The original concept of *perestroika* was economic. Government planning and ministerial control were to be greatly reduced, and industrial enterprises and the enormous collective farms were to become mainly self-managing and self-accounting. Some foreign trade was also to be devolved from the centre. But apart from the imprecision and inadequacy of the idea, perestroika met with enormous bureaucratic resistance, and suspicion from those quarters used to being cared for from the cradle to the grave and afraid of the personal consequences of major change.

Glasnost was therefore looked upon with hope as a means of exposing the recalcitrant who might simply be protecting their own positions or hiding their past. But while *perestroika* marked time awaiting the right circumstances, it was different with *glasnost* which began opening up all sorts of historical crannies and creating demands for political reform of a kind undreamt of even by hitherto clandestine radicals.

The widening public discussion raised a host of probing questions about the past, about Stalin's misdeeds, the victimisation of Trotsky and Bukharin and, going further back, the role of Lenin himself. While this helped to undermine the Party elite opposed to *perestroika*, it also began to challenge the raison d'etre of the Party itself. Gorbachev therefore found himself increasingly forced towards democratising Soviet politics in order to restructure the economy, and modernising the Party in order to help it survive in a democratised society. That was why he called a Special Party Conference in June 1988 and conducted it through a reform debate in front of television, an event that excited the media and public in the West almost as much as in the USSR itself. It enabled him to remove or downgrade the more conservative members of the Politburo in September, and to reduce the size and influence of the Central Committee the following year, moves designed to bring the Party in practice into line with public thinking.

However, as the debate continued, he felt constrained to put further pressure on Party bureaucrats and to meet popular demands by reforming what purported to be the Soviet Union's parliamentary structure. What he came up with was a very large Congress of Deputies, elected on a restricted franchise and itself electing a small Supreme Soviet. The Congress that he chaired in June 1989 lasted for three weeks, not three days as he had hoped, and turned into a critical analysis of the Soviet system before a television audience of millions. Soviet politics would never be the same again. When the Supreme Soviet met, it assumed powers of deciding policies and of appointing or not appointing ministers. And in the course of 1990, through a protracted struggle, it assumed the ultimate power –

the right to decide between alternative economic policies and their respective champions.

Gorbachev was influenced, not overcome. Having summoned the Supreme Soviet to help him press *perestroika* on the bureaucrats, he was himself forced to accept a more radical version of his original reform. But as the process continued, Gorbachev remained in command. In the spring of 1990 he agreed to become an executive President, no longer leader of his country simply in virtue of his role in the Party, but as head of a broader government that might ultimately emerge from multi-party elections. Having moved the 28th Party Congress forward from 1991 to 1990, he managed in July to defeat its anti-*perestroika* wing and to produce a centrist majority. But in the event he lost the radicals, who left the Party to swell the ranks of the multi-party lobby. A month later Gorbachev accepted the inevitable, allying with Boris Yeltsin who by an electoral process had become President of the Russian Federation and who, by walking out of the Congress, was able to act as radical spokesman. Carried forward on the tide of *glasnost*, Gorbachev seemed by then to be committed to a much more extreme *perestroika* than he had originally envisaged. On the other hand, during the Congress he further downgraded the Politburo and Central Committee by moving all his senior colleagues from the Politburo to the new Presidential Council, a kind of super cabinet. This move made it clear that, as Soviet politics were rapidly moving from being the pressure of one Party to being the battleground for many, he intended to stay democratically on top, in charge of *perestroika*, but acknowledging that, as a result of *glasnost*, he could do so only as executive President and no longer just as General Secretary of the one-time monopoly Party. And as an emerging democrat, he had to watch some of his decrees effectively challenged in the new constitutional court.

In the meantime, Gorbachev had been on another learning curve. Like many members of the establishment, he had been brought up in the easy belief that socialism had solved the Soviet nationalities question. After all, there were no troubles but lots of ethnic cultural events. But *glasnost* soon changed the picture. Some economic or political grievances quite naturally took a nationalist form, notably in the Baltic Republics. Elsewhere, inter-ethnic squabbles were able to surface and even led to fighting, as for example in and between Azerbaijan and Armenia where Soviet troops had to intervene. And clever politicians like Yeltsin used Russian grievances to recoup his early reform failure within the Party. Gorbachev was slow to appreciate what was happening – or else was preoccupied. With 15 union republics, 20 autonomous republics, 8 autonomous religious and 10 autonomous districts, embracing among them more than 100 different nationalities, he could not avoid the issue once it came to a head in Lithuania in December 1989. But just as he recognised the need to move from single Party rule to a properly constituted government, so he came to appreciate that it was essential to change the form of the Union and allow autonomy in at least economic matters. Fortunately this coincided with the latest version of economic *perestroika*, a market-type economy, and also provided a suitable basis on which to agree with Yeltsin. He was on the road to a hopefully successful political *perestroika* as well.

In this way, correspondents who have viewed Gorbachev as a peacemaker have come to appreciate him as a domestic reformer, and felt able to offer him help and advice and seek his guidance. Some began to worry about his future as his authority increased but his difficulties mounted. He had finally produced more radical reforms showing his ability to adapt to a changing situation but his policies still had to produce results.

Bill Wallace

25 September 1981

Dear Mr Gorbachov,

I thank you for receiving me during my recent visit to the USSR.
My visit with you was an honor and interesting.

The agriculture of each of our countries has enjoyed success and
currently has difficulties. US agriculture suffers especially from
inflation since agriculture is capital intensive, and that inflation is
worsened by the meteor like rise in petroleum costs reflected not
only in fuels, but all farm fertilizers and chemicals. In addition we
face a change in grain storage and transportation in agriculture as
a result of constriction of the railroad system. The USSR has the
immediate sadness of a very bad drought following a poor crop last
year. Both countries face the problem of minimal population growth
which will affect our work force.

You know that at the invitation of G. A. Arbatov of the Institute of
the USA and Canada I visited your farms for several weeks with the
idea of reporting my observations and suggestions to an audience at
the Institute upon my return to Moscow.

The agricultural production of the Soviet Union has grown
fourfold in the past sixty years, and a large part of that increase
has come in the last twenty years. That increase from sixty years
ago has been used to provide a stable food supply instead of times of
hunger, then to provide a richer diet, and then like most countries to
meet the ever increasing demands for an even richer diet. You now
are users and producers of modern farming machines and products.
The progress has been made while rebuilding from a devastating
civil war and then the Nazi invasion in which you lost sixty lives for
each American life lost in WW II plus the destruction of the physical
economic plant of your country and the homes you lived in. My
country has enjoyed about the same percentage growth, but enjoys
a great deal more rainfall, a longer growing season, and of course,
has not suffered the physical damage. As I traveled in Southern
Russia, I could not but be struck by the progress made by sacrifice
and hard work.

There were three subjects I discussed with you at our meeting.

Protein. Soviets and Americans feed about the same amount of
grain to animals raised for slaughter. Soviets feed, to balance this
grain ration, only a fraction of the protein that Americans feed.
The result is that meat production in the USSR is between one-half
and two-thirds that of the USA. Because of an unbalanced ration
the grain cannot be digested and is passed out in manure. This
is a terrible waste of grain – especially in years of drought. My

176

suggestion is that you ought to form a national protein industry which gathers in to its processing plants all the protein of the nation (sunflowers, cottonseed, rape, fishmeal, soya and single cell) process it and distribute the result on a practical basis. I believe that while you still would be short of protein as a nation, you would get more efficient use of grain as a result. I must warn you that this program would surely require the construction of a good many dispersed protein processing plants.

On-farm storage. The USSR has little or no on-farm storage. Thus harvest time is a crisis with grain having to be hauled long distances for storage and handling by a sometimes inadequate trucking system. The result is a severe loss of grain and grain spoilage between the combine and the consumer. I suggest that metal bins be built on the farm which have cleaning, drying and ventilating systems. This removes the crisis aspect of the harvest, insures high quality grain, and lets delivery to the terminal be at a time of lessened work load. You ought to manufacture these bins and equipment in your country. If I or my associates can be of help in this matter or others such as a grain sorghum seed plant or seed, let me know.

Agricultural infrastructure. The Soviet Union has progressed wonderfully in the past twenty years in agriculture. Because of farm machinery and chemicals and agricultural industrialization, the Soviet Union has achieved, I suspect, the greatest off-farm movement of people in history. Now they are at a level of sophistication which requires more than simple inputs. A sophisticated economy increases interdependence. Russia needs to guarantee that farms will have timely, dependable, high quality delivery of goods and services into agriculture. Such things as chemicals, fertilizer, spare parts, gasoline, trucking, etc. High and uniform quality of fertilizer means that it will work easily in machines and thus be used eagerly instead of reluctantly by workers. Timely and dependable delivery of agriculture inputs means less inventory in the 'pipelines' and thus greater utilization of annual production with less storage necessary. To not have this infrastructure at this level of development means that farms will tend to drift into fiefdoms hoarding or gathering necessary materials to protect their own production. I am sure that if this infrastructure is not developed, Soviet agriculture will plateau and have a much slower rate of growth. Every farmer must believe that he can expect timely, dependable, high quality products delivered when desired for maximum production.

One last suggestion – The Soviet Union guarantees work and thus wages for everyone. If a job has extraordinary success, there are bonuses. You do need to have economic penalties for poor jobs or failures in quality, or quantity, or timeliness that could have been avoided. These penalties, of course, should not hurt the ability of a family to nourish or house or clothe itself, but interdependence requires good management at more than just the top level.

Mr Gorbachov, I appreciate the opportunity I was given to look at your country. I admire the economic progress created by investments made possible with the self sacrifice of your citizens. It has not been an easy road. I am a proud American whose agriculture has been blessed with a better climate and two oceans for borders - so I congratulate you.

What I have suggested in this letter are investments that cost a great deal of money. Both the USSR and the USA are spending too much for defense against a possibility that I believe both are too wise to initiate. How much more wonderful if those funds could be spent for the betterment of mankind.

If I can be of help to your agriculture commercially or otherwise, I stand ready.

I have sent through Victor Lishchenko of the Institute of the USA and Canada an invitation to you to speak at the Iowa Bankers Convention on 20 September 1982. Mr Lishchenko is an outstanding, hard working, devoted citizen of your country. I hope you can accept the invitation he extends.

Sincerely,
John Chrystal, President
IOWA SAVINGS BANK

As can be seen in John Chrystal's letter of '81, while the two superpowers were locked in the Cold War, certain individuals and politicians were involved in the programs of what we now know as perestroika *and* glasnost.

In 1980 Gorbachev became the newest and youngest member of the Politburo and was the Party Secretary responsible for agriculture when the letter was written.

South Strafford
Vermont, USA   20 April 1987

Dear Mr Secretary,

We would like to urge you to include discussion of a Soviet-American high voltage power link across the Bering Sea on the summit agenda. The establishment of a scientific and economic task force to study this proposal has been proposed by the United Nations Natural Resources Council, Robert Muller (former Under-Secretary of the UN), Senator Ted Stevens of Alaska, E. P. Velikhov, Lee Nunn of the Alaska Power Authority, and many others. By sharing power resources, we can increase the amount of energy available to both countries, while decreasing superpower tensions.

Originally the concept of Buckminster Fuller, he called a transglobal power grid 'the highest priority' project in the world. It is the focus of a worldwide network of business people called GENI – the Global Energy Network, International. The Siberia-Alaska link is the easiest and most significant first step. If we link the world's energy grids into one continuous line, maximum efficiency and maximum reliability are achieved. This proposal is totally possible right now with existing technology.

The essence is this – the trend of history demonstrates the convergence of peoples into larger cooperative wholes. The only reason we are still playing by rules that are 200 years out of date is that each of us have not yet personally felt that interconnection. This proposal would very rapidly have people experience their reliance on the well-being of everyone else worldwide. The major threshold toward a world without war will be crossed in a way that is elegant and exciting. The peace that we all are working for is at hand. Thank you, and I look forward to your response.

Sincerely,
Peter A. Orgain

RUTGERS
New Brunswick, New Jersey, USA

5 November 1987

Dear Mr Gorbachev,

May I offer a few comments on your speech of 2 November, in which you reviewed the history of the Soviet Union? Naturally, I found the discourse of very great interest, and hope that I have understood its significance.

I think that I understand the reasons why you tended in your speech to 'rehabilitate' Nikolai Bukharin and Nikita Khrushchev, and equally why you did not see fit at this time to treat Leon Trotsky and his one-time allies Gregory Zinoviev and Kamenev in the same way. I certainly would appreciate hearing from you whether my observations on this are correct.

It makes eminent sense that you should look kindly upon Bukharin, who opposed many of the same things to which you are now opposed – the forced collectivization of agriculture, from which the Soviet Union is still suffering, and the form in which Stalin carried out forced industrialization. Similarly, Nikita Khrushchev was your predecessor in trying to bring about fundamental changes in the system originally established by Stalin and so your friendly view of him is understandable.

On the other hand, given your present situation, you could not politically rehabilitate Leon Trotsky. The fact was that once Stalin had defeated Trotsky, he put into application the policies which Trotsky and his economic associate Proebrazhansky had advocated in the polemical struggle with Stalin. Hence, to rehabilitate Trotsky at this point, would be to reinforce many of the things about Stalin's program with which you are in disagreement.

However, may I suggest that in your recasting of the view of Soviet history, there are at least two important things which would make that effort more credible for those people outside of the Soviet Union who have some understanding of that history. One would be to more frankly admit the monstrosity of the tyranny of Stalin – for example, the fact that he killed more communists than anyone else in history. The other would be to give recognition to Leon Trotsky as the person who organized the Red Army and led it to victory in the 1918–21 Civil War.

Yours truly,
Robert Alexander
Professor

On November 2, 1987, in a three-hour address celebrating the 70th anniversary of the Bolshevik Revolution, Gorbachev delivered his most radical and comprehensive criticism of Soviet Society since he gained power in 1985. He strongly attacked Stalin and the great purges of 1937-38. He also repeatedly stressed the need for democracy and freedom of expression, glasnost, as a precondition for economic reform and development.

HILTON HOTELS CORPORATION
World Headquarters, Beverly Hills, California, USA

11 December 1987

Dear General Secretary Gorbachev,

I very much appreciated the opportunity to speak to you and to participate in yesterday's meeting at the Soviet Embassy in Washington, DC.

I congratulate you on the signing of the INF Treaty which is certainly a positive step in Soviet-American relations and I hope further discussion on nuclear arms are similarly productive.

I found the meeting at the Soviet Embassy to be particularly enlightening on improving the economic relations between the Soviet Union and the United States. As you know, Hilton Hotels Corporation's subsidiary, Conrad International, has been having talks with the State Committee for Foreign Tourism about a hotel deal in Moscow.

As indicated to you, my brother Eric Hilton, who is an executive vice-president of Conrad International, was in Moscow speaking with Mr Konovalov and his representatives at the very time of your visit to Washington. We sincerely hope a relationship between Conrad International, named in honor of my father Conrad Hilton, and the State Committee for Foreign Tourism can be consummated.

I was pleased you mentioned tourism and the hotel business during your remarks at the Soviet Embassy meeting. Well-run hotels can do much to contribute to economic progress. My company has had a long and powerful record of performance in the hospitality field and I would personally see that any relationship with Soviet interests proves to be a successful enterprise.

Sincerely,
Barron Hilton
Chairman and President

Madrid
Spain   January 1988

Dear comrade and friend,

I am a Spanish woman, militant member of the P.C.E. (Spanish Communist Party), admirer of the Soviet Revolution and your country. Last summer I visited the Soviet Union and fell in love with the Soviet people and your beautiful country. (I saw Moscow, Leningrad and Kiev.) At the moment, I am reading the book that you have written on perestroika. I have nearly finished it and like it very much. I have decided to write to you because in the book you say that you read your letters and pay attention to the suggestions of all friends who write.

The new revolution which you propose seems outstanding to me . . . all that the Soviet Communist Party want to do to revitalise socialist society. We are unable to understand perestroika in the West because the press distorts everything, socialist countries are always talked about with contempt, they insist that capitalist society is the happy one. I know what this consumist society means to many people and neither journalists nor politicians can mislead me.

Felipe Gonzalez, President of my country which is social-democratic, explained perestroika by saying that the USSR was going to copy capitalist society. Luckily I have bought your book and am finding out myself what you want: socialism, but without corruption. Your book reveals so much sincerity and honesty. How different the politicians are in Spain and it is because of this that they do not believe in your sincerity, because they always lie!

But there was one thing I did not like about Perestroika, the chapter on family and woman. Communist revolutions have freed woman from her slavery (Mao ordered that little girls' feet should no longer be bound). Capitalist and Islamic societies, also many African religions continue to keep women oppressed. Communist countries have succeeded in allowing woman to be people who are able to succeed in their studies, in research and athletics, etc.

Now you must not regress. There are no specifically feminine tasks. The education of one's children and the work in the home must be shared between both partners. The woman must be able to fulfill herself as a person just as much as the man, to study and work and have positions of power etc, while at home, sharing everything; rights and duties.

Thank you Gorbachev! Go forward with everything, including the rights of women.

Yours,
Maria del Carmen Hitos Natera

AMERICAN EXPRESS COMPANY
American Express Tower World Financial Center
New York, USA

11 January 1988

Dear Mr General Secretary,

It was indeed a unique honor and pleasure for Mrs Robinson and me to be among the guests at the historic dinner at the White House on 8 December. May I again offer my congratulations to you, as I have to President Reagan, over the success you were able to achieve that week. The positive momentum you have set in motion offers great hope for a more prosperous and peaceful tomorrow for all mankind.

When I was introduced to you by President Reagan as Chairman of American Express Company, you asked if we were doing enough business together. I responded that we were doing 'some, but not enough' and that your new initiative 'needed a greater two-way flow of people, goods and services'. I was very heartened by your positive response and I promised to accelerate efforts within American Express to contribute to that objective.

Subsequent to our meeting, I discussed this with my senior executives and asked them to review the current status of their respective business relationships with the USSR and to consider ways in which we might enhance our current business relationships.

Perhaps some background would be useful for you. American Express Company has had permanent residence in your country for over twenty years through our Travel Service Office, now located on Sadovo-Kudrinskaya in Moscow. In close cooperation with Intourist and the Bank for Foreign Trade, we arrange for the provision of travel and financial services to our clients from around the world who visit the USSR. I was particularly pleased, when in June 1986 an agreement was signed with the Bank of Foreign Trade whereby a branch of the Bank was opened on the premises of our Moscow office to provide our clients with the full range of travel financial services which they expect worldwide, such as Travelers Cheque Refunds and Emergency American Express Card Replacement. It is also gratifying that we now have a small office in Leningrad. These recent positive developments can only help to reinforce the commitment of American Express to promote the USSR as a travel destination.

In summary, all of our activities have on-going business relationships in the USSR with working contacts established at various levels. We will continue to support these efforts while actively exploring ways in which these relationships might grow substantially over the next few years.

My associates and I applaud your initiative, including your New Year's message to the American people. We believe we can contribute to relations between our two countries through expanding the flow of people and financial services and thereby help weave what you have called 'a tangible fabric of trust and growing mutual understanding'.

Sincerely,
James D. Robinson III
Chairman

Minami Saitama-gun
Saitame-ken, Japan   27 January 1988

Dear Sir,

I have been engaged in foreign trade company dealing with machineries and equipments for exporting them to USSR and other countries in East Europe, and through my experience, I have visited several times your country and others wherever my business opportunity required me to go there.

If allowed to tell you very frankly, I do not have a good impression on your country, not to my knowledge just through ideology

183

through my experience of spending several months each year continuously in Moscow, one of the biggest cities in the world. Compared with even those cities under the communist regime, in East Europe like Berlin, Prague and Budapest, the capital city of the USSR, Moscow is most behind in advancement those of capital cities in standard of living, convenience of every day life, efficiency and management, products quality in market, environment and so on. Almost everybody except some scholars, journalists or top-management people flattering to USSR with unhealthy interest in western countries takes that such situation derives from the communist rule. I do not think so. I think it comes from the nature of the Russian people accustomed to the regime of communist party for seventy years.

Naturally and historically, the Russian people should have been most humorous in life, most courageous against any difficulty facing to them and most cultural, I think.

However, there is no sense of humour (though there exists anecdotes which are not spoken openly), good smile among human communication, especially with foreign people living in Moscow, and endurance (the endurance so thought presently is to be rather defined as resignation to the situation), but exists only stubbornness arising out of bureaucracy piled through the period of seventy years of communist rule . . .

Faithfully yours,
Masayoshi Yoshida

WORLD PUMPKIN CONFEDERATION
Collins, New York, USA

19 February 1988

Dear Mr Gorbachev,
On behalf of the World Pumpkin Confederation I wish to congratulate you for your courage in strengthening Soviet/US relations. Collins is a mere forty miles away from the Chautauqa Institute where the international conference was held last summer generating a great sense of communication between our countries. This was only surpassed by your later visit at harvest time.

Enclosed is information about the WPC. With your agricultural background I hope you find this interesting and perhaps you would be instrumental in helping us form an international competition involving your countrymen. Of particular interest to you may be the giant cabbage challenge. The US State of Alaska is famous for their cabbages and I will contact their Department of Economic Development to see if there is interest there. The UK is keen for this now as you can see in the enclosed newsletter. It is a fact that the USSR produce more cabbage than any other country and surely large ones can be grown too! The fertile area of the Ukraine could also produce giant pumpkins as well.

We welcome your friendly competition. If you would have a representative contact me, I will be more than grateful to work with them. Pumpkins for Peace!

Sincerely,
Ray Waterman
Vice-President

London
England   19 February 1988

Dear Mr Gorbachev,

Forgive the liberty of writing to you directly, but having just finished reading your book in which you mention that you do not mind ordinary people writing, I felt emboldened.

I think a lot of the views about your country are based on total ignorance – which breeds paranoid fears – and a fertile propaganda machine of the Western leadership. Uniting a people against a common enemy – as you are probably well aware – does tend to divert attention from internal ills. (In this latter respect I think the Falklands War provided such a focus for both Britain and Argentina!) Some of this suspicion is breaking down, although ignorance is still there. To digress for a moment, I note that whenever Moscow is shown on British television it appears dark, cold and forbidding. Part of this is because usually we are shown the May Day Parade and the October Revolution celebrations, thus we see Red Square and its pavement of cobbles. I visited your country with my elderly mother some two years ago, in the summer. I will never forget her face when she said, 'Oh how *green* everything is!' – I might add that she now (aged seventy-three) tells virtually anyone who will listen that behind that cold facade of the Kremlin wall it is all green with beautiful flowers! The more subtle nuances of reporting thereby became obvious!

One point in your book struck me forcibly again and again, and that was the level of overview of the total world system that you had. Too often politicians' views are limited – in the West sometimes by the apparent necessity of winning an election – to about two or three years. Your book grasped the necessity of long-term solutions to endemic problems. A time-span of at least into the next century would seem the minimum we should all aim for. (On another digression, I wonder whether this is not because for the first time in a long time we have a leader of the Soviet Union who is younger than those of the United States or Britain!) There has been some research done in Britain that indicates the time-span of managers is a direct correlation of their ability to problem-solve. I wonder therefore whether the time is now ripening when leaders – be they factory managers or world statesmen – will, of necessity, be those who can overview a long time-span, thus also highly complex processes, and be able to make appropriate long-term responses.

Another point which struck me forcibly – I think it might be concomitant upon the longer time-span – was both your determination and optimism that the world's problems are solvable. I wonder whether part of the problem of most people's inability to think long-term is coloured by the fear that there might not be a longterm. The threat of world annihilation is so grave that it appears to me that a lot of people hide their very real despair of any future by a round of 'busyness' in the present. However, part of the problem of the so-called peace movement is that it plays upon those very fears of annihilation, thus making the situation worse. Whilst our Campaigners for Nuclear Disarmament go around telling everyone we are only a few steps away from oblivion – without the necessary 'clout' to be able to change anything – it merely makes people scared. Scared people, in my experience, regard 'defences' as totally necessary. So although what CND is saying is valid, society as a whole feels more, not less, secure and therefore is even more unwilling to make rational decisions calmly. Our national leaders, picking up the 'scaredness' of our society, merely wish to be better defended.

My work involves working with individuals and groups who are 'defended' and closed down from other people in certain areas of their life. We sometimes describe them as people with a lot of fear, like a reservoir of water behind a dam. Draw attention to the dam, try and remove it by force and all you do is get a flood of fear. Ask what they are afraid of, sort out what caused this in the past, get them to recognise that the threat does not exist in the present, and the person as it were releases the sluice gates slowly, controlledly, until the dam is no longer needed. Defences, it seems to me, are indicators of fear.

On a simplistic analogy, it appears also that countries behave in a similar manner. Defences are there because the people were once faced with a situation they could not control and they got badly hurt. Obviously your own country has been badly hurt in its recent (and not so recent!) past. Your defences are there to stop your country having to sacrifice its people's blood in order to prevent a rape of the country. Similarly, I think Europe's defences as a whole are like that.

I wish you every success in the task you have started, both within your own country and in dialogue with the other nations. Though our elected leaders speak for our nations they do not, always, speak for all of the people all of the time. A lot of ordinary people in the street watched the televised summit in Iceland with hope, and also for once the recognition that maybe, just maybe, something concrete and historic would be achieved. The sense of disappointment and frustration was therefore very real. However, realising that you both came very close to solving some of the world's basic problems has at least fired again the hope that solutions are possible, even if they take longer!

Yours sincerely,
Evelyn L. F. Tovey

MPL
London, England

8 April 1988

Dear Premier Gorbachev,

Firstly, I would like to praise your recent efforts for world peace in your arms reductions negotiations with the USA. We in the West have often hoped for this kind of initiative.

As you may know, I was once part of a group called The Beatles. I believe our music is quite well known to the people of the Soviet Union, possibly even to you and your wife.

It occurred to me that it might be a good idea to release a record exclusively in Russia as a gesture of friendship towards the Russian people. With this in mind, I have prepared an album of rock and roll tunes and would be very pleased if you and your colleagues would assist its passage in any way you see fit, assuming of course the release of this record is acceptable to you.

Thank you for your kind attention. My family and I send our personal best wishes for the future.

Paul McCartney

In 1989 the album 'Back in the USSR' was recorded in England for special release in the Soviet Union. The album's jacket is in Russian and the lyrics to all of the songs are in English. An estimated 500,000 copies sold for roubles in the Soviet Union within a few months.

Sacramento
California, USA   15 May 1988

Dear Mr Gorbachev,
   Please forgive the English. I know no Russian.
   Being age sixty-four, and restlessly retired on a small pension, I vividly recall as a teenager reading the newspaper accounts of the massive German invasion of Russia in World War II; the painful Russian scorched earth in retreat (the magnificent Dnieper dam, etc, etc, etc); the savage German brutality toward soldier and civilian alike (Hitler: 'The rules of war don't apply on the Russian front'); the stubborn, courageous stands at Leningrad, Moscow, and Stalingrad that turned the Germans back. My own Army Air Corps service in the Western Pacific 3-43 to 2-46 prevented my following the Russian sweep back across Europe, but I recall my utter disbelief after the war at reading of an estimated twenty million Russian people lost (twenty million!).
   Considering Napoleon in 1812, WWI, and WWII (all ravaging storms that came from the West), it seems somewhat understandable that the Soviet Union might want to lower an 'Iron Curtain', heal its wounds, rebuild itself, and become so strong – at any cost – that no one would ever dare attempt such a horror again (our own General Patton was making speeches at war's end, 'We should fight the Russians now').
   We've had forty years of mistrust, misjudgments, antagonism, and confrontation. Perhaps we can, as a smiling Soviet official said of a recent naval side-swiping in the Black Sea, 'let bygones be bygones'.
   And now:
– Margaret Thatcher (about Gorbachev): 'Now here is a man I can do business with' (and believe me, the whole world noted her remark).
– Gorbachev to Reagan: 'What gives you the right to judge us?' (Marvelous!)
– Gorbachev leaping from his car in Washington, DC, unplanned, and shaking hands with ordinary people on the sidewalk (Americans loved it).
– Raisa gracefully out-maneuvering Nancy Reagan to talk longer with reporters; charmingly done, and without malice (Americans were delightedly amused). I somehow feel that Mrs Gorbachev will be the consummate gracious hostess at the Moscow summit.
– Western reporters bussed into the Kremlin (good).
– Gorbachev - *Time* magazine's 'Man of the Year' (it all helps).
– A top Soviet general walking confidently into our Pentagon (by invitation).

– 'The first art auction in Moscow since the Bolshevik Revolution' (Hooray! The world is interested).
– Russian officials converting munitions factories to proudly displayed bicycles, baby buggies, washing machines (wonderful; the Soviet people will love that).
– 'Go Gorby!' shouted in the streets (you are only a man, but you have become the symbol of the finest hopes of men).
– Glasnost and perestroika.
– Etc, etc, etc.

Every week some exciting new development in the Soviet Union. A friend of mine now greets me with, 'Well, what is Gorbachev doing today?' (I guess the 'cult of personalities' cannot be avoided altogether, because a leader is the spokesman and the symbol of his nation, and when he becomes the symbol of an idea that has universal appeal his stature goes beyond national boundaries) . . .

I am respectfully,
Robert S. Higginbotham Jr

Milan
Italy

24 May 1988

Dear Mr Gorbaciov,

Aside from any religious or political convictions, I believe, along with many Italians, both communist and non-communist, in your desire to preserve peace in the world.

You may laugh, but I pray that your enemies both inside and outside your country may not triumph and that you may realise your plan to restore the human rights of your people and of all peoples, whether they are tied to Russia or not.

I believe so firmly in the reality of the hopes which the world is placing on the new Russia that I am looking forward with great enthusiasm to spending ten days there in August. During this time I shall even try to establish a relationship between my pupils and the pupils of an elementary school in Leningrad and/or Moscow. In fact I have already written a letter to the head of the Italian school no. 318 Padjesdonoi Per. 12 in Leningrad.

This is not all. Although I have not yet received a reply, I am getting my pupils to do some pieces of work which I can leave at your school with the aim of setting up a cultural exchange between the two groups of pupils. I shall surely find a teacher in Leningrad or Moscow who is sensitive to the problems of fellowship and cooperation between people and who wants to communicate these ideas to his or her pupils!

God bless you for all you are doing and will do for the well-being of your people, whom I love more than any other.

Giuseppina Gezzi

Encino
California, USA   3 June 1988

To the People of the USSR:

[With] the summit now behind us, I write to you as a common American citizen in the spirit of the peace and friendship which can again be, as it once was, the natural state of our relations. I also write to you of the challenge before you in the necessary restructuring of your great nation. These two things are one.

As you now learn much of the real history of your nation and your revolution, permit me to say that the principal cause of enmity between our countries was less the conflict of the nineteenth century ideologies than the behavior of your former leader, Djughashvili [Stalin].

It is the American perception, rightly or wrongly, that his actions immediately following WWII (the Great Patriotic War) represented a new threat to peace, and we reacted – and perhaps overreacted – accordingly. This has created the climate of fear, suspicion, and the incredible cycle of economic waste which we have come to call the cold war.

More importantly to you today is that Djughashvili betrayed your revolution as it was envisioned by Ulyanov and the 'real Bolsheviks'. As he was dying, Lenin prayed to his followers to prevent the succession of power to Stalin. He failed, for Stalin controlled the party agenda.

Where would your country, and the relations between ours, be today had Lenin lived a few more years, and had his natural successors such as Bukharin succeeded him? We'll never know. But we all know – with due respect for his wartime leadership – that Stalin also created within the Soviet Union a degree of centralized party power which created fear, allowed oppression, all but eliminated initiative, subverted the freedoms inherent in your constitution, and built a nearly aristocratic bureaucracy, which, in the course of human nature, will resist change to preserve itself, as did that of the Czars.

Further, we as nations and as people can cooperate in solutions for the next century's enormous environmental problems, and in health, scientific and space programs which will benefit mankind for ever. Isn't that better for both of our countries than building bombs and missiles? . . . and for our children? Just think!! . . . the

190

USSR and the USA cooperating 'across the board'! Can you imagine what we could do?!

There is a problem, however. And it is a problem which only the people of the Soviet Union can solve. Those who would stifle your present leadership will exert every possible effort at the forthcoming All-Union Party Conference to prevent 'restructuring'.

If that happens, you will answer to yourselves for continuing living standards abysmally below those which the wealth of your country should permit, and you will answer to your grand-children for the fear in which we will all continue to live. If the Party Congress defeats the ideas of our present leaders, both of our nations will be insignificant in the affairs of the next century – if we're lucky enough to avoid a stupid and suicidal war.

However, if the Party Congress upholds the restructuring policies announced by your present leadership – 'the revolution without bullets' – we can offer a world to our children which is good as mankind can do.

The key is that at this moment in time, it is your leadership rather than ours, which will set the course. If it succeeds, and it won't be easy for you, you can be sure that we will respond favourably – including huge 'Western' economic inputs. You see, we capitalists think we can buy you, and you socialists think you can use us, and that creates a game in which we all can win ... compared to the present game in which we all lose.

Sincerely,
Carl G. Hokanson

Djughashvili is the real surname of Stalin, and Ulyanov that of Lenin. Some authorities say that Stalin and Lenin are names which they initially took to shield their true identities because of their illegal revolutionary activities.

Elm Grove
Wisconsin, USA 6 June 1988

Dear General Secretary Gorbachev,

I followed the events of the recent Soviet-American summit with a mixture of uneasy feelings. My one clear feeling was admiration of you – of your intellectual energy, personal strength, and dignity.

Hearing our President's well-intended but often condescending lectures to the Soviet Union's people and political leadership, I embarrassed for my country. The various remarks of our President seemed to me to obliquely represent that part of my country that President Reagan typically glossed over: our shortcomings. We Americans, proud of our economic achievements and huge amounts of personal freedom, sometimes look at the world the way a spoiled child does. We tend to see everything in terms of ourselves, in relation to our particular standards and desires. And while there is a great deal that is valuable and exemplary in the American system, our faults are such that we should not posture as an absolute ideal to the world, especially as guests on such a crucial occasion.

Your term of office, General Secretary Gorbachev, has been marked by a straightforward commitment to address the world we really live in, and to improve it. I admire your combination of pragmatism and idealism, which permits you to work for progress while dealing practically with the regressive elements present in any large political system.

It was very frustrating for me – and for many of the world's citizens – to see this recent opportunity for a significant reduction in militarism largely missed. Our President seems to feel that grandiloquent speechmaking invoking his idealized image of America is the true summit of progress. Of course, he is the elected representative of our nation, but many loyal and patriotic Americans like myself have come to realize that this Hollywood perspective on good, evil, and the fate of the earth is profoundly and dangerously unrealistic.

While I have absolutely no sympathy with communism, and deplore international hegemony exercised by your country as well as my own, it seems that Americans could better recognize the historical and cultural factors that differentiate our countries. It would be helpful for both our countries to recognize that we are struggling at opposite ends of the spectrum that runs from one extreme of individual freedom to another of social obligation. Of course it seems to us in America that the Soviet system, as it evolved under the tragedy of the Stalin era, has not left nearly enough room for private initiative and individual expression. But one could very well observe that at the fringes of America's private and competitive system, many experience mainly the unfortunate right to live without a home, in proximity to millions of guns wielded by 'freedom-loving' sociopaths, in the midst of a plague grown out of some dubious personal freedoms.

Now, that is a highly fragmentary and inaccurate perspective on a large, complex society. It is not how I see my country. But it is no less accurate than the notion that the Soviet Union is only represented by the plight of your citizens who are denied immigration, or that its progress should be measured by how closely it comes to resemble the United States.

A recent American President evinced this manner of national neurosis, bemoaning the prospect of our becoming a 'pitiful, helpless giant', at a time when we were unable to understand or defeat Vietnamese nationalism. I can well imagine that you have to face strong-willed and powerful individuals in the Soviet government and military who, like their American counterparts, insist on defining the rest of the world in terms of selfish, hegemonic interests, and equate national power with overloads of weaponry. It seems to me that you face internal obstacles greater than any American leader does, but perhaps the Soviet system has provided more groundwork for perestroika than is clear to Americans.

The 'tightrope' that you yourself are walking, balanced between certain difficult traditions of your society on one side and Western pressures on the other side, seems a great and exhausting challenge. But I ask you to remain strong, and to remember that you are not walking it for yourself alone. My wife and I have a child due next January, and like so many others throughout the world, we see the Soviet-American arms race as a stupidity unaffordable by our countries, by our children, by the earth itself.

Very truly yours,
David Bittinger

Corte Madera
California, USA   9 June 1988

Dear Mr Secretary General,
Time magazine recently published an article on Soviet women, including an article on Mrs Gorbachev which I am sure you have seen. After reading this article it occurred to me that fifty-three per cent of the Soviet population suffers over-exhaustion from coping with day-to-day living. How can you have increased productivity and reform the economy when over half of the population is too tired to enthusiastically participate? It is a rare and exceptional individual who will consistently produce at top capacity without some kind of personal incentive, yet this is precisely what is expected.

In political terms the Soviet system becomes more successful in having increased productivity, the capitalist system benefits from expansion of its market place, and most important each has a vested interest in the other's economic welfare, which decreases the risk of conflict. A reading of history shows that economic problems are often solved by military means. Not only did the Second World War bring the United States out of the Great Depression and begin a technological revolution here, it also graphically demonstrated the dogged endurance of the average Soviet citizen and the determination of the American GI. Both of our nations talk peace yet we are also arms suppliers to the world. Our economies are based upon the premise that there be strife and conflict somewhere in our world. The question is can we wage peace and prosperity with the same gargantuan capacity that we can wage war and human suffering?

Sincerely,
Lois A. Vos

'I spent most of my time in the kitchen or shopping. I spent hours looking for clothes and food. There are no kitchen appliances - mixers, graters, dishwashers, clothes dryers, appliances that make women's work easier. I get tired a lot. Really tired', is a quote from a young Moscow woman taken from the Time magazine issue of June 6, 1988, and which sums up the idea mentioned in the letter.

The Soviet Union and United States are the two leaders in major weapon exports. The New York Times reported in December 1988 that the Soviets gathered 35% of the market share, with the United States following at 32.8%. These percentages are based on 1987 exports, in 1985 dollars. In 1987, deliveries of weapons to foreign countries for the US amounted to $11.6 billion, just behind the Soviet Union, which added to $12.3 billion worth.

Andheri (East)
Bombay, India

1 July 1988

Respected Sir,

I, a citizen of India, very heartily congratulate you on the giant step you have initiated towards a more human and presidential form of government.

I have already read a lot about glasnost and other policies you have been introducing from time to time in your country. We as humans can proudly say that there is one leader who is genuinely concerned about welfare of humanity, world peace and nuclear disarmament. Since your appointment you made an earnest and sincere effort to bring the SALT treaty with USA by peaceful means. Your handling of the Afghan issue and the final withdrawal of the troops in itself speaks of your laurels.

Your sincerity, straightforwardness, foresight, capabilities, fearless nature, an eye for minute details will set a shining example for centuries to come and you will go down in the golden annals of history. You are a shining star on the horizon. The sapling which you have sown will become a tree for others to climb.

Yours sincerely,
Naren R. Bhuta

Naren R. Bhuta's wife informs us that on 21st June, 1990, he disappeared from his house and has not been heard from since.

Ostiglia
Mantova, Italy   12 September 1988

Mr Gorbaciov,

I am an Italian, forty years old, a bank employee. One day I decided, with some trepidation, to buy your book *Perestroika*; I say trepidation because I was sure it was one of the usual works of propaganda on the communist world which could have no connection with the problems of the Western system.

I am truly happy to say that I was wrong. Yours is a book of wide-ranging – indeed universal – interest; a book which can be read equally by an Italian, a Russian, a German or an American because the concepts which it expresses are truly valid for all these people, whatever their level on the social scale, who want to contribute to the good of their country according to their abilities. I am a Catholic and I am very glad to have found many principles of our faith in *Perestroika*: absolute respect for one's neighbour, the greatest tolerance for others regardless of the colour of their skin or their political or religious beliefs, the rejection of the use of force and above all enormous faith in the potential of dialogue.

These are all very important judgments but they would not on their own have persuaded me to continue in my reading, had I not found between the lines something of fundamental importance: *sincerity*, that is, I am convinced that you, Mr Gorbaciov, would not have been able to publish your book had you not been truly convinced, in the depths of your being, of the truth of the words you were writing.

The concepts which you express are not new because they have been inherent in man's nature from the very moment of his appearance on earth, but we have forgotten them all too often.

In every part of the world there are areas of conflict, states which seek to dominate their neighbours; so that the fact that a person of your importance has put the whole world on the same footing, with no more differences between black and white, European

195

and African, Russian and American, capitalists and communists, with the sole aim of achieving peace, is in my view, an event of fundamental importance.

Artiade Ravagnini

Naples
Italy
6 October 1988

My dear Mikhail Gorbaciov,

I am a lady, a hateful aristocrat by birth. I am an Italian, in fact a Neapolitan from the Vomero area of Naples. I hate politics and in a moment I'll tell you why. I am a tireless worker. I was born a socialist. I adore work and those who work well. I am on the side of the workers, and of those who respect their rights. Human, social, economic and legal rights. I think that those who offer their hands, their brains and sometimes even their lives have a right to human dignity for themselves and their families.

This is the first time in my life I have ever written to a politician. I am not some kind of obsessive, nor a fanatic. If I don't love politics it is because it's often about lying and deceit. I love things which are true and sincere.

You wonder why I am writing to you? It's hard to explain, very hard. I'm writing to remind you that someone said fairy tales never come true. You, Mikhail Gorbaciov, have shown this to be false. I have to tell you this, for love of the truth. You are the most beautiful fairy tale come true. All my life I have been observing your wonderful country, and loving it. I love its history, its culture, its magnificence. For me, Mother Russia had only one defect.

The only thing that was lacking was you, Mikhail Gorbaciov! You, the new man. You emerged from the millennia like a dream. You have broken barriers, crossed mountains, hurled down taboos with the force of a mythical giant. Nothing could stop you! And you came to us. You entered the house like a dear old friend. You, Gorbaciov, you are the Messiah of the great Mother Russia. The consciousness of the ground you tread on emanates from you. We were waiting for you, the real man, the strong man. You are the salt of the earth. You are the one we all watch with feelings of safety, of faith. You are the real man in whom we all believe. Perhaps there is a dream hidden in your great heart. Perhaps at night, when you are about to fall asleep, you too dream of a fairy tale, you dream of creating perfumed gardens in place of those terrible deadly weapons.

My dear Mikhail Gorbaciov it is time for me to say goodbye. I can do nothing for you, so from this enchanted country of mine I send you our Neapolitan hearts, our melodies, our most beautiful songs to lull you to sleep. Together with my blue sea we will whisper to you as you sleep: courage, Mikhail, courage, tomorrow another new day awaits you, a day which you will have to fill with your efforts, your responsibilities, your intelligence!

My dear President, forgive me if I have gone too far, but you see, this was an impulse, a rush of faith and affection that I neither could nor wanted to repress. I think that if the truth be told, this testimony was due to you. The world needs many men like you, but miracles do not happen every day.

May I extend to you and your wife my very highest regards and warmest wishes for the future.

Yours,
Flora Pinto d'Albavilla Capaldo

SOFT DRINK WORKERS UNION, LOCAL 812
International Brotherhood of Teamsters
Scarsdale, New York, USA

17 October 1988

Dear Mr Secretary,

This letter is a follow-up to my letter dated 27 May 1988 in which I asked for help in a worker's struggle with Pepsi Cola. Since that time I have had the opportunity to watch on television American singer Billy Joel's concert tour in the Soviet Union.

In one segment of the concert tour an elderly Russian woman whose poet son was a hero to the people, invited the Joel family to her home. When Billy's baby daughter acted up, the Russian woman's face showed immediate, genuine concern. She instinctively acted to soothe and comfort the infant. My wife, who was also watching the program remarked that maternal instincts are universal.

The next day I was still haunted by the sincerity expressed in the Russian woman's face as I listened to a tape recording of *Les Misérables*, the musical which was adapted from the classic novel. In one of the songs were the words: 'to love another person is to see the face of God'. I immediately made the connection with the Russian woman and thought how great it would be if this emotional and human concept could be shared among ordinary people of different countries.

Our countries compete in Olympic sports, but there is little personal contact. There are exchanges between musical and dance stars, by they are not typical working people. There is nothing for the common people of our two countries to connect with. I propose a connection.

I ask you to consider a worker exchange program for a period of time to be worked out. As president of the Soft Drink Workers Union, Local 812 of the Teamsters, I represent over five thousand workers. I would like to propose that soft drink workers at a Pepsi Cola plant here in New York swap places with Pepsi Cola workers in Russia.

The work Soviet and American soft drink workers perform is similar so that acclimatization to the job, albeit in a foreign country, would represent no problem. If you believe as I do that there is intrinsic value to the idea, my union is prepared to make whatever arrangements are necessary to carry out the people exchange program.

Respectfully yours,
Anthony Rumore

San Antonio
Texas, USA   1 November 1988

Dear Mr Secretary,

I am impressed by your efforts to open Soviet life to all peoples of your country. Informed Americans worry about you and the ultimate outcome of your efforts. We worry that you are changing the whole of your nation too fast. The Pandora's box which you are opening can never be closed once opened; there is no going back to rethink and to moderate changes. You are a brave man, Mr Secretary!

Respectfully,
James E. Wysong
Major, USAF (Retired)

Houma
Louisiana   8 December 1988

Dear Mr Gorbachev,

I heard your speech yesterday at the United Nations, and I was very pleased to listen to every word.

As I listened to you saying that 10,000 tanks and 500,000 men would be pulled back, my mind began to think of ways to utilize them and not waste anything you people worked so very, very hard to accomplish.

Please bear in mind, I'm not trying to nose-in or suggest anything, I'm only writing to tell you my thoughts. Listed below is what I was thinking, and possibly, it could be more:

10,000 tanks = 10,000 tractors

a. Remove turrets, guns, heavy armour plate;
b. improvize for cultivation and harvest;
c. two engines = plenty power for hydraulic power;
d. can also be used for construction and roadworks;
e. 10,000 jobs for 10,000 drivers already trained;
f. additional jobs for mechanics, helpers and many more.

These tractors could be used to pull large V-shaped ploughs to either irrigate or drain large sections of land in the north for rice or other crops that are needed. With this in mind, millions of acres of land could be cultivated, planted, and harvested for much-needed food and agricultural products.

I listen to all your speeches and think highly of them. I would like to say so much more, but perhaps I should hold my tongue in place.

Sincerely and God bless you,
Lawrence LeBlanc

Canvey Island
England
                                            26 July 1989

Your Excellency,

Please excuse a letter from an Englishman, just reached the age of seventy.

I normally live in Zambia and before you came to power I wrote to the Ambassador there (Mr Solidnikov I believe his name was) to say that USSR needed a much younger cabinet to rule the country, that as you are a world power there should be much more freedom for people to come in and out of the country.

I never thought I would see the day when that would happen, so I do congratulate you on all that you have done, and are doing still.

As a Christian I am also glad to see that most of the prisoners who were jailed for religious reasons have been released. This is the one side of Russian policy I could never understand. Even if the top people, including yourself, decide that there is no God, then it is very wrong to make this an issue at Russian schools; as every person should be able to judge for themselves whether there is a God, and act accordingly.

I understand that your dear wife Raisa went to St Paul's Cathedral in London and saw the famous painting 'The Light of the World' where Christ is shown knocking on a door, representing the heart of a man or woman. Christ never forced his religion on anyone. We – you and I – can decide for ourselves whether we open that door. But it is very wrong for your education department to make people believe that there is no God – even as it is equally wrong for any government to force religion on its people (for example, Iran).

So, Your Excellency, carry on the good work. Don't ever be downhearted at the apparent failures and setbacks. There are magazines even in England that forecast that your policies will not last and that you may even be forced to abandon them. Don't do it Your Excellency.

The people of Britain are behind you.

Yours respectfully,
Ted Blackmore MBE

Saarbruckenerstr
West Germany   21 October 1989

Dear Mr Gorbachev,

I am convinced that many monopolist and capitalist forces in the United States of America and in the German Federal Republic are doing all they can to present your government and the Soviet people in a bad light. I can only send this message to you and the Soviet Union: in spite of all economic reforms, do not let yourself be lured into introducing capitalism into your country. Work honestly and decisively to improve your country, as you have done up to now, within the philosophy of socialism and in accordance with the principles of socialism. Here in the Federal Republic, the people have everything they could possibly want in the economic sphere, but nevertheless, in my opinion, the culture is utterly decadent.

There is no individual and personal solidarity within the population, and everything is determined by commercialism and the pursuit of profit. Oppression by capitalism is a very secret, seductive form of oppression, with the result that the people in such countries no longer know what they should do or what they are living for. Only the common will of all people to live without the exploitation of nature or of other human beings, can help save this world from ruin, and is not that a basic tenet of communism?

I am not a member of the German Communist Party nor do I belong to any workers' organization, but I believe, like you, in the historical mission of the working classes; at this time of great confusion, it is very clear that work is one of man's greatest benefits, and that the mentality of the working class, based as it is on solidarity and not on arrogance, points the way for all levels of society.

By profession, I am a trained chiropodist; I am a very spiritual and religious person – I devote much time to prayer, to Indian Hatha

Yoga and to meditation, and have also had considerable success as an athlete in the spheres of football and cycle racing.

Please be aware that a simple man like me shares your hopes, and prays for you and for the Soviet Union.

Long live peace!

Yours sincerely,
Ingbert George

Durham
North Carolina, USA

April 1990

Dear Secretary Gorbachev,

When I was a young boy friends of ours who were actors, directors, and lawyers lost their jobs because of the fear of some Americans in the early 1950s, created by our perception of the Soviet Union as a threat to our freedoms.

Last week I heard a former Russian citizen, now at the Carnegie Endowment for Peace in Washington DC, claim something I found very disquieting. He said without more power your quests for glasnost and perestroika would never be realized. Only with power could you accomplish these goals. But he said that with such power your control over the Soviet state would exceed that of Stalin, and carried with it the possibility of accomplishing great evil.

You are not responsible for that Russian citizen's opinion – he may be quite mistaken. I remember, however, only too vividly the fear under which we lived in the United States during the last part of Stalin's life, whether or not it was exaggerated or justified. Moreover, it may have paled beside the fear that, I gather, actually existed in your country. You and I did not create that fear; we only lived through it.

I have a desire I think you have, and which your countrymen and my countrymen share. We all want to believe there are honorable men whose deeds and ideals are worthy of emulation. You stand, as much as our President does, to substantially shape the world in which we shall all live for the remainder of the twentieth century, and well into the twenty-first century. I appeal to you to create for your countrymen that image of honor, by your deeds and by your ideals, just as I believe it is important for honorable men and women throughout the world to serve as examples for others in their own countries.

Very sincerely yours,
Mr and Mrs Heath Tuttle

EASTERN EUROPE
Voices From a Changing World

LOOKING BACK over five years it is impossible not to conclude that what was in effect a vast transformation in Soviet life and policies was the most important influence in international history in the period and may well remain so for quite a long time. Yet on the face of things, the East European Revolution of 1989 must surely rival it. The balance of power in Europe was completely changed as the entire communist system disintegrated in a few weeks and, with it, its military alliance and close economic collaboration with the Soviet Union.

Yet although he was not the architect of the East European forms of *perestroika* or the instigator of the quick revolts that swept the communists from power, his behaviour in other matters and his approach to the area itself were of tremendous importance. In the early stages of his arms talks with the West he used his Warsaw Treaty allies to reinforce his arguments by calling special meetings of their Political Consultative Committee. He also listened to their advice which on balance favoured a steady acceleration of the disarmament process. In December 1988 Gorbachev told the UN General Assembly that he intended cutting Soviet forces unilaterally; and although this had other objectives, its eventual result was to challenge the legitimacy and authority of the East European governments and to encourage opposition to them. For the fact of the matter was that in the last resort their power depended on Soviet military force.

Gorbachev cannot but have been fully conscious of this. Stalin had sent his army in to defeat Germany and he left it in to contain America. He also used it to help promote a Soviet-type revolution that he believed would then flourish on its own. But in 1956 Krushchev had had to use the Red Army to crush a popular revolution in Hungary, and twelve years later Brezhnev had had to authorise the Czechoslovak invasion as the only means of putting a stop to the Prague 'Spring'. All that had prevented Soviet military intervention in Poland in 1981 was the willingness and power of the Polish army to defeat Solidarity itself. By 1988 the Polish army was unhappy with its role and inadequate for it; and there was no other East European force competent to contain a rebellion should one arise in its own country. So the more successful Gorbachev was in pursuing disarmament, the stronger the signal he sent to East European reformers that they would not be blocked.

It would in any case have been futile for him to promote reform in the Soviet Union and at the same time discourage it, still less intervene to stop it, in Eastern Europe. In fact, the evidence points to his understanding of this. In receiving a range of leaders and in visiting their countries he extolled the merits of *perestroika*. He was frequently impatient with them, notably with Honecker from East Germany and Ceausescu from Romania. And in behaving in this fashion, he had the additional reason that he needed reformers in high places in Eastern Europe to assist him in the struggle with his own Party.

That certainly does not mean to say that he looked to the overthrow of East European communism. Raising the price for Soviet oil and gas had reduced what some had argued was a Soviet subsidy to Eastern Europe. And there were political advantages in having like-minded socialist neighbours. To begin with, Gorbachev's approach was very positive. He tried to convert the Council for Mutual Economic Assistance into what it was supposed to be, but clearly was not, the East European equivalent of the European Community. But the so-called Complex Programme on Science and Technology he introduced in 1985 ran into national bureaucratic barriers, and by 1988 all that was left of his vision was a series of bland resolutions.

Even so, Gorbachev did not write off the value of Comecon, as it was called, since it provided important foodstuffs and some high quality industrial imports for the Soviet market. But he turned his attention increasingly to the European Community. His predecessors had refused even to recognise it, but Gorbachev gradually realised the part it could play in the regeneration of the Soviet economy by providing investment, technology and quality industrial and consumer goods. In 1988 he authorised an umbrella agreement with the European Community that enabled all the members of Comecon to negotiate trade treaties with it. In due course this will undoubtedly benefit the Soviet economy. But one of its immediate effects was to loosen already weak Comecon ties by encouraging the East European states successfully to set their sights on developing their economies through association with the West, with all that such an arrangement implied politically.

In India and elsewhere he had already preached the doctrine of non-interference in the internal affairs of other nations, and this was completely at variance with the so-called Brezhnev Doctrine that had been used to justify intervention in Czechoslovakia in 1968 and, by implication, was still to force twenty years later. This was also at odds with his approach to Western Europe. The Brezhnev Doctrine was clearly ripe for repeal. But the push came from another Gorbachev initiative. The idea of a 'common European home' was not wholly new. It had emerged under Brezhnev as an essentially anti-American ploy. But in 1987 Gorbachev began to use it positively, looking to possible economic and political co-operation that would generally assist a Soviet revival. In this context the Brezhnev Doctrine was a millstone around his neck; and the prospect of the Single Market in Western Europe in 1992 made its removal in good time all the more essential. It was significant that it was in addressing a West European audience in Strasbourg in July 1989 that he declared the Doctrine dead: 'Any interference in internal affairs, any attempt to limit the sovereignty of states - both friends and allies or anybody else - is inadmissible'.

In a way it is surprising that it took the East European revolution a good few more months to materialise. The gap in fact testifies that it was not all down to Gorbachev. The East European governments first had to realise that they were on their own and should accommodate with the demands for reform. And the reformers in Eastern Europe also had to appreciate that the Soviet government would not intervene. Gorbachev had to take action - to ensure that the East German forces would not open fire - and perhaps even to organise the actual revolt in Romania. When the people did come out on to the streets, they won. They had waited through decades of fear, but in the end they proved what the human spirit can do.

Bill Wallace

Crowds surge forward to witness the opening ceremony for pedestrian crossings at the area of the Brandenburg Gate on the boundary of East and West Berlin.

Demonstrators in the centre of Berlin demanding creation of free trade unions, the right to strike and the participation of workers in the resolution of production problems in January 1990.

Farewell! The Thirty-second Guards Tank Division from the Potsdam area in the USSR leave the German Democratic Republic amidst cheering crowds in May 1989.

At a meeting of the citizens of Brno, Czeckoslovakia, in the centre of the town, voices are raised in now familiar support of perestroika and democratisation. December 1989.

The revolutionary crowd in Bucharest, Romania, December 1989.

The question of the restoration of 'nationality' – the rights of the Turkish speaking and Muslim population of Bulgaria – evokes an uneven reaction amongst the 10,000 people who have come from all parts of the Republic. January 1990.

Gorbachev talks with onlookers in Vilnius, Lithuania, in January 1990.
Photorgraph: B. Babonov

Gorbachev taking the oath of office as he is elected President of the U.S.S.R. on March 15 1990 at the third extraordinary Congress of the People's Deputies of the U.S.S.R. *Photograph: B. Babanov*

Mikhail and Raisa Gorbachev in an early photograph.

Gorbachev enjoying a rare moment of leisure with his family.

President Gorbachev enjoys one of the more informal award ceremonies.

Mikhail and Raisa Gorbachev rub shoulders with children at the Artek pioneer camp. *Photograph: V. Musaelyan*

Mikhail Gorbachev. *Photograph: Tom Stoddard/Katz*

Blackburn
Lancashire
England

8 February 1988

Dear Mr Gorbachev,

I am writing to you for two reasons. Firstly, I should like to congratulate you on your presidency to date, particularly with regard to the reforms being introduced in your own country, and the very significant contribution to world peace resulting from the recent arms agreement.

The second point concerns President Ceausescu of Romania. I seem to have read quite a lot about him recently in the Western 'quality' press, particularly in connection with him and his destruction of historic and beautiful buildings to be replaced by hideous new ones. Furthermore the revelations in the book *Red Horizins* by the former Romanian minister Ion Pacepa indicate that he and his family are completely unfit to be in charge of any organization larger than a flea-circus! Even allowing for some exaggeration, it is clear that the man is doing considerable harm to the country and its people.

In view of the considerable influence which your government has over Romanian affairs, may I request that you do all in your power to rectify the position quickly.

With every hope for your continued success.

Yours faithfully,
Michael A. Loveridge

Kosmická
Prague, Czechoslovakia

March 1988

Dear Mr Gorbachev,

Could I be so bold as to trouble you by writing this letter. I am convinced that only you can contribute significantly to the revival of Czechoslovak society, the Czech and Slovak nations and the Communist Party of Czechoslovakia. Please, trust me that I am judging the current situation objectively and that it is not my intention to deceive you in any way.

As you no doubt know very well it was not possible in the Soviet Union to criticise Party officials before the advent of perestroika and glasnost, and this resulted in social and economic distortions. However, in my country we can only hope that our Mikhail Gorbachev might one day appear. The leading forces in the CPC embrace ideas identical to those of the Stalin and Brezhnev eras,

207

and they can hardly be expected to renounce these ideas as they reach the end of their political careers.

In Czechoslovakia they profess to keep the public informed. In fact, what we get is partial information and misinformation. Individuals and groups of people are denounced as anti-socialist without having the right to defend themselves in public. The press has not even publicised the initiative of many prominent writers and artists who call for reform, thus expressing the views of the majority of the nation. The nation is silent as past experience has taught it to stay silent; individuals look after themselves only. But still, was this not the case in your country before the introduction of perestroika?

Mr Gorbachev, our nation trusts you. Even those people who demon-press, in order that their future might be brighter; in order that the whole nation might decide public affairs; in order that a minority should no longer decide the fate of the whole people. This longing is directed neither against socialism nor the right of the CFC to exist.

The current system of briberies and black marketeers: the disregard for socialist property and failures of the economic mechanisms are to be blamed on those who have managed our society so far. Therefore, new people have to replace them, but this has not yet happened. You yourself will know how difficult it is even within the party to introduce new ideas. Please, do help our campaign for change. Let the leadership of the Communist Party of Czechoslovakia honour its promises of a dialogue, a dialogue with the whole nation. Let the party inform us fully, and not hide itself behind the notion of glasnost, which we have not yet experienced. Let the party cooperate with the whole nation in restructuring our society. Otherwise this reconstruction will only serve the narrow interests of a minority group, as we have known until this day.

Mr Gorbachev, Czechs and Slovaks place their hopes with you.

Jaroslav Kainek

Bolivar
Tennessee, USA   4 July 1988

Dear Sir,

I am a veteran of twenty-five years' service in the US Air Force. I retired with the rank of E9 Sergeant in 1968.

I have just returned from West Berlin where three hundred of us were given an official reception and dinner by the Berlin government. We came by invitation for a forty-year reunion of the Berlin Luftbrucke. I flew 130 missions from Frankfurt to Berlin hauling food and necessary supplies to the hungry Berliners.

Sir, I did not make those flights to oppose the Russians but to feed the hungry mouths of children. It was a dangerous operation. Seventy-nine of our side gave their lives.

One of the highlights of my trip to Berlin was being invited to tour East Berlin. Three places I visited there have given me cause to write to you.

Sir, I am sure that when the wall was built it served as a useful political tool and more. But you must be aware that this can no longer be true. Now it costs a great amount to maintain, i.e. routine maintenance, police, guards, dogs, surveilance equipment, etc. Even more are the hidden losses such as the free flow of commerce, ideas, work and development and so much more! Surely, the time has come for the wall to disappear. Rest assured the people of East Berlin will not attempt to escape when they have nothing to escape from. A few may move at first but many will return to their home. A small fence will make friends but a wall will make enemies.

Sir, the present wall openly invites people of the world to doubt the sincerity of your glasnost program.

It is my belief that you personally want to remove this wall of separation between East and West Berlin, nay, between Russia and the world.

Sincerely,
Martin I. Allin

Hempstead
Gloucester, England   17 August 1988

Bravo Comrade Gorbachev,

Bravo for releasing Herr Mathias Rust from custody after he had served but a short term of the four years' sentence passed at his trial, following his foolhardy flight over your country during which he violated the air space and territory of the Soviet Union by subsequently landing his aircraft in Red Square, the very heart of Moscow itself. Such an act of clemency shows not only compassion and humanity, but also diplomacy and statesmanship.

In the year 1992 all existing barriers, of whatever kind, will be removed within the European Economic Community. This organisation now includes virtually the whole of Western Europe, with the exception of one or two countries. But, whether within the EEC or not, all the countries of Western Europe are free and independent, even allowing that NATO forces are stationed in some of those countries.

With the Soviet people enjoying a certain relaxation of restrictions due to your policies of glasnost and perestroika, to be able not only to think more freely, but to act, talk, write and express more freely, and perhaps, in time, even move more freely, both within and without the Soviet Union, would it not be wonderful if these policies, and the changes they bring, were to be extended throughout the other countries of the Soviet bloc in Eastern Europe.

Would it not be wonderful if East Germany, Poland, Czechoslavakia, Hungary, Bulgaria and Romania were fully and truly independent and free to govern themselves. Without the control or occupying forces from another country, whether welcomed by the peoples of those countries, or not.

But by far the most wonderful and desirable of all, would be to see all the barriers between East and West removed, and to be replaced by a total European unity based on friendship, understanding and patient tolerance.

As 1992 is the year in which all barriers will come tumbling down within Western Europe, would it not be a great achievement if all barriers could be brought tumbling down in Eastern Europe by the same year, including those between East and West, leading in time to the removal of NATO forces from Western Europe, and of Soviet forces from Eastern Europe.

This may seem an idealist's dream, but the reality is not impossible.

My sincere regards,
Edward James Williams

Tunbridge Wells
Kent, England   26 August 1988

Dear Mr Gorbachev,

I am a socialist and friend of the Soviet Union. But as a friend I am not an uncritical one. I found the Brezhnev years terribly depressing. I had hoped that it would be possible to look to the Soviet Union as an inspiration after Khrushchev had denounced Stalin. Then came the invasion of Hungary. I was just a student at the time and this came as a bitter blow. I did not see Imre Nagy and Pal Malater as a threat to socialism in the USSR or elsewhere. After the downfall of Khrushchev, I hoped that the new leaders of the USSR would allow the development of socialism in each country to proceed in its own way, and in due course recognise that they had made a terrible mistake in Hungary and would rehabilitate the executed Hungarian leaders.

In 1968 many of us looked with new hope to Czechoslovakia, where it seemed that the leaders of that country were building a form of socialism which would have tremendous attraction for us in the West. We did not think that the Soviet leaders would move in to crush it. I booked a flight to Prague and arrived in the city on 16 August so I was there when the tanks moved in on the night of 20 August. That was a black day for all socialists and did incredible damage to all those who were serious friends of the USSR. Perhaps you do not realise what it did to the way ordinary people in the West view the USSR. I also am convinced that it did a lot of harm to people in the USSR and in Eastern Europe and in its way contributed to the economic difficulties faced by the USSR today. Furthermore it did a lot to strengthen reactionary forces in the West, including those who might pay lip-service to peaceful coexistence, but in practice are bitterly opposed to it. They welcome the invasion of Afghanistan, because they could stay very pleased that the present Soviet government has agreed to pull out and is in the process of doing so.

There are many socialists who are delighted at the way your government has persisted in its efforts for peace and disarmament since you personally became Communist Party leader. We welcome glasnost and perestroika. We are pleased that there are now people allowed to demonstrate freely about things which concern us in the West as well. We strongly welcome increased contacts between East and West and particularly the INF Treaty for reducing the quantities of nuclear weapons. We feel that our government in Britain is out of step, because it is increasing the number of warheads it possesses when Trident is built. Yet there are two factors which make us reserve our judgment at the moment:

a. While recognising that private enterprise might have a greater role in the Soviet economy and that multinational corporations will be involved in joint projects with state industries, we would be extremely worried if capitalist development went too far. The Soviet Union has existed without a Stock Exchange for seventy years and we hope that it can continue to do so. We would regard its introduction as an important step backward, which could undermine the socialist economic base.

b. We do not feel that the USSR has fully come to terms with the nightmare of the Stalin era and the dreadful years of the Brezhnev era until it can freely write a truthful history of itself with nothing to hide. Personally I would like the Soviet Union to do the following:

1. Repudiate the invasion of Czechoslovakia, and recognise the injustice done to Alexander Dubcek and other Czechoslovak leaders of the time.
2. Repudiate the invasion of Hungary in 1956 and rehabilitate the executed Hungarian leaders.

211

3. Investigate thoroughly the massacre of Polish Officers at Katyn with a view to establishing the date and who was responsible. Then tell the people of Poland the truth.

4. Rehabilitate all the Bolshevik leaders and others murdered on Stalin's orders in particular Trotsky, Zinoviev, and Kamenev.

I think it is now time to expose all skeletons in the cupboard to the light of day. This, I believe, will strengthen not weaken the Soviet Union, and perhaps awaken the socialist conscience of many of us in the West.

Perhaps you will say that my demands are impossible or ignore what I have had to say. But I am an optimist and hope that one day we can have peace and socialism all over the world. Thank you at least for reading this,

Yours sincerely,
Patrick G. Funnell

Charleston
South Carolina,   5 February 1989

Dear President Gorbachev,

I am a retired radio braodcaster in my very late fifties, and so I am old enough, while I did not participate in fighting in World War II, to remember so clearly the dream so many imagined then of a post-war peace and freedom we supposed was to come.

In those times, while some quarters here may even then have secretly been suspicious of Stalin – the people surely had a vision of coming cooperation in that imagined world ahead which they so fervently and with such sacrifice groped toward through the dark night of war.

The shattering of that vision with the cold war which began to emerge within weeks of the end of fighting, indeed by the time of the Potsdam Conference – I believe left a great philosophical and spiritual scar in my own society which never healed. What a precious dream it was to lose. How ironic that the very chair President Truman sat in at Potsdam - today faces directly the site of the wall which has symbolically divided the two sides of post-war Europe.

In a way that wall brought peace through reduction of tensions; but how much better a quality of Peace can be imagined. Alas – so far, only imagined.

What had been envisioned as peace during the war never came into being. Instead, from one unimaginable hell, we came to dwell on the everlasting brink of another even worse; and the mushroom cloud seemed always ready to step on stage like an actor awaiting an expected cue.

As I say, sometimes it was better and at other times worse; but never was genuine trust and possible cooperation achieved or the hope present – which has since been felt not only here but in Western Europe since you have headed the USSR. My daughter lives in London and is an actress and not long ago saw the Bolshoi Ballet there and has been so impressed by the change. People wonder almost in unbelief if the vision of the ancient Hebrew prophet Joel might truly be reversed; with swords now turned back again into plowshares, and threatening spears into pruning hooks.

Both societies – and the whole earth – so long for leadership which would accomplish this – to give all societies a chance toward devoting productivity and energies to a better life on this planet; and that above all we do not destroy it entirely, as a few individuals have held the capacity to do.

I have never seen your country except through music and literature, although I would sincerely like to; just as I wish more citizens of the USSR might know firsthand what I believe to be the real America – not just tall buildings or tourist postcard views, but the actual nation and people beyond. As a person semi-retired, I cannot now afford travel; but in 1986, I spent a month in Eastern Europe, going in at Frederichstrasse station in Berlin, and coming out a month later on the Bulgarian border with Greece.

Along the way, I saw and experienced Krakow, Warsaw, Auschwitz, Gdansk, Prague, journeyed beside the Danube to Budapest, walked streets in Sofia, and viewed at monuments to Dvorak, Smetana, Josef Conrad, and Chopin; and the Elbe, Moldau, Baltic and Vistula.

I also experienced Soviet soldiers – not as the perceived threat which so many unconsciously outside the East bloc imagine them, but as young people so much like our own here. I think of those Sunday throngs of enlisted men in brown overcoats who were passing through the Goethe House alongside me in Weimar; or the pair of considerate Soviet officers who without being asked one night helped me place my luggage aboard a street car at the railway station at Potsdam; or the Soviet officer standing beside me as we looked at paintings in the Zwinger Museum.

As I looked at those canvases, I wondered about his uniform and what his rank was, and where he lived, and about his family. He became a human being to me then, not something existing only in precious imagination. How little we know of each other and how awful at times the fruits of unsupported fear and imagination.

I looked at stationary Soviet rail coaches outside my own train rolling through the yards at Warsaw and wished that I knew what those who rode them there were like, and about that territory they traversed – where the great war had been fought with such blood and agony between there and Moscow.

It was those battlefields, of course, above all, holding the graves which determined the fate of Hitler.

What I saw I enjoyed deeply and shall never forget; whether in booming bells of Russian Easter from the Alexander Nevsky Cathedral at Sofia, or patiently and lovingly rebuilt facades of Gdansk and Warsaw, and the horror and guilt I felt as an American as I took my first view outside the Dresden train station. I thought as I looked with anguish at those empty spaces and wondered why they had been created in place of art treasures and palaces; and of an admonition of Frederich Nietzsche, loosely translated: Take care, ye who fight with monsters – lest ye become a monster!

My trip to the socialist countries in the spring of 1986 was made possible by a wealthy wife who the moment I returned from such a journey divorced me. She thought anyone who even wanted to see such places had something wrong with them.

Good luck, President Gorbachev. I hope that you and our own new President can do great work to create and realize for all the world that post-war peace which so sadly eluded us all and the whole world forty-five years ago.

Sincerely,
Paul Bailey Mason

Prague
Czechoslovakia

7 February 1989

Dear Prime Minister,

I have decided to write to you because I cannot be indifferent to the fate of our country. I cannot also be indifferent to the fact that in this country the meaning of the words is misused. The pages of *Rude Pravo*, the Communist Party daily, continually call for democracy; for dialogue; for the public to be kept informed and for restructuring of society. Why do we go no further than words, as before? What sort of game are we playing? Why is it that the Soviet Union of the Stalin and Brezhnev eras remains our model despite the fact that we pay lip-service to the Soviet Union of Mikhail Gorbachev? Is it not evident that the one-party monopoly of power is fundamentally opposed to the Marxist law of 'negation of negotiation'; that if there is no criticism distortions follow, the degeneration of everything; and that this monopoly of power has not ever been proved correct? Are you not aware that this offered dialogue has been with us since 1948, but despite this our society urgently requires restructuring?

Could you, please, explain to me why we can suddenly see all around us black marketeering, alcoholism, prostitution, bribery and a disregard for socialist property or green issues?

You call for a dialogue but in reality you do not intend to participate in it. You call for the public to be kept informed but you publicise only those things which suit you. Do you really want to lose the remnants of public trust or do you want to regain it? I would like to ask you, Prime Minister, to use your position to implement the sentiments expressed above. Begin a dialogue with the whole nation concerning matters of public concern; keep the nation informed about all the issues, as you can either keep the public informed or not informed at all. At present the public is not informed. Begin restructuring of society in earnest for the benefit of both the whole nation and the Communist Party of Czechoslovakia. Unless your deeds match your words there is no hope of success. The nation is no more interested in half-hearted attempts concerning economic changes initiated by the very same people who repeat hypocritical declarations about a new era calling for new people. Keep your promises! Let the nation express its views, and stop calling those who speak out anti-communist or anti-social elements, if you do not even allow these people to defend themselves in public!

You wondered at the appearance of young people in Wenceslas Square. Do not be surprised. They find all these phrases in which words and deeds conflict alien. If they had not been worried about reprisals they would have turned up in even greater numbers. Even though . . . one never knows whether the majority of young people are apathetic to social events. But is this not the same? Young people nowadays find these bombastic words of the fifties about the class struggle completely alien. They only want to have a better life. They are even willing to work hard to that end but without slogans about capitalism and socialism. They are only interested in achieving results, and not in the history of slogans. They are interested in reality, not in promised goals. If you want them to be on your side, you must radically change your approach. If it is still possible! I am sure, however, that young people nowadays, and not only the young, have the same aims as perestroika itself, and they would be deeply grateful if you directed our society in the same way; but if you really led a dialogue and enabled the public to be kept informed honestly through the freedom of the press, if would mean a genuine restructuring of society.

Jaroslav Kainek

215

Am Weinberg
West Germany   15 June 1989

Dear Mr State President,

I was very moved today when I followed the television report of your speech to the workers of the Hoesch steel works. You must have felt the warmth of those people's response, the genuinely rapt attention with which they listened to your words and the goodwill they expressed in their applause. When one considers what the Russian people (all the people of the Soviet Union) suffered under Hitler's fascism, this day must have been a great experience for you and Mrs Gorbachev.

I come from a family in which we listened to Radio Moscow throughout the whole of the Second World War (under the Nazi-imposed threat of the death penalty). We were horrified at Hitler's attack on the Soviet Union, at the great human and material losses suffered by your country, and we did what we could to help the Russian prisoners of war. In doing that we were risking our lives every time we tried to throw food accross the fence into the prisoner-of-war camp.

Meanwhile, almost fifty years have passed since those terrible events. The fact that people here (from wide circles of the population) acclaimed you so warmly, also has its psychological reasons. You as leader of the Soviet state made an approach to your former enemies – and that is something that must win our deepest admiration. You have spoken of a 'new start'. And the people here believe you, they have faith in your sincerity, your goodwill, the realization of your intentions and promises. With the exception of a very few hidebound ultra-reactionaries and anti-progressives, there are so many people here today who look to the future and who want nothing more than that the long and close friendship that existed for many centuries between Russia/Soviet Union and Germany, should be renewed and become a powerful factor within Europe.

For years I have asked myself why does not the Soviet Union reverse this negative 'post-war' position and ensure the removal of the weapons from the Federal Republic.

Why not now (at a time when everything is in favour of it and it would be entirely to your advantage) take a decisive initiative and demand as soon as possible a 'Conference to put an end to the post-war condition in Europe'.

When Stalin offered this some thirty-five years ago (Stalin made the offer!) , the Western powers refused it brusquely – supported by their lackey, Adenauer. If Stalin's plan had gone through, you would not now have been paying 60–80 million roubles per year in defence, or had a German state stuffed full of weapons, all directed against you and your country, forcing you into an arms race and making it impossible for you to carry through your plans and to ensure a higher standard of living for the people of the Soviet Union.

Why do you not do away with the occupation and at the same time with the associated partition of Germany, even if that means dissension with your former allies of the Second World War? It is, after all, these former 'allies' who are threatening your country with many thousands of nuclear weapons, most of which are stationed here in our country.

It is high time to end the 'war', to hold a conference and to conclude a State Treaty with Germany (in which you could win for yourself all the advantages and privileges of intensive cooperation with a free Germany) and to live in peace in the 'European home'. Nobody believes that this could be possible unless Germany regains its sovereignty and is a really free partner, enjoying self-determination.

You are wiser than the Western powers. Draw your own conclusions: it is impossible to deny an entire nation the freedom of self-determination for almost fifty years, to keep it occupied, to divide a metropolis like Berlin into two parts (what madness that was and still is!) and at the same time to cry out that one wants 'to live in peace with one's fellow men'. You have it in your hand to alter this post-war state of affairs.

But of course, it cannot succeed unless you also attempt and achieve something new in the German question. Any initiative you make in this direction will win great approval here (and even more in the GDR), and will ensure at the same time that:

a) the huge armament build-up against the Soviet Union that is the result of the partition of Germany (and therefore of Europe) can at last be reduced (and it should be reduced one hundred per cent), and,

b) as a result you get a free hand (especially financially) to carry through your programme to the benefit of the people of the Soviet Union and therefore the whole of Europe.

Mr President, today (1989) your true friends no longer are in Washington, London and Paris. You have more sincere, better, more straightforward friends in the entire German people.

Prof. G. Muller

Konrad Adenauer (1876–1967) was the Chancellor of the Federal Republic of Germany from 1949 to 1963. He successfully presided over the creation of a Western-oriented German state after World War II, aiding the astonishing recovery of West Germany and its acceptance into the Western bloc during the cold war.

Paris
France   June 1989

Dear Mr Gorbachev,

This is a message from a group of Romanians living in the West.

We find from newspapers, radio and television broadcasts about the bad situation in Romania (hunger, cold and terror), a situation which is not caused by the Romanian people but by the mistaken policy of Mr Ceaucescu.

You know better than us that the October Revolution in Russia was caused by hardship and terror.

This is exactly the situation in Romania now. We found out from Romanians arrived in the West as tourists or for business that it is possible a revolution will happen in Romania aiming to overthrow the Ceaucescu family.

We think the bad situation in Romania is due to:

– Nicolae Ceaucescu, a good for nothing, sclerotic Stalinist, having no university background (former apprentice of a shoemaker) who brought Romania to the verge of disaster with his major decisions.

– Elena Ceaucescu, also having no university background, a former worker who became academic, doctor, engineer, scientist of international reputation (her books being written by others) and who imposes regulations which can only harm the Romanian people. What are the names of the schools she went through and who were her school friends?

– The deeds of the crown prince Nicu Ceaucescu, were like heavy losses in foreign casinos.

A 'securitate' officer from his personal guard shot Ducadem, the goalkeeper of the football team 'Stau', in the shoulder because he didn't want to give the 'prince' the car given to him as a present by the King of Spain.

The slapping of the cosmonaut Prunariu (Romanian) because he didn't want to leave a restaurant where the 'prince' went for a party.

We heard the 'prince' committed a crime in USSR; if true, for what price was he released? One of us was in Romania when you were in Bucharest. We suspect you know about the trick they performed in the case of the food shops shown to you. After you left these shops, the food was loaded in lorries and moved away.

A friend of ours witnessed that in a square in the south of Bucharest.

Why is your policy of reforms and reconstruction appreciated and used in all other socialist countries apart from Romania?

218

Our Romanian group has monthly meetings in Paris, has conversations about the Romanian situation and we have reached the following conclusion:

Because we don't want a revolution in Romania, which means bloodshed, the only solution is Nicolae Ceaucescu and his family should be isolated.

We believe that you (yourself) are not in favour of a revolution in Romania.

Would it be possible to isolate Ceaucescu politically and economically within the Eastern bloc Common Market, Caer?

A first stop towards isolating Ceaucescu could be to publish this letter of ours in *Pravda* and *Isvestia*.

In the USSR, we hear the press is free now. The Russian public should find out the real situation in Romania.

Do you think such a letter, sent by some Romanians, could make a contribution towards involving the Russian Communist Party and the government of the USSR?

The publication of such a letter in Russian newspapers could have some effect and make a contribution towards Ceaucescu's isolation in the West as well.

A group of Romanians living in the West

Greenbelt
Maryland, USA   1 September 1989

Dear President Gorbachev,

On your actions today hangs the fate of all mankind.

Fifty years ago, as a boy of eleven, I saw Stalin's panzers roll into my home town. Helpless, I cried when they came. Estonia became a Soviet Republic, but against our own free will. Later, during the final battles of World War II our family escaped to Germany (I was sixteen then). Many years later we were able to come to the United States of America, where we started a new life.

Fifty years have passed since Hitler and Stalin signed their infamous pact and World War II started, bringing untold suffering to the world. And the country to suffer most was Russia.

Mr President, isn't fifty years enough, even on the scale of the history of mankind? Both Hitler and Stalin are dead. But their curse still casts a shadow over the world. Mr President, your stunning ideas of glasnost and perestroika should signal the end of the Age of Stalin. You have the power to change history. You can restore the honorable name of the Russian people. You can denounce Stalin. You can create a new Europe where East and West meet as shapers of a better future.

219

The young Estonian boy who cried when Stalin's tanks rolled into his home town, has grown into a grey-haired man. Mr President, that grey-haired man still has a vision: Estonia at the end of this century – a new, open gateway between Eastern and Western Europe. A small, independent country (not unlike Finland) through which the trade of goods and knowledge freely flows, almost like in medieval times of the Hansa League. Hamburg, London, Copenhagen, Paris – connected to Leningrad, Novgorod, Moscow, all through Tallinn, through the ice-free ports of Estonia. A new beginning, a new start for a new open Russia, a new Europe, a new gateway to a new, open century.

Sincerely yours,
Jyri Kork

Neubrandenburg,
East Germany   5 November 1989

Dear General Gorbachev,

I would like to express to you my personal thanks for your farsighted, progressive policy which unites both people and peoples. By your visit on 6 October, in your behaviour and your words, you have shown yourself to be one of us, the comrades in the SED (Socialist Unity Party), the working classes. And there is no doubt that we, the people of the GDR, were able to understand you better than we do a number of our own leaders.

I suppose, Mr Gorbachev, that when you get a letter like this, you would also like to know something about the person who is writing to you.

Perhaps you can already guess from my name that before the end of the war, I lived near Königsberg, having been born in 1943; I am married, have two children (a daughter of twenty-one, a son thirteen years old); I took a diploma in engineering and specialized in production engineering; since 1958 I have been a member of the DSF and FDGB and since 1963, a member of the SED.

My son's respect for you shows itself in a rather different form. Since he is a person who loves nature and mankind, he respects you because you bring peace to the world. He is very proud to wear two stickers, one of them showing you with Ronald Reagan, and one carrying your portrait. He was a member of the so-called 'R-Class' (Russian class) and now attends the Sports Academy for children and young people (KJS), where he hopes to train as a wrestler (at the Luezenwalde KJS).

I consider you to be among the greatest politicians of the twentieth century. For me, you are on a level with Bismark and Helmut Schmidt of the Federal Republic. But I am convinced that you are going to be the greatest politician of peace that humanity has ever produced. We are proud of having seen you personally from a distance, and of having had the experience of seeing weapons of mass murder destroyed without ever having been used against other people. Together with Mr Reagan, you have already written and created world history.

There is a second reason for writing. Until 31 January 1989, I was an independent worker in the Local Planning Commission of the Council for the Region of Neubrandenburg. At my own request, I resigned from the Council and went into industry. The reason, as a member of the party, I did not want any longer to offend against the interests of the people and the statute of the SED; I no longer wanted to be a state official.

I was ashamed that we, who had for years heard about and acted on the principle that what 'big brother' does is the right thing to do and must be imitated (learning from the Soviet Union means learning to be victorious . . .), for the most part followed along the path which the KPdSU (Communist Party of the Soviet Union) had been travelling since 1985. So resignation or silent protest became widespread, the government officials drove 100,000 of this country's sons and daughters out of their fatherland, and would have gone the same way, irrespective of the losses incurred.

On 6 October 1989 you, Mr Gorbachev, spoke to the press, in words to this effect: . . . politicians who govern without taking the people into account can fall . . . It was the signal, a signal from Moscow to the people of the GDR – we, the Soviet people, will not act against you with tanks and soldiers as in 1953.

Unfortunately none of the more than twenty speakers on the Alexanderplatz in Berlin on 4 November 1989 mentioned your name, Mr Gorbachev, or the KPdSU [Communist Party of the Communist Party] as one of the essential primary causes. Yet every citizen of the Eastern bloc who is at all honest knows that, without you and the KPdSU, socialism would unquestionably have landed on the rubbish heap of history.

Where did Stalinism lead us?

Mr Gorbachev, you are needed at home in the Soviet Union, otherwise an offer would have been made: become the leader of our state! You would win every election, and you would have comrades and a people inspired by a will to become a better Germany, both politically and economically.

General Kreuz has not many supporters even in the SED, a man who travelled to China instead of to Moscow, and that at a critical phase: how can one have confidence in him?

The people are marching silently with candles, against the Stasi and against old ineffective politicians, along a long road. Could you help us again? I realize it is presumptuous to ask you and the ZK (Central Committee) for help.

I wish you, your wife, your comrades, your people great success in solving the problems that face you.

I hope you and your wife have as much success in the USSR as you have had in the international arena.

Yours sincerely,
Uwe, Beate, Christine and Peter Jurkschat

Kirkheim-Teck
West Germany   11 November 1989

My dear Mr Gorbachev,

Forgive me please when I address you as 'dear Mr Gorbachev', but I cannot do otherwise. I would like to thank you from the bottom of my heart for your action in opening the border between East and West Germany. We can still hardly take it in.

I was born in 1934 in Dresden, now the GDR. In a bombing raid on that city in February 1945, we lost everything, escaping with only our lives. We had to leave our home town at once, and ended up close to Stuttgart. Because I am very attached to my native home, I have gone back there every year since 1967 to visit my Dresden friends, most of whom are younger than I am. They have suffered very much, as I have, from not being able to visit me here. We followed the events of August 1968 with close attention and were deeply shocked by the invasion of Czechoslovakia. I mention that only so that *you* should understand the depth of my present gratitude – our gratitude – which is extreme.

We sincerely wish you the strength you require to carry out your reforms, and the trust and support of your people, for whom I have a deep love.

Helga Stecher

Achères
France   20 November 1989

Dear President,

I know that it is not your official title, but I like to give it to you in the current European and world political context.

I am seventy-two, a retired teacher, and I must confess that I have never been tempted by communism, especially in my communist-run town where Stalinist practices are still in favour, if I dare say so. I have visited several countries in the East, as we say, and I have realised that capitalism has made the majority of the inhabitants happier than the communist regimes have done, from the point of view not only of freedoms but also of equality and justice.

Without doubt communism has been a brutal way of moving from utter destitution to poverty, just as a surgical operation leaves one with scars? But men are born to live, not to suffer.

Since you have been at the head of the USSR, we in the West have felt that you were neither an out and out ideologue like Lenin nor a criminal like Stalin, nor a joker like Khruschchev, nor a ponderous oaf like Brezhnev, but a man.

Many of your proposals and your actions have been well received here: the Berlin Wall is open! It was just a loathsome symbol, but it did so much harm to your country. And then Poland and Hungary, tomorrow Czechoslovakia? Everybody here knows that it could not have taken place without your consent: we thank you.

I hope that my letter is not thrown into the waste-paper basket and that you will be aware of it; so many useful things could be done for the whole of mankind if the billions of francs, roubles and dollars devoted to the manufacture of weapons and espionage were used for the building of schools, hospitals, motorways or libraries . . .

My letter just wishes to encourage you to go on with what you have begun so well in your own country and for the whole world. The mistake of the Communist system (in my opinion) has been to neglect the welfare of people and to have suffered dramatic economic failures. Otherwise the whole world would have long since been a communist paradise.

I even admit that your personal appearance is that of a man-like-everybody (excuse this formula) and not that of a fanatic.

I have written to you to give you the courage to persevere: General de Gaulle used to speak of a Europe 'from the Atlantic to the Urals'. Who knows? The day after tomorrow, perhaps?

I feel much better for having told you what I think: I wish you a long life and good health, happiness for your country and peace in the world.

Yours sincerely,
Roger Bélis

Aschaffenburg
West Germany   25 November 1989

Dear Mr General Secretary,

An article in today's copy of the newspaper *Main Echo*, quotes remarks made by the President of the French Republic, to whom you are reported as saying that on the day on which German reunification takes place, the news agency TASS will carry a two-line announcement of the fact that your post has been taken over by a marshal of the Soviet Union.

This caused me great dismay. It shows, after all, that both France and the Soviet Union entertain fears that a United Germany could once again pose a threat to Europe or even to the world.

My dear Mr General Secretary, as a free citizen of post-war Germany without any party-political commitments (I am fifty-two years of age), I can assure you that there is not one fellow German known to me who thinks in that way. We are glad to be able to live in Europe in peace and freedom; most of my friends and acquaintances look upon our immediate neighbours in France (who were at one time described as 'arch-enemies') as true brothers, and we note with the greatest of satisfaction that the same feeling exists among the French (as well as other Europeans), even though in the past, many great wrongs were committed in the name of Germany. I cannot imagine that any dictator (in the First World War it was the Kaiser, in the Second World War, Hitler) could ever again seduce us into attacking another nation. We have, as far as we have been able and as far as it is at all possible, paid for what we did, and one element of the price we had to pay was precisely the partition of Germany into two states and the surrender of former German territories.

If there were to be a reunification, we envisage ourselves at most as equal partners within a united Europe (following appropriate elections and declarations of affirmation from both countries). My dearest wish is to be able to experience such a thing and to become a citizen of a United States of Europe, to which, of course, the Soviet Union would also belong.

Yours sincerely,
Werner Sachse

Belair
South Australia
7 December 1989

Dear Mr Gorbachev,

I like and praise you for what you have done to bring about change in the USSR and Eastern Europe.

It is, however, not enough for you to denounce the evil decisions of Lenin, Stalin and Brezhnev; you must be able to show that you have the ability to be a good administrator.

Your weakness is practical economics. You, and many East Germans, would like East Germany to remain separate from West

Germany but, it can't because the East German economy is too weak and unnatural. Food is subsidised, housing is subsidised, professional people – doctors, architects, etc – are paid not much more than workers, there are few consumer goods, food shortages and industry is too old-fashioned to compete with Western European countries. Above all, East Germany has not got the capital to change its economy.

East Germany is naturally part of Germany and the people of East and West Germany will be forced to come together by East German economic weakness. There are many East and West Germans who do not want to reunify Germany, but, it will happen anyway!

You must decide how you want the reunified Germany to function in Europe. A reunified Germany could not be a member of NATO or the Warsaw Pact.

Do you want reunified Germany to be a part of the Western European union of 1992 or a separate independent nation like Poland and Czechoslovakia?

You must decide now because the USSR has not got the economic strength to support East Germany.

Yours sincerely,
John Gilbertson

The Treaty of Rapallo (1922), between Germany and Soviet Russia, provided for the annulment of past war claims and restoration of diplomatic relations between the two countries.

Berlin
East Germany   December 1989

Dear Mr President,

As things are going now, the GDR will be changing over to capitalism sooner than was expected; certainly every effort to that end will be made in Bonn, since things are going too slowly for them. If there is a reunification, there will be an economic superpower, Germany.

The states such as Hungary, Poland and Czechoslovakia will associate themselves with the West, since they are also dependent upon Germany's economy; anyone who has once got into debt to capitalism never gets free of it. Up to now, only two countries have managed it – the People's Republic of China and the Soviet Republic of Romania, because they adhered to Marxism-Leninism and socialism; it is the only way to prevent the exploitation of people by other people.

In the new situation, the western border of the Soviet Union will run along the Ukraine: with perestroika as it is practised now, the

Soviet Union will very soon split apart into many small states, which would then in turn become dependent upon the economic superpower Germany. The Warsaw Pact would no longer exist, and capitalism would have reached its goal; in that way, the whole world can also be changed.

Yours sincerely,
Erich Gröhler

MAULIK CHEMICALS
Bombay, India

3 January 1990

Honourable Sir,

You have made practical the meaning of Universal Brotherhood. You have truly emphasised the meaning of freedom and most important of all – you have made the correct use of power so granted by your people.

It is pleasing to see Eastern Europe blooming with aspirations of freedom and democracy. Now everybody seems to be involved in his own progress which collectively will be the real progress of the whole world. Surely you are the push-button to it.

The reduction in arms, limitations to nuclear programmes, turning of tanks into tillers, concern for an individual, the basic realisation of living together in love and peace will be a history in itself for the human race and generations to come.

I am particularly happy about the timing as this change came into being when the world was on the threshold of destruction by way of power supremacy.

I am very happy to be living in the present generation and having an opportunity to see a worthy human sailing through the hard winds to reach the banks of glasnost and perestroika. May God be with you and blessing of scores of human beings be with you as the impending dark shadow of nuclear war is diminishing and the world is enjoying the fruits of freedom irrespective of the religions and principles they adhere to.

Yours sincerely,
Manish P. Sarvaiya

Pforzheim
West Germany 22 January 1990

Dear Mr State President,

On the basis of recent developments in Central Germany which make the reunification of East and West Germany inevitable, and raise the question of what is to be the military status of a reunited Germany, I venture here to express my opinion in the matter, particularly since I am convinced that you, as a reasonable man, will share that opinion.

1. I, like the great majority of Germans, am convinced that the only real possibility is for a united Germany to be neutral and logically this means that West Germany should leave NATO, and East Germany should leave the Warsaw Pact.

Any other possibilities are only wild fantasies dreamed up by the Bonn politicians or the Western powers, who have basically never been our friends.

You are quite right that the Soviet Union cannot be expected to hand over East Germany to NATO, nor is it feasible to do as Genscher suggests and leave West Germany in NATO and East Germany in the Warsaw Pact. In such circumstances I despair of the good sense of the Bonn politicians, the majority of whom are dependent upon NATO and who are frighteningly middle-of-the-road in their politics.

2. This could, on the other hand, be a unique opportunity for Germany and Russia to introduce a pan-European peace initiative.

The Federal 'Minister of Travel', Genscher, would be spared from attending his many conferences, which anyway nobody takes seriously any more, and Germans and Russians would save millions formerly spent on armaments.

To prevent pan-German neutrality by all kinds of tricks and subtle cunning is simply illogical and borders on a Babel-like confusion of tongues.

3. The argument that is always being dragged out that a reunited Germany constitutes a danger, is deliberate fiction, and only serves the purpose of keeping Germany in leading strings. In the course of two dreadful wars that ended in defeat, the Germans have learned their lesson, and for long enough, have given proof of their will to peace.

Moreover, the world should sensibly take note that the Germans have renounced nuclear weapons, although England, France and the Soviet Union are nuclear powers. In view of such facts, it is ridiculous to use catch-words like 'the German threat'.

4. In their demand that a united Germany should not be neutral, the Western powers including the USA are quite clearly acting

with the intention of preventing good harmony and understanding between Germans and Russians, on the lines of the Rapallo Treaty (1922). And I shall write a letter to that effect to the German Chancellor.

5. Because of its geographical situation, its size and its history, a united Germany could not adopt the sort of 'free fare tariff neutrality' that Switzerland, for example, practises. Therefore it is my opinion that the Germans have every reason to go beyond mere neutrality and establish a special relationship with the Soviet Union, and as far as possible to put their technological and economic potential at the service of the Soviet Union. In fact, the friendship between Russia and Germany has a long historical tradition that should be taken into consideration.

6. I am convinced that a strong and neutral united Germany can benefit the Soviet Union more than all the other possibilities.

7. The German people will appreciate it if Moscow gives the green light to the reunification without setting conditions. The important thing is the unification of East and West Germany, everything else can be put aside for the moment, and left with confidence to the further course of history.

If Germany and Russia remain at peace within the framework of an honourable balance of interests, there is nobody who can threaten them. That is the great historical opportunity.

8. Because up to now, the Western powers – our 'friends' – have shown themselves less than enthusiastic in agreeing to reunification (Thatcher!) and have merely placed obstacles in our path, the opportunity is all the greater for the Soviet Union to demonstrate who the true friend of Germany is.

Therefore I would ask you to bring all your authority, courage and far-sightedness to bear in order to achieve the realization of this unique and historical opportunity for the well-being of Europe. I myself, born in 1923, a serviceman who was twice wounded, will do everything that lies within my modest powers to contribute to this end.

Yours sincerely,
Günter Heinz

NB I do not belong to any political party and have never been in any National Socialist organization.

Seelingsstadt
East Germany   25 January 1990

Dear Comrade Gorbachev,

Because of the critical situation we are faced with in the GDR, I am turning to you with a sincere request. I realize that I am only a worker, but I too have my point of view, namely that in spite of all difficulties, our GDR must be preserved. Even though I left the party after thirty-eight years, it was not out of cowardice but out of bitter disappointment. Because I had a brother in the Federal Republic, I was denied any possibility of improving my position in any way. Now, like thousands of others, I too have made a clean break. And if we are looked down on as a result, we shall just have to go on, and we cannot simply crawl away and wait until everything is lost. We cannot simply endure in silence, and therefore I have formed an 'Initiative Group' for a neutral party.

It is to be called the 'Neutral Party of the GDR'. We are still in the process of formation, which is being made difficult for us by the press. We want to give all former comrades the chance to take political action and to make good what Honecker and Milke have despoiled. Many people lack the courage for this, and it will certainly require a great deal of strength for this work of reconstruction. If in our programme we want to disassociate ourselves from Marxism, it is only because this is not a time for any more experiments. It is not intended as a blow against the Soviet Union, but we want to create a policy for the present day which will allow us to live better. We have been getting a lot of stimulation and encouragement from your articles and writings published in the press. It was our own communists who made up the former SED (Socialist Union Party of East Germany) leadership and those of the Bloc Parties and the Trade Union who have damaged the esteem in which the Communist Party was held on an international level. With their egotism, their high-handedness and their personality cult, they have debased Marxist-Leninism. We also feel ashamed because we have followed them in blind obedience. We feel shame when we contemplate all the anti-fascists who were murdered, like Ernst Thlmann and Rosa Luxemburg. Through the Soviet Union, we were given the unique chance of making reality of Ernst Thlmann's dream, which was also the dream of thousands of resistance fighters, was trampled underfoot by the egoism of Honecker's party aristocracy. With arrogance and presumption, they showed utter disregard for the people and the Soviet Union. What kind of communists were they? No wonder that the people have become so angry.

It is a bitter pill to swallow. Forty years of our life have been stolen from us for 'Nothing'. The guilt with which we are loaded

229

down threatens to crush us. When we discuss things openly, we are often reduced to tears. Emotionally and morally we are at the end of our tether and everything is a struggle against despair. It was communists of the Stalinist dictatorship who plunged us into this misery; but one thing we know and genuinely respect – that you, as a communist, have acted with courage and have given back to us our dignity, freedom and democracy. I believe that I speak for thousands when I express sincere thanks to you for that. We are all anxious that your Perestroika should finally make a breakthrough and become the vehicle of hope for your country. That is what we want for you and your people.

If a neutral zone is created in Germany on the territory of the GDR, then none of our neighbours need have any fear of Germany. In such a case there will be reunification only when there exists one single free Europe. Perhaps here I have become obsessed with a possibility that cannot be fulfilled, but yet I have a deep inner conviction, as do many thousands in the GDR, that this step is a way to a better future.

Yours sincerely,
Karl Heinz Rathgeber

Berlin
West Germany   14 February 1990

Dear Mr Gorbachev,

You will undoubtedly be surprised that I am writing to you. I have been wanting to do so for some time, but was always rather nervous about it.

I have been deeply moved by the events that have taken place in this country since 9 November 1989. Today I read in our newspaper in huge letters 'Moscow clears the way for German unity'.

Dear Mr Gorbachev, I would like to express my deeply felt thanks for this, for, in the final analysis, it was you, with your policy of perestroika who set the heavy stone of politics in motion.

You can have no idea how many people in Germany revere you and consider you to be one of the greatest politicians of the present age. On that day when the people of East Berlin and of East Germany were able to come over to us freely, thousands of people shouted out your name 'Gorbi, Gorbi, Gorbi . . .'

The people fell into each other's arms and wept for joy, because at last they were free after forty-five years of suppression and authoritarian rule under a communist-Stalinist system. This dreadful wall and border, which was now being opened up and carried away stone by stone, cost many people their life, and was a source of bitter suffering for many families.

Many had to sacrifice their life simply because they wanted to live in freedom. And the people who could not reach this goal were made to suffer dreadfully, they were arrested, imprisoned, humiliated and even tortured.

The German Democratic Republic was ruled by terror. It was not us, the West Germans or the West Berliners, who were the 'enemies of the working classes', no, the enemies of the people were to be found within the country itself, they were members of the government with Herr Honnecker at their head.

Only through you, Mr Gorbachev, through your courageous political initiative, through the reorganisations within your own country, was it possible for something to be achieved here too, for an end to be put to the activities of a criminal government, for an entire people to rise up, a people which wants to live in democracy and freedom.

In addition, I hope that as a result of help from East and West, the shortages of food supplies and consumer goods in your country will be relieved, and that the words spoken by Mr Wjatsheslav Dashitshev on this subject will be listened to by all the Western heads of government, because the success of perestroika depends upon that too.

I hope you will get this letter and that it will not be laid aside in the secretarial office.

With every good wish for your personal wellbeing.

Yours very sincerely,
Roman von Kalckreuth

San José
Costa Rica   14 February 1990

Dear Mr Gorbachev,

Thank God, yours and mine, you were elected as number one of the Soviet Union on 10 March 1985.

What is happening now in the world but specially what is happening in East Europe, could positively change the present social, economic, ideological, commercial and religious condition of all of us in this long-suffering planet.

And all that, thanks to you, thanks to your great and historical ideas of your perestroika and glasnost.

You deserve to honourably become the man of this century and be sure that the history will always remember you as one of the best men in these one hundred years.

I hope that both Germanies, once united, do not have the crazy idea of the Fourth Reich or another German Empire because if that

231

happens it would bring disastrous and irreversible consequences against our own world and the worlds of a greater part of our Universe.

Be sure that God, the Cosmic Mind, the universal number one or whatever we may call him, will help and recompense you, your family and the people of your great country.

Very sincerely yours,
Carlos Blanco Castro

New Zealand   26 February 1990

Sir,

You will be probably surprised to receive a letter from the end of the world but I feel it my duty to write to you with a warning about German reunification about which there is a lot of talk at the present time. I have lived a long time in Austria and Germany and I think I know the German mind fairly well.

There is no doubt in my mind that a reunified Germany would soon attempt the reconquest of the territories she lost in the last war to the USSR and Poland by waging a Third World War. Therefore preventive action should be taken now, that is to say reunification should be prevented by all possible means, even military occupation of East Germany. History should have taught the world that Germany cannot be trusted. The only thing she respects is force. You will probably remember the Nazi slogan: today we own Germany – tomorrow the world. So the countries most concerned should act now before it is too late.

I have the honour to be, Sir,

Your obedient servant,
(name withheld)

Bad Oeynhausen
West Germany   1 March 1990

Dear Secretary General Gorbachev,

You may be surprised to receive a letter from a woman living in West Germany. I have always respected you greatly and held you in high esteem, but I cannot understand how you could have broken your word in respect of re-unification. If you or your staff have seen West and East German television, then you also know that we, as Germans, want to have one common fatherland, built up in peace and freedom. We have waited for forty-five years for the barbarous wall which has brought so much grief and sorrow to both sides, to be pulled down. The realization that this wall was in part built out of money paid by West German tax payers can still make me feel ill today. I do not know how many thousands of millions of West German capital have been poured into East Germany, but instead of helping the suffering population, splendid official buildings and magnificent avenues have been laid out and a Stasi [state security service] built up, which is without parallel anywhere in the world; for the present distressing situation in East Germany, the people have to thank Ulbrich and Hoenecker, who promised the people over there heaven on earth.

When you, Mr Gorbachev, came on a state visit, the red carpet was rolled out and you saw only the splendidly imposing streets of the Democratic Republic, but what you did not see was what it looks like everywhere behind those streets – as if the war had come to an end only yesterday. The houses are decrepit, the factories outdated, they are still the same as they were in the First World War and are responsible for a great deal of environmental pollution. But we in West Germany also had to pay reparation costs and had to start all over again from scratch.

And now, Mr Gorbachev, I would like to talk about the Polish western border. From what we have seen and heard on television and radio, you are insisting upon the recognition of the Oder-Neisse border as the western border of Poland. I was born in 1922 in Lower Silesia in the village of Vogelsdorf, in the district of Landeshut, and I am well versed in the history of my local area. My native area has never been Polish. The places of cultural interest which still exist today are of purely German origin. Our family tree stretched right back to the thirteenth century. Old monasteries, such as Gruessau Monastery are among those places of interest. Gravestones which, as I found on my visit three years ago, are inscribed in the German language, date back to the eleventh century. I have taken photographs of them. Sadly the cemetery has fallen into ruin. I could give you many such examples, but they would make the letter too long.

And why is it there is only talk about Poland's western border, why not about Poland's eastern border? This area was, after all, also simply taken away from the Poles by Stalin as their wartime ally. The people there were resettled in my home district. They were second-class people. The first Polish mayor we got could neither read nor write. When I needed a voucher for my train journey, I had to write it out myself in his words, and as a signature, he made three crosses. I would be so happy if my dear home could become German again.

At the end of the war, we had three Russian officers billeted in our house which my father had built in 1936. All the officers always behaved very properly towards us, and in particular they protected us from the Poles. This changed after the Russian troops left our village. Together with other women, I was forced to dig up corpses with my bare hands, to remove their clothes and to wash the wasted corpses or skeletons with water. As a result I contracted ptomaine poisoning of the legs, and the scars are still visible today.

Mr Gorbachev, I speak for all my fellow countrymen when I say how much we would like to have our home back again. We would soon make this stretch of land blossom and flourish. The right bank of the Oder is very fertile. We used to have great estates planted with fruit and vegetables, it was the granary of Germany, and today the Poles have nothing to eat and are starving. When they took it over, there were unlimited supplies. We were not allowed to take anything with us, only the clothes we stood up in. You should just see what it looks like today, what the Poles have made out of our beautiful country, how everything is overgrown and delapidated.

I hope you will have sympathy with my letter.

With best wishes for you and for the success of glasnost and perestroika.

Yours
Dorothea Hoeynk

Prince George
British Columbia, Canada   1 April 1990

Dear Mr President,

Undoubtedly you receive great quantities of mail, both positive and negative. As you will have found, you cannot please everybody. I have decided today to give my opinion and especially to express my appreciation of your policy. There is no doubt that you, Mr Gorbachev, are the master architect of a new Europe. Without your policy of perestroika, we would never have got to the situation in which states under a dictatorship made the decision to adopt democracy.

However, what is happening at the present time in Lithuania is, in my opinion, going too far. There we have a small republic within the USSR that decides overnight to paddle its own canoe and be an independent state. For fifty years, Lithuania has belonged to the Soviet Union and now it is suddenly playing the fool. What would happen to the Soviet Union if all the republics that belong to it split off from their mother country? There would be chaos. I know you are a man who will not let himself be intimidated by other nations. You did the right thing yesterday, 31 March, when you expelled all Western journalists from Lithuania. They contribute a great deal to the manipulation of public opinion. What would happen if, in the USA for example, one state after the other were to leave the confederation of United States and to declare that from tomorrow, we are independent, and everything that has been constructed and invested by the government in Washington in the course of so-and-so many years, now belongs to us. What do you think would happen, Mr Gorbachev, if your soldiers were to behave in Lithuania as the British police did yesterday in London? All at once the Western press would be full of reports about the atrocities and brutalities of the Soviet troops in Lithuania.

Will you allow me a further word on the reunification of East and West Germany. What the NATO countries and also Federal Chancellor Kohl are planning seems, in my opinion, not to be fair. I cannot see why a united Germany should remain a member of NATO and why foreign NATO troops should remain stationed in Germany. In fact, what is the point of NATO being retained at all? When the whole world is striving for a lasting peace, and is entirely serious in this aim, there is no need for troops or weapons of attack, nor do we need missile defences in space. Of course, this is only if the desire for peace is genuine. In my opinion, Germany should remain neutral. Then all speculations about Germany representing too strong a power in Central Europe would be groundless.

You, Mr President, have already expressed this possibility, and I would be very pleased if you would insist upon it unwaveringly. Perhaps this decision would be the start of demilitarization in Europe, and the USA would have to go along with it willy-nilly. Canada would in any case be very pleased if it no longer had to belong to NATO; the high defence expenditure is the major factor in this. Those many millions would be better used in other sectors. And the same thing is true for the USA. Millions of people live on the poverty line while 300 million US dollars are shot up into space by the government in the form of a spy satellite, which then does not function and remains up there as useless garbage. Those 300 million would have given food to a vast crowd of poor people and a roof over their heads.

I hope my letter reaches its goal. As for the great goals that you have set for yourself and the Russian people, I sincerely wish you every success, so that the world can continue to live in peace, and so that your name can go down in world history, where it will hold a position far above all the other great men of world history. THIS ALONE IS WHAT I WISH.

Yours sincerely,
Hans and Karolina Haus

YOUTH
Carrying the Torch

I THINK IT IS FAIR to say that the youth of the world were among the first to grasp the gauntlet thrown down by Gorbachev. For too long they had been unable to comprehend what many of us saw as the madness of the arms race. What could be the point of having enough weaponry to destroy the planet many times over? Why were the two superpowers exporting deadly weapons as though there was no tomorrow? The Iran Iraq war of 1980-88 was a classic example of how destructive this policy of greed could be. And why were the industrial nations of the world not addressing themselves to the problems of pollution and global warming – surely the most pressing problems of our age?

In Gorbachev the younger generation found a leader who was addressing the issues that other politicians seemed afraid to tackle. On environmental matters they were pleading with him to do something about them not because his record in this areas was impressive but because they felt that only Gorbachev had the vision and influence to orchestrate global cooperation. Much was laid on his shoulders and it is still debatable whether he can ultimately deliver the goods. What is in no doubt however is that in Gorbachev they found a leader who shared the dreams of millions of young people, a man who was not too proud to compromise, lose face if necessary and 'go with the flow'.

To the youth of the Soviet Union, Gorbachev must have seemed like a breath of fresh air. He was only fifty three when he was elevated to the General Secretaryship of the Party. He succeeded Chernenko who was seventy two when appointed, only to die a year later. In short, leadership jumped a generation; and Gorbachev set about the task of getting rid of the old men who had ground the Soviet Union to a halt.

The elderly remembered all too well Stalin's dictatorship and Hitler's aggression and found it difficult to think imaginatively and take constructive risks. For Gorbachev such memories were little more than childhood whispers. His most active recollection were the frustrations and lost opportunities of the Khrushkev and Breshnev years. He was therefore not only young enough to act; he had objectives and was bent on implementing them. He wanted to get rid of past taboos and be creative.

Five years later the link was weaker. Komsomol, the Communist Youth Organisation, was in ruins, but that was all for the good in freeing young people to follow their own tastes. There were said to be unhappy sides to this liberation, particularly in crime and drugs. But perhaps the main problem for the young was the delay in the reforms they most wanted. With consumer goods and hard currency in short supply, videos and Western travel were not as accessible as they had expected. And by 1990 Gorbachev's economic restructuring was in the mire.

As some of Gorbachev's correspondents seem to imply, Soviet youth, like young people elsewhere, was preparing to create a new future whose characterisation in due course only they will be able to describe. Bur Gorbachev will have given them their opportunity. And they, after all, are our future.

Lloyd S. Fischel

Dear Mr Andropov,

My name is Samantha Smith. I am ten years old.

Congratulations on your new job. I have been worrying about Russia and the United States getting into a nuclear war. Are you going to vote to have a war or not? If you aren't please tell me how you are going to help to not have a war. This question you do not have to answer, but I would like to know why you want to conquer the world or at least our country. God made the world for us to live together in peace and not to fight.

Sincerely,
Samantha Smith

Samantha Smith was invited to the Soviet Union by Soviet leader Yuri Andropov after writing a letter to him asking why he wanted 'to conquer the world'. Then eleven, she visited the Soviet Union in the Summer of 1983 with her parents. Samantha died on August 25, 1985 in an airplane crash at the age of thirteen. In reporting on her death, a commentator on the Soviet television news show, 'Today in the World' said: 'It is difficult to believe that the voice of this wonderful American girl will not sound again.'

МЕЖДУНАРОДНАЯ

МИНИСТЕРСТВО СВЯЗИ СССР

ТЕЛЕГРАММА

П Р И Е М:	ПЕРЕДАЧА:	
го 46ч. 657	го ч. м.	Адрес
Бланк № 611	№ связи	

RMS779 WDR248 IOC003 4-0000568152
SUMS CV UDNX 308
TDBN SAN FRANCISCO CA 331/322 01 0021 SECTION 1 OF 2

GENERAL SECRETARY OF THE USSR MIKHAIL
GORBACHEV
THE KREMLIN
MOSCOW

DEAR MR GORBACHEVCHILDREN AS THE PEACE MAKERS HAVE TRAVELED TO MOSCOW
9 TIMES SINCE 1982. EACH TIME WE HAVE MADE A REQUEST TO MEET WITH THE
GENERAL SECRETARY. NOW CHILDREN FROM SIX COUNTRIES WILL BE JOINING ME
IN MOSCOW TO PARTICIPATE IN THE OPENING CEREMONIES FOR THE
INTERNATIONAL CONGRESS OF WOMEN.
IN MARCH OF THIS YEAR I WAS IN MOSCOW WITH MANY OF THESE SAME
CHILDREN. WE WERE ON A PEACE TRIP AROUND THE WORLD.
ON THAT TRIP WE MET PRIME MINISTER BRUNTLANDAND KING OLAF OF NORWAY,
PRIME MINISTER RAGIV GHANDI OF INDIA, SIR DAVID AKERS-JONES IN HONG KONG.
CHILDREN AS THE PEACEMAKERS WILL BE IN MOSCOW JANUARY 19 1988 UNTIL
JANUARY 24. THE CHILDREN WOULD VERY MUCH LIKE TO PRESENT YOU WITH THE
INTERNATIONAL CHILDREN'S PEACE PRIZE AWARD SCULPTURE FOR YOUR WORK
FOR WORLD PEACE. THE SCULPTURE IS USUALLY GIVEN TO CHILDREN FROM
AROUND THE WORLD AT OUR INTERNATIONAL CHILDREN'S PEACE PRIZE CEREMONY
WHICHHIS HELD EVERY YEAR IN THE UNITED STATES. WE OCCASIONALLY GIVE
THE PEACE PRIZE TO A WORLD LEADER. YOU WOULD BE THE SECOND WORLD
LEADER TO RECEIVE THIS PEACE PRIZE. AND WHAT BETTER BAROMETER OF YOUR
WORK THAN TO BE RECOGNIZED BY THE CHILDREN OF THE WORLD.

WE WILL BE GUESTS OF THE SOVIET PEACE COMMITTEE AND MR BOROVICK WILL
BE ABLE TO GIVE US ANY APPOINTMENT INFORMATION.

YES, WE ARE INDOMITABLE.

SINCERELY,
 PATRICIA MONTANDON AND THE CHILDREN OF THEWORLD
  950 BATTERY STREET
   SAN FRANCISCO CALIFORNIA 94111

The children did eventually meet Mr Gorbachev!

Cleveland Heights
Ohio, USA   27 August 1987

Dear General Secretary Gorbachev,

My name is Camilla Taylor and I am a sixteen-year-old girl from Cleveland, Ohio, USA. In the autumn of 1983, I began a petition for young people, aged sixteen and under, that read:

'We petition the governments of the United States and the Soviet Union to agree to a mutual and verifiable Nuclear Weapons Freeze.'

Since then I have collected 110,000 signatures from 43 countries, including approximately 96,000 from the USSR.

Would you please accept these signatures, which are expressions of hope from young people worldwide? Would it be possible for me to deliver the signatures to you in person? My thirteen-year-old sister, Imogen, would help me bring the petitions over to the USSR. Maybe two young Soviets would like to help us present them? I have enclosed a statement which I thought would be appropriate for the occasion. I would like to say it in Russian and I am hoping that one of the Soviet young people might like to say it in English.

I apologize if this letter, and my suggestions, appear presumptuous but I have been hoping for this presentation, and planning it for so long.

I would also be very grateful if you could find the time to accept all the signatures. But, most of all, I am sure that the signers of the petition, and many other young people around the world, would be very encouraged to hear that you had acknowledged their concerns.

Yours sincerely,
Camilla Taylor

telegram

camilla taylor
cleveland heights ohio
usa

dear camilla, soviet peace committee received your letter adressed mr gorbachev which says that you collected 110000 signatures petitioning young people in many countries stop we want inform you that big delegation of our committee headed by its president mr genrikh borovik going be washington jan 27 - feb 5 1988 for conference organized with center for soviet american dialogue tel (202) 543-7301 stop you may deliver signatures to our delegation

242

and discuss all questions related to it best wishes soviet peace committee

STATEMENT TO BE GIVEN AT THE WHITE HOUSE AND AT THE KREMLIN DURING PRESENTATION OF THE SIGNATURES

President Reagan/General Secretary Gorbachev

We young people (110,000 of us from 43 countries), are giving you our signatures in the hopes that you will understand how great our desire is for peace. The names come from: Angola, Australia, Austria, Belgium, Bulgaria, Canada, Chile, Colombia, Cuba, Cyprus, Czechoslovakia, Denmark, East Germany, England, Finland, France, Greece, Hungary, India, Ireland, Israel, Italy, Japan, Luxemburg, Mauritius, Mexico, Mongolia, The Netherlands, New Zealand, Norway, North Korea, Poland, Reunion Island (Indian Ocean), Romania, Sweden, Switzerland, Syria, Tunisia, Turkey, The USA, The USSR, West Germany, Yugoslavia. Not only our futures, but the future of all life on Earth is at stake. Please save this planet. Come to an agreement with General Secretary Gorbachev/President Reagan and halt the nuclear arms race.

SOVIET PEACE COMMITTEE
MOSCOW, USSR

19 November 1985

Dear Camilla,

Today I have received your letter dated 21 October. I was pleased to know that you are doing a great job participating in the struggle agains the nuclear arms race.

Unfortunately it took too much time for your letter to reach us by post. When I received your letter Mr M. S. Gorbatchev had already left Moscow for Geneva. Yesterday I saw on TV a delegation of American children presenting the Soviet delegation a collective message of an antiwar children organization. Mr Zamyatin, who received them, highly estimated the fact that American schoolchildren together with their parents are participating in the struggle to put an end to the nuclear arms race.

I hope that together with you we shall find means to deliver to Moscow the letters you have collected and to present them to the Soviet leadership. But this we'll have to do after the Geneva summit meeting.

For the time being I advise that you should continue to collect signatures. From the depth of our hearts we wish you good health and success in your studying. Please, convey my cordial regards to your parents and relatives.

Respectfully yours,
Yuri Zhukov
President

Thanjavur
Tamil Nadu State, India   September 1987

Respectable and Honourable Soviet Leader,

   This is a letter written to you by an Indian girl. I go by the name D. Geetha. I am seventeen years old. I am a college student.

   I hereby bring to your kind consideration about my opinions and wishes regarding world peace. Sir, I thank you first of all for having made arrangements for the removal of your troops from Afghanistan. I read in Indian Express paper dated 9 Saturday 1988 which is published in India that you have assured Indian women that you would do the maximum for the removal of nuclear weapons. I felt so glad when I read it through. It shows your boldness and broadmindedness towards world's peace. I appreciate your glasnost programme.

   . Sir, why should you compete with each other in the creation of nuclear weapons, which will one day or the other eradicate our entire human race from this earth. Scientists discovered nuclear components for destructive purpose. If your nation and US start eradicating nuclear weapons then it is sure that the whole world will cooperate with you.

   It was only during the past men were greedy for holding vast territories. Now most of the countries are independent. But think over how many nations are perfectly enjoying independence? It is very few. I now worry why civilization has progressed. If it had been like the past we would have been content with what we have. It is all due to the advances of science that we face many crises nowadays. You have helped us launch Insat IC. This progress in science is a welcoming progress but not the progress of nuclear weapons. Due to the advancement in fighting, in the future world history it can be noted as follows, 'there were many pairs of enemies during the twentieth century. They were US and USSR, Iran and Iraq, India and Pakistan, etc.' So, please try to use scientific discoveries for the progress of mankind.

Yours sincerely,
D. Geetha

Hammond
Oregon, USA   7 December 1987

Dear Mr Gorbachev,

Our class is writing letters to famous people and I decided to write to you because I remember the Russian fisherman who came to our house for lunch. First we went to the column which is a big tower on a hill that you could see all of Astoria from. They gave us a real Russian flag and a big bottle of grape juice from Russia. It was good.

I was reading about the summit. I don't understand why we are enemies because they were friendly and when they came to our school they gave us Russian candy.

I am ten years old and live by an army fort that was built during the American Civil War. The column was built in 1922. It has the history of Astoria painted on it in the shape of a spiral. Thanks for taking the time to read this. Please write back with a signed signature.

Sincerely,
Adam Gannaway

Piazza Marconi
Pero (Milano), Italy   16 December 1987

Dear Gorbaciov and Reagan,

We are nine-year-old Italian children, pupils at the Pero elementary school in the province of Milan.

We saw on television and read in the papers about your meeting, during which you came to an important decision: to begin to destroy a small part of your nuclear weapons. We want you to know that we all heaved a sigh of relief, because we think that all weapons are dangerous, useless, damaging and producers of violence, death, fear and destruction and that their only purpose is to do evil.

We want you to know that we are happy about your initiative, but we also want to tell you that it is not enough. For there to be true peace all arms must be destroyed.

We children think that it is better to help the peoples who are suffering from hunger and who live lives of poverty and misery, instead of spending money on arms which can destroy the whole world. All of us desire and choose peace only and for ever, and we hope that this desire will be realised. Carry on meeting each other, and talking, and deciding and signing: set a good example to the whole world and, perhaps, those nations which are now at war will understand that their problems can be resolved only by peace.

245

We wish you, your families and your peoples a happy Christmas and a peaceful New Year.

With love from all of us and from our teachers.

Fourth Year Pupils
Marconi Elementary School

Appleton
Wisconsin, USA   8 January 1988

Dear Secretary General,

My name is Jodie Unger, I am a sixteen-year-old girl, a tenth grade student at Appleton High School East in Appleton, Wisconsin.

I feel compelled to write to you since the horrible disaster of the earthquake in your country. I want to extend my sincere sympathy to you and your fellow countrymen.

I was very glad to see in the *US News and World Report* magazine that when the Yerevan airport opened, the United States was the first to be there and provide aid to your people.

We've been raised to be fearful of the power of the Soviet Union. We've worried that the US and the Soviet Union would someday destroy each other, our families and the world, but certain incidents lately have made me confident that this will not happen. I feel now that we are alike, with the same hopes and dreams for the future, similar fears and courage.

I was awed by the newspaper article telling of the courage and bravery of Susanna Petrosyan, who was trapped for eight days under the rubble. She had been trapped in darkness, flat on her back, only able to move from side to side, cold, hungry and fearful for her life and that of her child. With little clothes that Susanna had on she took them off to give to her child. She knew her death was imminent and was struggling to save the life of her child. Susanna also tried to sustain her daughter's life by cutting her own fingers with a piece of broken glass and allowing her child to drink her blood.

I know many people criticized you for leaving the US so early, but I feel you did what any other leader of his country should have done in your place. I admire you for wanting to be with your people during this time of hardship.

I am hopeful that the communication that has begun between our two great world powers will continue and flourish, so that we all may live and grow in peace.

Sincerely,
Jodie Unger

246

'Marceliano Santamaria'
Burgos
Spain   30 January 1988

Dear Mr Secretary,
   We are a group of eighth-year EGB pupils in the Marceliano Santa
Maria State School, Bda. Inmaculada, Burgos. Our parents are
simple workers, some unemployed, who are daily struggling to
support their families and to give their children what they were
unable to have themselves.
   We are writing to you because it is the day of peace, in memory
of that great, although small, man Gandhi. Firstly, we would
like to thank you for the Reduction of Arms Treaty, signed by
you and Mr Reagan. But we are not satisfied with this alone
and ask you to embrace the 'O' option as supported by our
president, Felipe Gonzalez. This treaty must not be the end of
it. There have to be others, so as to eliminate all weapons
and the danger of extinction of life on earth. For the good
of humanity Sir, Star Wars must be avoided. Take courage, Mr
Secretary!
   Our Social Science teacher has explained a little to us about your
policy in perestroika, which we think to be excellent since it means
a step forward in the democratisation and progress of your fellow
countrymen. We all know that this could not be achieved in
the twinkling of an eye as there will, no doubt, be many who
disagree with these projects. Even so, from here, we encourage
you to continue towards bringing about these changes which we
see as ideal.
   We would like to say that instead of spending so much money on
weapons, set it aside to help the development of the Third World.
So many people are dying of hunger! Think of Africa, Asia, Latin
America, etc.
   As you ask for the freedom for each nation to govern themselves in
perestroika, we ask you to withdraw your troops from Afghanistan
and help them towards being free.
   Now that we have said all this, we thank you once again and hope
that you continue with your projects. We hope that these will bring
peace and friendship to all peoples.
   Many thanks, Sr Mikhail, for all that you are doing for the good
of humanity. We wonder whether you and Mr Reagan will secure
the peace yearned for by the whole world, as well as total nuclear
disarmament. Courage!
   A kiss from all the children in the group.

                            Signed by delegate and three members

Elverum
Norway   March 1988

Dear Michael Gorbatsjov,

I am writing this letter to you, because I believe that you, as one
of the leaders of the world's big powers, can do something about the
problems in the world. I hope you can take some time to read this letter.
The pollution in the world makes it difficult for people and animals to
live here. The ozone layer is so thin that ultraviolet rays which may
burn everything living, have begun to come through.

These are problems which occupy me and many others. As the
Soviet Union occupies such a large part of the Earth, I believe
that it would be a great help if you did your utmost as well, to
protect the environment. Nuclear power stations can be changed
for hydroelectric ones. If the hydroelectric power stations had been
big enough, enough energy would have been produced. After the
accident in Chjernobyl, which claimed many lives, I think it is about
time that something was done. Factory discharges make it difficult for
the fish to live. To prevent this, cleaning plants and adding lime to
the lakes are needed. Because we do need the fish. The factories also
emit poisonous gases into the air which makes plants and trees die.
In Germany almost all forest has been wiped out because of pollution
from factories. The trees and plants make air which we breathe in. So
if they disappear we will not have anything to breathe any longer. If we
don't do anything about this, the future looks dark.

Something I appreciate about the Soviet Union is that all the public
transport is so well developed.

Then fewer people need a car and the air becomes cleaner. Because
the car pollutes badly. Many cars have a catalyst, but the exhaust
never gets to be absolutely clean. Cars have been made which run
on electricity and electricity pollutes very little. In the future we shall
have to resort to that.

It is going to be quite a job to exchange the old petrol cars
with the new ones. And if people are going to be able to afford
these cars, the prices shall have to come down. The prices of
environmentally friendly products should be lower than the prices
of products that pollute. Then it will be easier for people to take care
of their environment.

I keep asking myself this question: Do we not care about our
earth? It seems we have not considered what is going to happen
if we continue in this way. Children who are born today, what is
it going to be like for them when they are grown up? What is the
earth going to look like then? Are there going to be any flowers
and trees, sun and water left at all? Let us hope so and let us do
something now!

I hope you will take this up with other countries when you meet the president or the prime minister and I hope you will get them to look after their country in the same way as you will want to look after yours.

So let us save the Earth, as we have after all only one!

Environmentally friendly greeting.
Aud-Ingebørg Barstad
(A Norwegian schoolgirl)

Clearwater
Ontario, Canada   March 1988

Dear Mr Gorbachev,
How are you? I'm fine. My name is Wayne Smith. They call me Wiener. They know me by athlete at school. I have a dalmation. His name is Spike. We named him that because his hair would spike when he was a little puppy. I have one brother and one sister. My brother Tony is living with his girl-friend in Toronto. My sister Jacqueline is still living with us. My parents' names are Tony and Irene. Do you like your job? I would love it. Please stop acid rain all over the place. My favorite sports are soccer, baseball, basketball and hockey. They are all fun. Got to go now.

Your friend,
Wayne Smith

Zaandam
Netherlands   May 1988

Dear Mr M. Gorbatrjov,
I have heard on the TV news that you will talk again with Mr R. Reagen about peace and wapen controle on 29th of May 1988. That is also for me a special day because it is my birthday. I become than ten years old. I have written a letter to Mr R. Reagen and I hope that there will peace very soon.

I wish you very nice days in Moskow.

Christiaan de Bruin

Trier-Filsch
West Germany   12 May 1988

Dear Mr Gorbachev,

I am a girl from West Germany, sixteen years old, I go to secondary
school and am very interested in politics. I have read your book
Perestroika from start to finish, which has been published in West
Germany and in many other countries. It prompted me to write to
you, to tell you my impressions and to assure you that you have my
support.

There are parts of your thoughts about the United States of
America which I cannot accept. Certainly you know a lot more
about politics, but I think you cannot just see the entire American
nation as being against the Soviet Union. Especially in the USA you
have received much praise for your policies of restructuring and
won much recognition through your appearance. The American
people also want peace, and perhaps you should see the positive
sides of American politics and the attempts that have been made by
the USA.

I would also like to tell you something about West Germany.
Especially in our country you get much support and admiration
from all people. We, the young people, see your proposals with
great pleasure, because we are afraid of the future. We do accept
the Soviet Union and her different system and we try to deal with
that. I would very much like to learn more about this country, more
than I know from the media. The West German people hope that you
will succeed with perestroika. Not so long ago my Latin teacher
said, 'In the history books of the future you will not read about Mr
Kohl, you will not read about Mr Mitterrand and you will not read
anything about Mr Reagan. There is only one politician you will read
something about, and that is Mr Gorbachev, because perestroika is
a historic turning point.'

Something that I am very concerned about just now is the divided
Germany. During a recent visit of our school class to East Berlin I
and some of my friends from my class spoke to East German people.
I talked to an old lady, who like all the others complained about the
terrible lack of freedom. When we left she said to me, 'I hope you
will have a lovely and free life.' I was very moved by this because
I realised that many people cannot so easily travel to all countries
of the world. It is very sad that along the border between the two
Germanies the order to shoot people is still in operation.

Yours faithfully,
Katja Schmitz

Fort Collins
Colorado, USA   27 May 1988

Dear Mr Gorbachev,

I am writing to you, somewhat distrubed, as a result of a Foreign
Policy class I am attending at Colorado State University. Currently
we are studying the history of US-Soviet relations, including those
views of Sir Winston Churchill and George Kennan, who wrote
'Sources of Soviet Conduct' (by Mr X in the July 1947 issue of the
Foreign Affairs Journal). I have come to the conclusion that this
world has had a lot of foolish, irresponsible and naive people in
the past, with the United States claiming more than its fair share
of them. As you may be aware, a poll was recently taken, showing
you, Mikhail Gorbachev, to be more popular among United States
college students than our own President, Ronald Reagan. I find this
to be a particularly honorable achievement.

An American philosopher, Robert Nozick, once said, 'Because we
value someone's particularity, we know that makes it appropriate to
aid him rather than another, and through moral advance we will
eliminate this.' I contend that humanity is on the doorstep of
this advanced state where we no longer need be afraid of our
fellow man.

Sincerely,
Jon K. Farris

*Under the byline 'X' in Foreign Affairs, July 1947, George Keenan wrote
that the US policy towards the Soviet Union should be one of firm dealing
and 'containment' until the USSR either enters into cooperation with the
US or experiences internal collapse. Keenan believed the USSR could not be
approached on Western terms since they held capitalism to be incompatible
with communism. Consequently, he believed, the USSR must be suspicious
of capitalist nations and oppose their moves without merit or justification.
He believed the Russian aim was a 'world Soviet.'*

Carmel
California, USA   November 1988

General Secretary Gorbachev,.

I am a nineteen-year-old American from California. I am now
studying politics at Sonoma State University in northern California,
and would like to visit your country sometime in the near future.
I consider myself very fortunate to have been born into this era,
during which you have attained the position of General Secretary
of the CPSU, and have been able to implement the policy of
perestroika. I believe what you are now doing is the single most

important step towards world peace, unity, and universal human rights of this century.

Although I am not a Soviet citizen, as a world citizen I urge you to continue the reforms that you have started, and to introduce as many new policies as you see fit, in order to bring the people of this world closer together. I know this may be difficult, but I believe that the traditional, conservative faction of the Party will soon see the urgency and the necessity for perestroika, and will support you in your quest for more freedom for your fellow countrymen, as well as in the drive for peace in a more complex and troubled global situation.

Soon, the United States and the Soviet Union must be able to join together to try to solve some of the problems of the underdeveloped countries, and to promote peace throughout the entire world. One of the problems with a growing number of Americans is their refusal to believe that things really can change, and their belief that world peace is merely an immature, uneducated person's view of an idealistic situation. These people need both hope and proof that peace is possible. Mr Gorbachev, you have the power to give both of these necessities to the American people, and I hope that President Bush will work with you to promote peace, and to break down many of the invisible barriers that some Americans tend to see as separating our two nations.

I urge you to continue to disagree with our 'Star Wars' defence systems (SDI). We must not escalate the arms race any further. As we should have learned by now, this problem must be solved by cooperation between human beings, not by new and more modern ways of trying to kill each other.

I know this must be a difficult time for you, domestically, but I want you to know that you have my full support. With over a hundred ethnic groups in one country, not even Superman could be expected to have control over all of them, especially when the policy of perestroika is being implemented. I really hope that these groups will soon realize that the road to peace is found through inclusion, rather than through isolation. Once these people can say they are Soviets first, and Armenians, Estonians, Lithuanians, Latvians, Azerbaijanis, etc ... second, then the peoples of the world will be one giant step closer to peaceful coexistence.

As neither a communist, nor a capitalist, but as a democratic humanist, I hope you will consider this letter as a token of my appreciation for your hard work at home, and for your unrivaled committment to peace on our planet.

Thank you Mr Gorbachev,
Greg Harrison

252

Vicenza
Italy   9 December 1988

Dear Mr Gorbaciov,

I'm a student, studying Economics and Business at Venice
University, and I wanted to write to you (but perhaps I am being
presumptuous because you will probably never read this letter)
to tell you how pleased I am to learn from the mass media of
the courageous positions which you have taken over armaments
in Europe. Here, contrary to appearances, our news is heavily
'filtered' and those few gleams of peace which glow here and
there are invariably interpreted as a cover for who knows what
devilish schemes of conquest: perhaps possession of the whole
world renders one omnipotent or eternal? At least, that's what some
people here seem to think.

It is clear that the economic model based on free exchange has
been a failure, not least because it is always built on the backs of the
poorest: the South of the world is dying of hunger and internecine
wars fought with weapons made in the North and bought with
money lent by the 'rich' nations. But if the resources wasted on
the making of arms were used for other, much more important
purposes, the situation might perhaps improve.

The time is ripe for radical change, many of us young people
recognise this need and keep alive hope for a peaceful future; there
are all too many situations which have been dragging on for years
without finding a valid solution for humanity. The Middle East,
South Africa, Afghanistan, Namibia, the Ukraine and many more
. . . we must 'rediscover' the fact that the fundamental value to be
respected is man himself; we are no longer interested in 20,000 tanks
or 15,000 planes! The roads towards a future of peace and solidarity
between nations are different ones. But a fresh wind is blowing from
the East . . . perhaps it is bringing spring.

I would like to thank you from the bottom of my heart and wish
you a happy Christmas and a peaceful 1989.

Best wishes,
Paolo Pomi

PS How could our hearts not go out at this time to the tormented
people of Armenia?

253

Surabaya
Republic of Indonesia   13 December 1988

Dear His Excellency Mr Mikhail Gorbachev,

This letter I make purposely because I want to tell something to
you Mr Mikhail Gorbachev. I'm sorry this letter I write with English,
because I can't speak Russian.

I am Hentje Alvy Pongoh AI. I'm a boy sixteen years old, I'm a
student of second grade of SMAN 3 Surabaya (SMAN is a similar
senior high school). I was very amazed with your simplicity and
Mrs Raisa. From your simplicity I believe you are a good leader
and wish and loving peace. I'm very amazed with development
and progress state of USSR, especially since you have become
General Secretary for PKUS and President of USSR. And with this
letter, I wish to express my deepest sympathy and my anxiety on the
disaster that fell on your country (the earthquake disaster that fell
on Armenia). Please accept my condolences, His Excellency, Mr
Mikhail Gorbachev.

I like to collect about datas, name cards, photographs, signatures
and biographies of the famous personages in the world who loving
peace. And I like to be friendly and to correspond with them. Would
you give me a name card, signature, photograph and biography of
yours? And I want to be friendly with you and your people and
to correspond with you His Excellency Mr Mikhail Gorbachev. I
want to study Russian language, therefore would you give me and
send me some guide books to study Russian language? If you His
Excellency Mr Mikhail Gorbachev agree to give me and send me all
souvenirs, I thank you very much beforehand. I think my letter stop
here. I beg pardon if there are words that don't be pleased. Well, I
think it is enough for this time and I'm waiting for your reply. Excuse
me for my English is rather poor.

May God always bless and shelter you Mr Mikhail Gorbachev and
the USSR. I offer peace and love to all persons in the world.

With love and peace,
Hentje Alvy Pongoh AI

Jilin City
Jilin Province, PR China   1 January 1989

Dear Mr Gorbachev,

Allow me, in the name of an ordinary Chinese youth, to extend
my congratulations to you on the arrival of the New Year, to
congratulate you on your efforts and contributions to world peace

in the past few years, and I hope, through you, to pass my best wishes to your wife and family.

Due to your unusual courage and insight in your time as General Secretary of the USSR Communist Party, you have made remarkable changes to your country, have made much-needed and indelible contributions to world peace, and have played a positive and decisive part in the improvement of Sino-Soviet relations. All these have been welcomed and highly appreciated by peace-lovers all over the world and by we, the Chinese people.

Since you became General Secretary, it was you, together with the American people, who determined courageously to destroy medium-range missiles; to withdraw troops from Afghanistan to free its people from the sufferings of war; it was also you who decided resolutely to reduce the armed forces of the Soviet Union by 500,000. All the above are contributions you have made to world peace. Of course, this is only a part of your efforts. There are certainly a lot more international problems still remaining to be solved which will require further efforts from you, e.g. the problems of Cambodia, the four nothern Japanese islands, etc. Moreover, your efforts towards the improvement of Sino-Soviet relations are known to all. The withdrawal of troops from Mongolia, negotiations between the Foreign Ministers of our two countries are particularly memorable to the Chinese people. But it will be very difficult and will need much more effort to solve all the problems which exist between China and the Soviet Union, since some of them are relics of history, sometimes dating back decades or even centuries ago. These are all achievements of yours in the field of international affairs and are much appreciated by me and by the Chinese.

However, what you are most admired for is not all these things I have mentioned but your style of work which is brave and resolute, vigorous and swift, and full of the pioneering spirit. As a Communist Party leader, your style of work has fully reflected the nature and quality of a Marxist, and the disposition and insight of a party and state leader. Your style of work has also dealt a heavy blow to dogmatism and bureaucracy. Since you became the supreme leader of the Soviet Union, I and all the Chinese people, and our leaders, too, have been looking to you. You have not only created a new atmosphere for your people, but also a new atmosphere for world peace, a new atmosphere for Sino-Soviet relations, and a new atmosphere for the future.

We Chinese have an old saying that final judgment can be passed on a person only when the lid is laid on his coffin. But in my view, you are an exception.

Let the whole world unite, bid 'farewell to arms'. Let's join hands in the struggle with the common enemy of mankind –

natural calamity, and strive for a better environment for mankind to exist in.

I wish your family a happy New Year and every happiness.

Yours sincerely,
A Chinese Youth

Mr General Secretary, it is an unhappy fact that my father has contracted cancer of the liver, which is already in its final stage. He is completely unable to look after himself. He is not long in this world. He is a retired worker, and a Party member of thirty-four years' standing.

Chiswick
London, England   19 January 1989

Dear Mikhail Gorbachev,

I am a sixteen-year-old student, in England, and I study, both in school and outside school, international politics. I am deeply committed to the principles of pluralist socialism; that is I am convinced that the socialist principles and doctrines are those that are the most humanitarian, and just, but I believe in the choice of electorates to choose the philosophy they believe in. However, at this time in history, the British and American electorates have chosen paths that are not to their benefit, and ones that are steeped in reactionary rhetoric. The fact is, though, that what doctrines a country chooses to represent it is of only passing significance, and one that will not be historically important. What history will judge this epoch by, is how the governments and peoples of this world combat the unique menaces of the nuclear arms race, with the resultant threat of the extinction of all life on this planet, and the ecological time bomb that has been created for short-term profit-mongering and exploitation of natural resources. The future peoples will also examine the period and ask themselves why it is that at a time of such great technological advances and scientific leaps, the scourge of povery was not driven off the planet, and why instead these scientific gains were turned to making 'better', and deadlier weapons of mass murder and destruction.

Whatever happens in the international arena in the next few years, never stop the processes that have been instigated. They are the most fascinating, and the bravest that have occurred since the end of the war, and the people of the world at last see a glimmer of hope for the future of mankind; at last the arms race is being challenged by a political leader, and the idea of common humanitarian needs is starting to rise above ideological differences. Your book stresses the need to live in peaceful competition and cooperation between the different social ideologies, and that surely is an imperative in the interconnected world that we live in. But that glimmer is still not quite reality; people still are not sure whether that glimmer is going to turn into a picture before their eyes. That is not your fault; the peoples of the different Western countries view you as the best political leader out of all the major powers and the one most genuinely driven by the goal of international harmony, and justice for all. In the next few years, the prospects for major arms reductions, and the securing of effective treaties to stop the proliferation of the nuclear and chemical weapons trade can turn into actual realities.

The moral leader in this course is you, and your entire country. In the eyes of the majority, the Soviet Union is democratising, and the perceived menace (caused by the great mistrust of Stalin) no longer exists in the minds of most intelligent people.

Glasnost and perestroika must never be allowed to stop, and the humane socialism that is the hallmark of the Gorbachev era must remain the true representative of socialism. Distortions in the international view of socialism have been caused by figures such as Stalin, and only now do people understand how great and just a movement it really is. I believe that socialism is the right course for countries to pursue, but above all, more important than ideological differences, the world must learn to live in peace. War cannot be afforded, because of the human suffering it causes, and it should therefore be banished as a means of resolving differences. Even if only one life were lost in a conflict, then that conflict would still not be worth pursuing.

This is how I view the new revolution that is taking place in Russia. It is more than just a passing interest; I am very interested in it not just because I love politics, and find it especially stimulating when it is put to good use, but also because all of my grandparents were Russian Jews: they fled from the country during the pogroms at the end of the last century, and settled in the USA and England. One of my grandfathers actually grew up in Russia, until the 1930s, when his family left the country. His father was a prominent rabbi, Rabbi Abramsky, and under Stalin he was sentenced to the labour camps. He was freed to the West in an exchange for some convicted communist spies, and my grandfather, with his mother and younger brother (his other two brothers left Russia after them) also were let out of the country to join his father. My grandfather, Professor Chimen Abramsky, settled in England; like many people in the 1930s he became a committed communist, and stayed dedicated until the late 1950s. He bacame one of the leading historians on

Marx, especially in relation to his role in the English movement, and together with his friend, Henry Collins, wrote: 'Karl Marx and the British Labour Movement, Years of the First International.'

Anyway, this letter is to tell you that I am very pleased that at long last someone who is interested in the preservation of justice in the world, and has ideas that are so new and different, has finally emerged as a leader. The opportunities for humanity are great, and can be forwarded by the knowledge that eternal liberty and justice are the hallmarks of a civilised world, and that peace and security for all are the situations that must be strived for. I hope that the ideas put forward by you in the 27th Party Congress, and the June 1988 Party Conference, and most remarkably at the UN in December, bear fruit, and that the west finally changes its tune, and stops moralising to a country that has shown itself to be far more determined than the West to solve humanity's problems. I also hope sincerely that those whom Stalin persecuted are posthumously recognised and reinstated; apart from the ordinary millions, surely the next step should be to reinstate Trotsky, and to stop the fallacies that Stalin perpetuated against him; he was Lenin's right-hand man, and from reading your book I realise how much you admire Lenin's aims and methods. Surely this step would be the logiclal conclusion of the discrediting of Stalin's terror, and the measures of reassessing and opening up Soviet history to criticism and self-analysis. Trotsky was not a traitor to the communist cause, and certainly did not deserve to be hounded out of the Soviet Union.

Yours sincerely,
Sasha Abramsky

Takapuna
Auckland, New Zealand   8 February 1989

Dear Mr Gorbachev,

The recent initiative which you have taken for the reduction of chemical weapons is a very cheering sign indeed. Chemical weapons are an atrocity and should be eradicated. I am glad to see that you (and from the favourable response, Mr Bush) feel the same way as I do.

On the subject of nuclear weapons and nuclear power it appears we disagree. I believe that of all the issues facing us today, such as ozone depletion, the greenhouse effect, and pollution, the nuclear issue is the most important. Many world leaders seem to regard the nuclear problem as a joke, an excuse for propaganda, or even as harmless.

I would like to see the eradication of all nuclear weapons and nuclear power. I believe that while there are some benefits the risks involved in having nuclear weapons and nuclear power (even for 'peaceful' purposes) far outweigh any advantages.

The nuclear arms race is a totally futile exercise in self-destruction. As a deterrent it can hardly be called efficient, the numerous wars and terrorist incidents since 1945 are testament to this. As a method of offence nuclear weapons are highly unsatisfactory, they wipe out your allies and your enemies quite indiscriminately. Surely a strong conventional force would be sufficient for self-defence if greater efforts were made with diplomacy.

Aside from these arguments there is another question which I am unable to find an answer to. Why is the nuclear arsenal of your country so huge? Why is it necessary to have so many arms and even continue building them when you have enough not only to destroy yourselves, your opposition and everyone else, but to do so many times over?

The reductions recently made by both the Soviet Union and the United States are insignificant on their own. Without further efforts they will become an exercise as pointless as removing a bucket of water from the Caspian Sea and expecting it to disappear.

While nuclear weapons are still being built the problem won't go away. The frightening thing is that one day, be it by equipment failure, terrorist attack, human error, or even on purpose, that nuclear stockpile could blow, taking most, or all, of our unique world with it. You may not be around then, I may not be around then, but would you wish that fate on your grandchildren, or their children? Now is the time to start making sure that that never happens.

You may think that it will never happen, but can you read the future?

I am begging you to work towards a reduction and eradication of nuclear weapons and nuclear power before it is too late. While you may consider nuclear power when used for peaceful purposes to be no more dangerous than a hydro dam or any other conventional form of energy generation, I am unable to agree. Had a hydro dam collapsed at Chernobyl the leukaemia rate would not be increasing in Scotland, food supplies over much of Europe would not be contaminated and where reactor four once stood, there would not be an immense tomb designed to seal the reactor for hundreds of years.

Complacency could lead to further disasters in the Soviet Union, in Europe, the United States or anywhere nuclear power is used. A small mistake could destroy so much. The risks are too great. Surely it is not worth it.

Again I beg you to consider my plea. At seventeen years old I can do nothing about it except write letters and say how I feel; you are in a position to really do something about this terrible threat.

Yours sincerely,
Melanie Newfield

Kengeri Satellite Town
Bangalore, India   20 February 1989

Dear Mikhail Uncle,

I am a sixteen-year-old girl student and have just completed my class ten.

I write to wish you A VERY HAPPY BIRTHDAY.

I have often watched you on the television when you come to India. Your photos in the newspapers are very good and I keep them. Our Prime Minister Rajiv Gandhi has said that you are his best friend and the word 'Drushva' is loved by all Indians.

The happenings which led to the disaster in Hiroshima and Nagasaki can never be forgotten. We remember your signing the Delhi Declaration with our Prime Minister in November 1986. We also thank you for your support to the six-nation peace initiative and the Non-Aligned Movement. I admire your bold steps taken recently to end tension in Asia and Europe. Your unilateral ban on nuclear weapons testing was a very positive initiative. These days another kind of arms is spreading terror. The chemical weapons have ruined cities, families and children. In a recent programme on the TV, I was horrified to see the burnt faces of small children during the Iran-Iraq war. Chernobyl in Russia and Bhopal in India experienced unspeakable destruction when chemical gases leaked accidentally. But to know that people make such things to kill each other is unimaginable. The Soviet Union has taken strong steps to eliminate such arms and save the generations of tomorrow from elimination.

Your great country has stood by India through thick and thin and you have helped us all through our developing years. Our beloved leader, the late Indira Gandhi, always admired the Soviet Union for its frankness and courage. Pandit Nehru fought for our freedom enlightened by the Great Revolution in your country, under the able stewardship of mighty Lenin.

We are indebted to you and grateful to your tried and tested friendship. The Soviet Union and India are not only friends but also brothers. The Festivals of India and Russia have succeeded in bringing the peace loving people of two great and historic cultures closer to each other.

I have read a little bit of your book on perestroika in a magazine. I like your philosophy absolutely but I don't have the book to help me read it fully.

I also congratulate you that all the brave soldiers of your country have returned to their homeland, after risking their lives for so many years in Afghanistan. I hope the Soviet Union and India will join hands together to lead the world to the twenty-first century in peace, hope, happiness and prosperity. The success – a great one in history – depends on your experienced shoulders and our Rajiv Ghandi's young shoulders. I know that you will fulfil the aspirations of millions. Dear Uncle, I wish to meet you once but I don't know how to do it. You are very far in Moscow but do, please send me an autographed photo of yourself and Aunty Raisa.

Yours faithfully,
Vijaya Moorthy

Seville
Spain   20 February 1989

Mr Gorbachev,
Before anything else, forgive my boldness in sending this letter to you. Allow me to introduce myself.

I am a young man, a Spaniard of twenty years of age, who feels deep distress at seeing the state of the world, hunger, poverty, war, drugs . . .

I will briefly explain the purpose of this letter to you.

I was reading the biography of Albert Einstein and read, that in the last years of his life he spoke of a few ideas that he had concerning the unification of states, but, regrettably, he died before having time to speak about this to the United Nations.

I thought about this fact and reached the conclusion that this form of government would solve many of the world's present problems.

If we stopped to think about this subject, having only one state and one government, all weapons could be disposed of and all the money spent on armies could be saved. All wars would be eliminated. Wealth would be more equally distributed and the trafficking and taking of drugs much better controlled. What do you think of the idea?

Galo Cano Cano

Falmouth
Massachusetts, USA   23 February 1989

Dear Your Excellency,

Environmental awareness is the first step in preserving the earth and its resources. The depletion of resources and pollution cannot be controlled unless world leaders comprehend the importance of immediate action. Cooperation and global peace are the means for the survival of all species on earth.

The ozonosphere, approximately twenty to thirty miles above the surface of the earth, filters out about ninety-nine per cent of ultraviolet radiation from the sun. Human activities have gradually decreased this protective layer. If this continues all the earth's beings will suffer. Skin cancer will increase. The world's crops (wheat, rice, corn) will decrease. Another problem is the heating of the atmosphere, which will result in global climate alteration.

No one country can be blamed. It is all the world's fault and responsibility to correct. There are many solutions to consider.

Stop improper disposal of toxic and other hazardous waste. Control and minimalize burning of fossil fuels. Develop alternative energy sources (solar power). Implement regulations to control carbon dioxide emissions via industrial smoke stack gas. Plant more trees to take carbon dioxide out of the atmosphere. STOP use of chlorofluorohydrocarbons! There are many more solutions, but not only one solution will suffice.

All the people on earth are responsible for its future. Please, as a leader of a nation, direct your energy in protecting your, your country's, and my future!

Sincerely,
Rebeka Rand
Biology student

Manheim
Pennsylvania, USA   1 June 1989

Dear Mr Gorbachev,

My name is Tara M. Ellinger and I am a senior at Manheim Central High School, Manheim, Pennsylvania. This year I have enjoyed learning about your country and style of government in my World Cultures class.

Not only have we read about the USSR, we have seen films and filmstrips centering mainly on Moscow and Leningrad. We also saw a video on your school system. I noticed similarities in the subjects studied; however, I did notice your children are taught more advanced concepts at a younger age than in our educational system.

How difficult and pressure-filled your days must be trying to meet the demands of your country. I have great admiration for you and believe you care about your people. While watching you on television, I have sensed this warmth and friendliness.

I have always lived in a democracy and have taken my freedom for granted, so it would be difficult for me to relate to living in a communist country. Maybe some of the young people in my country would have a less difficult time growing up if they had less freedom and maybe some of your teenagers would fulfill their full potential with more freedom. Who is to say who is right and who is wrong – we are all different with different personalities and different beliefs. However, one common element between our countries should be the desire for a worldwide peaceful existence.

I wanted to convey this message to you, because we all have so many individual problems to deal with throughout our lives, it would be nice to know our countries could accept each other's governmental and cultural differencies and learn to live together in peace. As a result, the money spent on the arms race would be available to help mankind with social, educational and health problems.

Someday I would like to visit the USSR, and if someone asked you what would be the highlight of this visit, what would you say? I thank you for taking time to read my letter.

Sincerely,
Tara M. Ellinger

Mannheim
West Germany   19 June 1989

Dear Mr Gorbachev,

I am a nineteen-year-old school pupil, who, like many other Germans, follows your political progress with great hope and trust, and I would like to encourage you to continue in the pursuit of your great goal with resolute determination.

A firm and enduring friendship between our countries is possible because we are closely linked by the ties of a common culture. Just as I do, there are many Germans who love the great Russian composers, and who, when they hear that music, feel a deep affinity with the Russian soul. In just the same way, European literature would be incomplete without the tremendous sensitivity of the dramas and novels written by Russian authors. I admire Tchaikovsky just as I do Beethoven, Chekhov as I do Shakespeare and Dostoevski as I do Thomas Mann. Marx too is a link between us, for without the German philosophers who preceded him, it would have been unthinkable for him to have developed his ideas, which Lenin then tried to transform into practical politics in the Soviet Union.

But today it is necessary to make a new assessment of this process. Old demands and principles are not to be clung to for all eternity. One should be ready, over and over again, to consider anew what view of things is the politically sensible one to adopt under the existing circumstances.

I am firmly convinced that if all sides examine their social systems in this way, there will no longer be any differences in principle. Because a socially equitable provision for the entire population – and that is what is necessary – can only come about when an efficiently functioning economy makes available the means that are required to achieve that end. For that reason, I hope very much that the economic reorganization that you are striving for will be successful. But I hope just as much that not only the economy, but at the same time policies as well will be reorganized, so that in your country, those people who are endeavouring to achieve political freedom will not be cruelly persecuted and oppressed as they are in China. In every period of history, man has striven for freedom, and Europe has come closer to this goal as a result of great revolutions.

A further characteristic of the European, and in the world of today certainly the most important one, is our common, and therefore unifying, longing for peace. As a result of the terrible experience of appalling wars that all the peoples of Europe have had to endure, we bear, indelibly printed in our hearts, the knowledge that wars are unnecessary, futile and worse than any other possible alternative. Because there are other nations that are not yet aware of this, we Europeans must unite together and take on the responsibility for peace throughout the whole world. European unification should not be restricted to Western Europe alone, because the Russian people in particular had to endure tremendous suffering, and are convinced of the necessity for peace.

But if, as you repeatedly confirm, you want to see the nations of the world living together in harmony, not only because that is economically advantageous but primarily out of honest conviction, I would ask you to give greater attention to ensuring that the borders between East and West are opened up; only then is it possible for people to live together in peace without fear of one another. The Berlin Wall in particular has become superfluous today; its continued existence endangers the credibility of your entire politics, whereas its destruction could be an extremely positive symbolic act.

I write this letter to wish you good fortune and success in your future work and to show that, as a German, I believe that the USSR belongs to Europe as an important member.

Yours sincerely,
Thorsten Critzmann

Arlington
Vancouver, USA   24 September 1989

I am a junior at the American University in Washington, DC and am writing to you to express my feelings and concerns regarding the Soviet Union.

I have personally been fascinated and even intrigued with the Soviet Union since I was in high school in Oak Ridge, Tennessee. I have always disagreed with stereotypes and attempt to refute them as much as possible. Therefore, I have continued to study the Soviet Union and upon graduation in December of 1990, hope to become a foreign correspondent there.

My concern is that the stereotype of the 'evil empire', although decreasing daily, remains strong in many parts of the US. Friends of mine that have studied the Soviet Union are as fascinated with it as I am. We see the falsity of the stereotype, and see the realities of the people in your country. We see that people have the same human emotions and general qualities wherever they live and whatever their political and ideological orientation. We plan to study more, and to do what we can to aid perestroika i.e. working to better relations between our two countries. There are many, however, who still believe in the old stereotypes. They almost question the humanity of the Soviet citizens. They mistakenly believe what our government tells them. They don't see the propaganda going on in the American media. These people are voters, and hence, inevitably help shape government policy. This concerns me.

My suggestion to you (as if you don't have enough on your mind) is to increase the educational exchanges between our countries. A professor at the American University has attempted for years to organize a study abroad program in the Soviet Union. The last I heard about it, red tape was still holding the program up. I feel that more educational exchanges would lead to greater understanding of the important differences – and similarities – between our countries. Exchanges would allow greater numbers of American students to learn first-hand about the people and the situations within the Soviet Union. This first-hand knowledge would, through time, greatly decrease the old stereotypes and suspicions; ultimately this will have a positive effect on US foreign policy toward the Soviet Union.

I will also make a suggestion to American educators – *Perestroika* is a masterpiece and should be required reading in all universities!

Kathy Harman

Takaoka-shi
Toyama, Japan .   December 1989

Dear Mr Gorbachev,

I am a Japanese girl of twenty-one years old. I go to university. I love you, and USSR.

We are products of very different histories, speaking very different languages. The decade of the forties found us in a tragic war.

However, a commonality of interests brought us back together in the productive partnership we share today. And while our cultures remain distinct, and our languages are different, we have made real progress in overcoming the physical and mental barriers of distance.

Now, by almost any objective measure – political, economic, or cultural, to name just three – what Japan and the USSR do alone and together is of tremendous importance to our two countries and to the entire world. And what keeps us working in harmony is that – unlike other bilateral relationships which, though important, are sometimes based on adversarial associations – Japan and the USSR are allies who have many common goals and objectives. This further reinforces the bonds uniting us.

We must not allow these bonds to become frayed or tangled because of friction or misunderstandings. Instead, we must ensure that our relationship will always be a productive and cooperative one, based on mutual trust, equality, and shared goals.

Indeed, the USSR-Japan relationship – its stability, reliability, and durability – will be a decisive factor in determining the future of most of the world.

Ideas do come to life. Possibilities do become realities. Dreams do come true. It is up to us.

Looking forward to hearing from you soon.

I am in good health. I hope you are in good health, too.

Yours sincerely,
Tomoko Iwahara

Enniscorthy
Co. Wexford, Ireland   December 1989

Dear Mr Gorbachev,

I hope you are feeling well after your journey to Rome to meet Our Leader, Pope John Paul II, with your lovely lady, Raisa. It was indeed a historical and memorable occasion. I want to thank you for all you have done. It is marvellous that the Berlin Wall exists no more and the people in Eastern Europe have been granted freedom. It is unbelievable how fast all these wonderful things are happening. We were delighted when the news reached our ears that the people in Russia now have the freedon to practice their faith.

It gives us great hope and encouragement to see the great powers showing such great example.

The starving millions in Ethiopia are in a terrible state. I plead with you to use your influence to open a road to allow the food through to these defenceless people.

Now, I wish you a joyous Christmas and a healthy and peaceful 1990.

Well done, Mr Gorbachev, you are indeed a marvellous leader.
Best wishes,

Yours sincerely,
Rosalee (aged 4 years)
John (aged 9 years)
Mary-Lucia Furlong (aged 11 years)
Thérèse (aged 12 years)
Patricia (aged 15 years)
Patrick (aged 16 years)
and Majella Furlong (aged 13 years)

Yahatanishi-ku
Kitakyushu, Japan

16 January 1990

Dear Mr Gorbachev,

We are Japanese high school students. We learn a lot about your country and foreign countries every day in class. Of course, we learn about your country, too.

We have studied world affairs in school and through mass media. We have become aware that big problems like 'environmental pollution' and 'shortage of food' are still unsolved, but that at last people have begun working on ways to solve them.

We, too, are thinking that perestroika of your country is very helpful to other unsolved problems like 'racial discrimination' and 'confrontation between capitalistic countries and socialist countries' and 'high rate of population growth', 'energy conservation' and so on.

All these problems can't be solved only by each individual country. We think that not only one country, but that all the countries of the world have to cooperate together to solve these problems.

We hope your country will play an important role to settle these problems!

The other day, many people came to Japan to have an international symposium on global warming. We strongly feel the mood of 'Let's save our earth' is rising to become the number one issue in the world.

Environmental problems are a matter of life and death for all of us; and they have a direct effect on the world food situation. Thus, the problems which we are talking about are linked with each other deeply and make things more serious and complicated.

We have studied the Soviet Union and the United States in school. Most nations of the world align themselves with either a socialist country or a capitalist country. A lot of wars have been fought between the two sides due to their differences in principles. Your country and the US have great influence in all the nations of the world. So we think that if there is no distance between socialism and capitalism, people can change the world in a good way!

Mr Gorbachev, we are really glad with your perestroika in the Soviet Union.

The 'Wall' was dismantled in Germany, and after the Tiananmen Square, a new leadership may arise in China. Our country, Japan, is being called 'the most powerful economic country' but this hasn't helped Japan to make changes for problems such as 'the ageing population', 'the bribery scandal of government', 'the foreign trade deficit' and so on.

We believe that we should not think solely about our own affairs now. Especially, at present, Japan should be on the contributor side. It is very important for each country to make efforts to do good for other countries, isn't it?

We think the first step to unite our countries is being taken by you, the Soviet Union. If the merits of the capitalist country is mingled with the merits of the socialist country, the world will change wonderfully!

Sincerely yours,
Misa Endo
Miharu Yoshida
Noriko Umisaki

Class 6
Falkenberg, West Germany   27 March 1990

Dear Mr State President,

We are pupils from two classes in a Bavarian school.

We were recently very disturbed to read an article 'Soviet Jews fear Pogrom on 5 May' in our daily newspaper (copy of article enclosed).

Various television programmes have also reported that for some time now, nationalist groups in the Soviet Union have been stirring up hatred against Soviet Jews.

In the course of school instruction, we have learned how in all periods of history, people have made use of scapegoats in order to divert attention from their own failures, and to direct the understandable minorities.

What we have read and seen, has given us the impression that this is exactly what is happening at the present moment in the USSR. Responsibility for the desperate economic situation is being laid upon the Jewish minority by a portion of the population, just as has happened so often before in history.

When groups of nationalist thugs at the Moscow Writers' Convention demanded a 'solution to the Jewish questions in Russia'; when the Panjat group talks about a 'Night of the Long Knives'; when threats of pogroms are made openly; and when it is reported that the police looked on without taking action, we are reminded with fearful clarity of events in National-Socialist Germany during the Hitler period. The terrible end of that drama is well known.

Mr President, we children follow with great interest the efforts you are making to achieve peaceful coexistence. Therefore we would like to ask you urgently to take appropriate measures to provide help to the Jewish citizens of the Soviet Union who are threatened by blind hatred.

Please ensure that those who are acting blindly in this way are given enlightenment through rational explanation, and please direct the police always to take action when peoples' rights are infringed. May we schoolchildren count on your support in this matter of concern, and hope for a reply?

Yours sincerely,

Bad Kissingen
West Germany   27 March 1990

Dear Mr Gorbachev,

I know there are more important things than the letter of a twelve-year-old girl, but nevertheless I would like to ask you to write to me. I'm the girl in the horrible photograph.

To get to the point straight away, I think you are a fantastic politician. I find it terribly boring that just now Lithuania wants to be independent. Without you the Republic of Lithuania couldn't even exist. They are dependent on you. If you don't put down your foot now they will all want to become independent and then you will be seen as 'unable to put your foot down'. And that the Americans now get themselves involved absolutely takes the biscuit. They should just keep their mouths shut. You didn't say anything either when they invaded Panama only because Noriega didn't do what they wanted. Mr Gorbachev, you musn't let THEM tell you what to do because you are absolutely able to govern such a big country. Hopefully, you will be in power for a long time, there should be more men like you. I know, when you read this letter you will think like most adults that it is not all that easy. But it is easy. You only have to tell people your opinion and put your foot down, and do the same with other politicians.

                                                        Lots of love,
                                                        Judith Matthies

PS Don't let yourself get bogged down!

Roxby Downs
South Australia   April 1990

Dear Mr Gorbachev

I am sixteen-year-old student from Australia and for a long time, myself and countless other adolescents have been worried about nuclear weapons and the risk that they might be used in the event of a war.

To the youth of the world (as well as many older people), however, nuclear weapons are seen in a totally different perspective. Being young, we have our whole lives ahead of us and hence the most to lose if a nuclear war were to occur in the near future. In such an event all our hopes and dreams would be destroyed in an instant and, if we managed to survive the actual bombings, we would be left with little more than the prospect of a slow, painful death from starvation or radiation sickness. In fact, Nikita Khrushchev summed up the whole grim scene rather well when he claimed that 'the living would envy the dead'.

270

Such a thought frightens me but it also makes me wonder at the sanity of so-called 'responsible' leaders. After all, from witnessing *Voyager 2*'s spectacular rendezvous with planet Neptune not long ago, there is every indication that the human race could go far in the future. However, we have also amassed enough weapons to exterminate our race in minutes! It makes me wonder whether or not that humanity has got its priorities right.

Then, of course, there is the fact that nuclear weapons are designed primarily to kill innocent people and leave horrible scars on the planet. True, chemical weapons may also seem fairly barbaric but at least there main use is on the battlefield where they leave no permanent damage. The majority of nuclear weapons, on the other hand, are aimed at the cities of the world where countless millions of ordinary people with no military importance whatsoever live. Not only that, but nuclear arms kill by incinerating their victims at a temperature in excess of one hundred million degrees Celsius as well as releasing lethal radiation and fallout that quickly kills off those not destroyed by the main blast. Such methods of killing people are horrible and inhuman ones and, worse still, the power to inflict such a terrible death on so many is given only to very small group of people. This effectively means that roughly one hundred men determined the fates of over five billion others and it shows that there is something horribly wrong with the way the world is being run.

This thought, however, does not seem to deter those in power from risking a global nuclear holocaust considering the number of times that humanity has been on the brink of annihilating itself. Consider, for example, the Cuban missile crisis of 1962. At this point in history there were roughly three billion people inhabiting the globe yet it seemed for several agonising days that two of them, Kennedy and Khrushchev, were poised to wipe them all out if they so desired to.

Another one of these was the bombing of Tripoli by the Americans in 1986. Now, if there wasn't so much tension in the world then I would have been surprised if anybody had made much of a fuss. After all, most people consider Libya to be full of terrorists anyway and such an attack would be seen as justifiable, even commendable. Yet, because the human race seems so intent on destroying itself, students in Australia were crying there eyes out because they were terrified that the situation could escalate into something much, much worse. And if this is the case then it shows that we need drastic changes in the way that this planet is governed.

The truth is that the arms race has gone out of control and the superpowers are now manufacturing more weapons than are necessary to maintain a sensible balance of nuclear arms. Deterrence has not stopped many wars at all. In fact, the only war that it probably has stopped is one between the superpowers, a war that wouldn't be so serious if there were no nuclear arms in the world anyway. Apart from that, other nations do not seem to hesitate in waging war on one another. Just look at the Gulf War, It sprang up virtually overnight and carried on for over eight years, all the while showing the rest of the world some of the most brutal wartime atrocities ever commited. During the course of the war, for example, the Iranians used young boys as fanatical suicide troops and human mine detectors whilst the Iraqis employed a whole host of chemical and biological agents in order to win their battles. And when peace was finally declared, very little had been achieved in the past eight years anyway. No side really won and in the course of the war, millions of people had been killed, tortured, maimed, wounded and mentally scarred.

Another disturbing aspect of nuclear weapons is the seemingly constant need to test and upgrade them. The testing of nuclear weapons is, in many people's view, unnecessary as well as showing a deliberate disrespect for the earth and its enviroment, two things we are now desperately trying to save. Besides, most people know how destructive nuclear weapons are and the testing of such armaments can only be seen as a costly and pointless exercise. And as for upgrading nuclear weapons, what can one say save that nuclear weapons are already lethal enough without being made more deadly at the public's expense. Even the atomic bombs dropped on Hiroshima and Nagasaki were destructive enough, each one killing hundreds of thousands of innocent people as well as reducing its target to nothing more than a heap of radioactive rubble.

However, this letter is not meant to be solely one of condemnation although much of its content has been of a critical nature. I am a realistic person and I know that all the damage done by the cold war cannot be undone overnight. However, now that we are well on the road to nuclear disarmament we must not delay in ridding the world of these weapons completely. We the youth of the world, congratulate you on the positive steps already taken towards peace and disarmament (e.g. the INF treaty) and give you our full support for any other disarmament plans you may have in mind. Above all, now that you've started, please don't stop.

Yours faithfully,
James Brazel

According to a United Nations' report there have been over 170 armed conflicts since the cessation of World War II. These have been characterized by the absence of any formal declaration of war or clear ultimatums with the result that 'the parties to the conflict have not felt bound to any rules of conduct' such as international law or treaties. Over twenty million people have been killed in armed conflicts since the Second World War.

Chronology of Events
March 1985 to August 1990

It is impossible, of course, to include all of the major events relating to the end of the Cold War within realistic space restraints. This chronology is intended to document the most important revolutionary changes and most of the major events of the period related to the demise of the Cold War, and to give the reader a feeling for the general tenor of the times. It is not intended to offer a complete historical accounting. Sometimes events are included because they had great press coverage in the West at the time of their happening. In this regard, it is hoped the entries will help give the reader historical reference points. To the layman, many events contained herein might not at first appear to have much significance. These should be read taking into consideration their historical context in relation to the country to which they belong, and in so doing their significance will be better understood.

Lastly, many in the West tend to think that President Gorbachev single-handedly laid the Cold War to rest. While his contribution is incalculable and his spirit infectious, as exemplified in the letters sent to him, this chronology offers a broader perspective and pinpoints the process which actually occured. In order to make reading easier, the events from 1988 are not necessarily listed in exact chronological order within a particular month.

1985

March The Central Committee of the Communist Party of The Soviet Union unanimously elects Mikhail S. Gorbachev its General Secretary after the death of Konstantin Chernenko. At 54, he is the youngest man to take charge of the Soviet Union since Stalin, who was 45. On taking office, Gorbachev outlines urgent agenda to improve the economy.

Vice President Bush headed the US delegation at funeral services in Moscow and delivered a letter from President Ronald Reagan inviting Gorbachev to visit the United States.

The U.S. Congress approves building twenty-one MX missiles.

April Presiding over his first full session of the Central Committee, Gorbachev emphasises the need to reshape the economy, *perestroika*, and refers to a need to restore the 'human factor', and reduce rigidity in the Soviet social system, *glasnost*. In the same session he elevates new members to the Politburo, including Yegor K. Ligachev, Chief of Party Appointments, and Nikolai I. Ryzhkov, Manager of the Soviet Economy.

The Soviet government publishes its decision to begin a unilateral 'moratorium on the testing of all nuclear weapons from 6 August

273

1985–the fortieth anniversary of the atomic bombardment of Hiroshima.' Continuing the cessation beyond November would depend 'on whether the US follows our example.'

White House Spokesman rejects a US freeze, saying the SU holds a ten to one advantage in medium-range missiles and that 'prior Soviet statements of intent to establish a moratorium. . . have been followed by continued deployments.' Reagan's national security advisor calls the offer propaganda and a political ploy.

May President Reagan orders a trade embargo with Nicaragua, the Central American nation to which the Soviet Union has been sending military hardware.

Referring to Reagan's visit to a cemetery in Bitberg, Germany where high level Nazi SS officers are buried, Gorbachev says there are 'political figures ready to forget or even justify the SS cutthroats and, moreover pay honour to them.'

After Liverpool soccer fans stormed a stand killing thirty-eight people and injuring more than 200, Prime Minister Margaret Thatcher declared, 'Those responsible have brought shame and disgrace to the United Kingdom and to football.'

June Announcing his rejection of a five-year economic plan presented to him, Gorbachev calls for massive reforms to combat economic stagnation.

Shiite Muslim extremists seize a Pan-Am airplane with 153 persons aboard and free the passengers seventeen days later. One American was murdered during the terrorist attack.

U.S. Congress votes aid for Nicaraguan 'contras,' those fighting a guerilla war against the government. President Daniel Ortega responds to the vote and proclaims that he will lift a moratorium on arms procurements.

During the flight of the US space shuttle 'Discovery' tests are conducted for the Strategic Defense Initiative (SDI or 'Star Wars').

July The Soviet Politburo removes veteran Soviet Foreign Minister Andrei A. Gromyko to the prestigious but largely ceremonial Soviet Presidency and Eduard A. Shevardnadze, previously Communist Party leader of the Republic of Georgia, is named foreign minister.

Gorbachev announces the Soviet decision to establish a unilateral moratorium on all nuclear testing starting 6 August, and calls on the US to follow suit.

A seventeen-hour rock concert, 'Live Aid,' broadcast to 152 countries raising an estimated $70 million for starving people in Africa.

August South African President Pieter Botha delivers a long-anticipated speech stating in part that 'one man, one vote' would

274

'destroy white South Africa' and mean 'strife, chaos, and poverty.' He attributed the violence to 'barbaric communist agitators.'

September Soviet Foreign Minister Shevardnadze holds a series of discussions in New York with US President Ronald Reagan and Secretary of State George Shultz.

Gorbachev meets eight US Senators who report he said the SU would. make 'radical proposals' to reduce nuclear weapons if the US agrees to curb the 'militarization of outer space.'

October Gorbachev visits France as his first visit to the West since becoming General Secretary; signs a Soviet-French Agreement on economic cooperation for the years 1986-1990, and also an agreement eliminating double taxation for Frenchmen conducting business within the Soviet Union.

Reagan addresses the General Assembly of the United Nations on the occasion of its fortieth anniversary and asks the SU to join the US in seeking settlements of five regional disputes involving regimes supported by Moscow. He also calls for a 'fresh start' with the SU.

November Meeting for the first time, US President Reagan and Gorbachev in Geneva issue a joint statement, declaring the inadmissibility of nuclear war and confirm that both nations no longer seek military superiority. During the meeting, Soviet Foreign Minister Shevardnadze and the US Secretary of State George Shultz sign a general agreement on technical exchanges and people to people contacts in the spheres of science, education and culture. It is the first time in six years that leaders from the two countries met.

December Great Britain and Germany agree to participate in various areas of the US SDI programme.

1986

January Gorbachev and Reagan exchange New Year's Day greetings on television within the other's country. Gorbachev states it is the 'duty of mankind' to create a climate conducive to the preservation of peace. Reagan notes the 'good beginning' towards better relations between the two superpowers.

Gorbachev publishes his programme for destroying mass destruction weapons and recommends that all nuclear weapons be banned by the year 2000.

Several political prisoners are freed in an exchange; Anatoly Shcharansky is among them. The warming of relations between the superpowers is said to have influenced the releases.

February Gorbachev calls for major economic reforms, including more autonomy for local managers and the linking of factory salaries to sales in an effort to encourage quality control and bring incentives in return for higher levels of performance.

February/March The Twenty Seventh Party Congress adopts a new edition of the Communist Party of the Soviet Union rules and basic guidelines on Soviet economic development for the Period 1986-1990 and in some areas until the year 2000. Mikhail Gorbachev again elected General Secretary.

The Communist Party Congress approves a resolution calling for 'truly revolutionary changes' in the economy as put forth by Gorbachev and Prime Minister Ryzhkov. The Party adopts the idea of an interconnected, interdependent world and drops the idea of a class struggle in foreign relations, the first such affirmation since the Communist Party took power earlier in the century.

The Presidium of the USSR publishes an appeal for the instant half of nuclear arms tests. Gorbachev airs the new Soviet proposals for halting nuclear tests on Soviet television.

April The US conducts its second and third underground nuclear tests of the year.

US warplanes bomb Libyan targets after the country was suspected of being responsible for a terrorist attack on a disco in West Berlin.

South Africa will no longer enforce the so-called pass laws that limit the movement of blacks within the country.

Vladimir Horowitz, the world's most acclaimed pianist, returns to his Russian homeland after an absence of sixty-one years, at the age of 81. His performances are well received, and they are a direct result of the cultural exchange programme approved during the 1985 superpower summit.

The Chernobyl nuclear power plant releases a lethal cloud of radiation after its core melts down. This event stimulates fear around the world as to the horrors of radioactive fallout. One leader called the incident 'by far the worst nuclear reactor accident known to mankind. . . beyond even the worst nightmares of nuclear scientists.'

June Plans to disband the SU's government censorship agency are announced amid other moves toward openness, or *glasnost*.

August Gorbachev speaks on Soviet television prolonging the unilateral Soviet moratorium on nuclear explosions until 1 January 1987. He asserts that the US can not use the verification issue as a justification for continuing to test, and he points out that a US environmental organisation has been allowed to conduct seismic monitoring near Soviet underground test sites.

The Reagan administration announces the US will subsidise

exports of up to four million metric tons of wheat to the SU.

September Special Session of the General Conference of International Atomic Energy Agency (IAEA) is held in Vienna with over one hundred nations taking part. The Conference adopts and signs the 'convention on the Early Notification of Nuclear Accidents' and the document 'Emergency Assistance in the Case of a Nuclear Accident or Radiological Emergency.'

Nicholas Daniloff, an American journalist in Moscow, is released after having been arrested in August for espionage. His arrest clouds the possibility that the superpower leaders would meet the following month. Daniloff's release clears the way for a confirmation that the summit will take place.

The US Congress passes a bill which will severely limit US trade with South Africa.

October Gorbachev and Reagan meet in Rejkyavik, Iceland. According to reports, Reagan refuses to consider limitation on developing SDI which Gorbachev has linked to any agreement he would enter into on offensive weapons.

November The USSR Supreme Soviet publishes 'To the World's Parliaments and Peoples' which contains a number of proposals on nuclear disarmament.

Gorbachev visits Prime Minister Ghandi in India, resulting in the signing of the 'Delhi Declaration on Principles for a Nuclear Weapon-Free and Non-Violent World.' The declaration states that confrontation and conflicts be resolved by political rather than military means.

December The USSR signs protocols related to the Rarotonga Treaty proposing nuclear free zones in the South Pacific.

The Soviet Union announces its decision to halt its unilateral moratorium on nuclear testing, because the united States has not reciprocated, and issues a statement which puts forth proposals to hold talks on banning nuclear tests.

Soviet dissident physicist Andrei Sakharov is released from exile.

Protests by Chinese students calling for more democracy spread throughout China. The government accuses the students of 'illegal actions' that 'will affect social stability and unity.'

1987

January Gorbachev opens the first Central Committee Plenum of the year with a call for democratisation; reforms include secret ballots and multi-candidate elections, bringing more women and

277

young people into the party, and permitting citizens to take grievances against party officials to the courts. He also criticizes economic failures during the rule of Leonid Brezhnev (1964-1982). The Central Committee approves his proposals for greater flexibility in elections within the ruling party.

The Council of Ministers enact legislation which allow firms, associations, and organisations to enter into joint ventures with foreign firms. This initiates a tide of foreign businessmen and tourists which helps to infuse the spirit of *glasnost* into the country.

Newspaper articles are publishing unfavourable economic news, including infant mortality rates, disasters, and social problems. Controls are loosened in the arts including music, books, films, and plays.

US Secretary of State Shultz meets for the first time with a leader of the principal group seeking democratisation in South Africa, the African National Congress. The ANC is deeply allied with the South African Communist Party and to the Soviet Union for military weapons and training.

February The US conducts an underground nuclear test in Nevada. It is the twenty-fifth after establishment of the unilateral Soviet moratorium on nuclear testing which began in August of the previous year.

An international forum called 'A Nuclear-Free World for the Survival of Humanity' is held in Moscow.

The SU ends its eighteenth month moratorium on nuclear tests by conducting a test, and the Soviet defense ministry proclaims that the USSR would resume its moratorium as soon as the US announces a halt of its own testing program. Gorbachev announces his country is willing to agree to various arms control issues even if the US continues development of SDI.

The 140 dissidents convicted of 'anti-Soviet agitation and propaganda' and held in prisons and labour camps are released. This is the largest number freed at one time in more than three decades.

March Thatcher confers with Gorbachev for eleven hours in Moscow, as the first British Prime Minister to visit the SU in twelve years. She supports Reagan's SDI research and asks for more progress on human rights. Gorbachev rejects her views on SDI as 'unrealistic' and suggests the debate over human rights be broadened to include millions of unemployed and homeless people in the West. On concluding her meetings she says, 'When I met Mr. Gorbachev in December, 1984, I said he was someone I could do business with. Well, we were able to do a lot of business yesterday . . . .'

In condemning artificial fertilization and generation of human life outside the body, the Vatican asserts, 'The one conceived must be the fruit of his parents love.'

April US Secretary of State George Shultz, in Moscow, signs the Soviet-US agreement, 'Cooperation in the Exploration and Use of Outer Space for Peaceful Purposes.'

Shultz is interviewed on Soviet television for thirty minutes, virtually uncensored.

The USSR agrees to purchase from the US the largest sale ever of sub-sidised wheat to one country – 4,000,000 metric tons, approximately worth $375US million.

Gorbachev visits Czechoslovakia and receives a warm welcome from citizens who appear to approve the economic, social, and cultural reforms he is promoting in the USSR. Noting that some East-block countries were reluctant to follow the new path of reform, Gorbachev says he is not asking anyone 'to copy us.' A letter from Czech reformers asserts that Gorbachev has revived hopes for 'Socialist democracy' in the country.

May The Soviet Union successfully tests the world's most power-ful rocket.

Gorbachev visits Romania and receives a cool reception; no applause as he addresses 5000 Communist Party officials.

A nineteen year old West German flies across four hundred miles of Soviet air space in his single engine plane, and lands in Red Square. The Soviet defense minister and commander of air defense are dismissed.

June Voting for local councils is held in the USSR, with multiple candidates running for office in over 5000 elections.

The USSR Supreme Soviet passes the law 'On the State Enterprise of Association,' 'On National Debates of Important Issues of State Life,' and 'On Restructuring Economic Management at the Current Stage of Economic Development.' Cooperatives, essentially small private partnerships, are allowed to compete with the state to provide consumer goods and services. Farmers are legally allowed to lease land in perpetuity to recreate the small family farm, and the legalisation of small-scale private enterprise. These developments signal a continuation of Gorbachev's plan for democratisation and lessen fears among his supporters of an overthrow of his policies and his ouster.

The US Congress approves $1 million budget for 1988. The Pentagon will get approximately $289US billion.

The new US Embassy in Moscow is found to be loaded with Soviet listening devices hidden in concrete sections prefabricated away from the site of construction. The building is deemed unusable.

Reagan at the Berlin Wall in the shadow of the Brandenburg Gate challenges, 'Mr. Gorbachev, open this gate. Mr. Gorbachev, tear down this wall.' Just days before, East Berlin youth attempting to hear a rock concert emanating from the Western side, were violently dispersed by police. The youth chanted in defiance, 'We want freedom!' and 'Gorbachev! Gorbachev!' Authorities later dismissed the event as 'horror tales' invented by the Western press.

Pope John Paul II visits Poland for the third time as leader of the Roman Catholic Church and gives unmistakable endorsement to the outlawed Solidarity labour movement which bolsters confidence amongst reformers.

Thatcher is elected to a third consecutive term as Prime Minister. This is the first time a British Prime Minister has been elected to a third term in office since the 1820's.

August   West German Chancellor Helmut Kohl offers to dismantle seventy-two Pershing missiles in order to clear the roadblock to a superpower treaty on intermediate nuclear forces.

September   Soviet Foreign Minister Shevardnadze meets with US President Reagan in Washington for talks on all aspects of bilateral relations. The Soviet and US governments sign an accord on centres to be developed for reducing nuclear dangers.

East German President Erich Honecker, who had presided over construction of the Berlin Wall in 1961, makes an unprecedented visit to West Germany and issues a communique outlining agreements in the fields of science, the environment, and nuclear safety.

October   The Soviet Union announces it will pay all of its debts to the United Nations. The US refuses to pay on all activities it does not support including $197US million owed for peace keeping.

November   On the seventieth anniversary of the Russian revolution, Gorbachev delivers a nationally televised report titled 'October and Perestroika: The Revolution Continues,' in which he sharply criticises Joseph Stalin saying, 'the guilt of Stalin is enormous and unforgivable,' and discusses the need to erase the 'blank spots' from Soviet history. This opens the way for a re-examination of the past, legitimising criticism of other organs of repression and loosening censorship. Armenians, Lithuanians and others use the occasion to vocally assert greater independence from Moscow.

Boris Yeltsin, who was elevated to the Politburo by Gorbachev, is dismissed as Moscow party boss by the Central Committee after accusing conservatives of blocking Gorbachev's reforms. Articles critical of *glasnost* are printed in official party news organs and the police harass informal political clubs, the origins of which began under Gorbachev's democratisation programme. These events signal Gorbachev's hold on his position could be totally undermined by adversarial forces within the country.

Gorbachev acknowledges the USSR is working on its own version of SDI – not to be built or deployed, but basic research.

First round of full-scale Soviet-US talks on limitation and the ultimate halting of nuclear tests is held in Geneva.

December Gorbachev and US President Reagan meet in Washington and sign the unprecedented Intermediate-Range Nuclear Force Treaty. This is the first time in history that the two superpowers enter into an agreement to eliminate nuclear forces.

1988

January Gorbachev and Reagan exchange televised good wishes for the New Year. Both men laud the INF Treaty signed the month prior. Reagan attempts to explain his view of SDI.

The new premier of Japan, N. Takeshito, pays his first visit to Washington.

March The US National Aeronautics and Space Administration announce that the ozone layer is declining in the northern hemisphere.

April Agreements on a political settlement of Afghanistan are signed in Geneva; this includes bilateral agreements between Afghanistan and Pakistan on the principles of mutual relations, specifically on non-interference and non-intervention, and also on the voluntary return of refugees. A 'Declaration on International Guarantees' is signed by the USSR, the US and other countries.

May Quadrapartite talks begin between representatives of Angola, Cuba, South Africa and the United States (as mediator), on a peaceful settlement of the situation in Southwest Africa.

French President F. Mitterrand is elected to a second seven-year term.

USSR and US representatives in Geneva sign an agreement regarding the implementation of the agreement on medium and short range missiles capable of carrying contemporary and new weaponry.

In line with the Geneva Accords dated 14 April, 1988, on the political settlement of the Afghanistan situation, a phased withdrawal of Soviet troops from Afghanistan begins.

May/June Fourth Summit between Gorbachev and Reagan held in Moscow. Ceremony to ratify documents putting into effect the

Soviet-US Treaty on Eliminating Medium and Short-Range Missiles is held on 1 June. Reagan's visit symbolically appears to be a divorce from his earlier cold war slogan in which he had labelled the USSR an 'evil empire.'

June The Russian Orthodox Church celebrates the 1000 anniversary of the introduction of Christianity into Russia with support by governmental leaders signalling a new tolerance of religion.

In a speech to the first special Communist Party Conference since 1941, Gorbachev declares that an overhaul of the system is essential for Soviet economic and social change.

A nationalist political organisation in Estonia becomes the first non-Communist political group to gain official recognition.

June/July The Nineteenth All-Union CPSU Congress held in Moscow adopts resolutions based on Gorbachev's proposals regarding measures for reforming the country's political system by approving a restructuring of the government into a system with a powerful president picked by the new legislature, the Congress of People's Deputies, fighting bureaucratism, dealing with inter-ethnic relations, *glasnost*, and other legal reforms. The atmosphere is characterised by unprecedentedly open and unrestrained debating stunning the nation to the fact that the democratic process is evolving in an atmosphere of non-violent dialogue.

August US and Soviet scientists conduct a joint nuclear test for the first time. The purpose is to define techniques for verifying underground nuclear explosions.

September A major Kremlin shake-up consolidates Gorbachev's power, and he is named President of the Soviet Union, replacing Andrei Gromyko.

October Two whales, trapped in ice off the coast of Alaska, are freed through international efforts.

November George Bush is elected the forty-first President of the United States.

Thatcher visits Poland and publically criticised their policies aimed at diminishing the influence of the outlawed Solidarity trade union. She flies to Washington and meets with President-elect Bush. In an interview she praises the policies of Gorbachev stating, 'We're not in a Cold War now.'

In Geneva an agreement is reached on a general package of agreements including the timetable for the withdrawal of Cuban troops from Angola, a guarantee for Angola's safety, and the initial stages of independence of Namibia.

Gorbachev visits India and signs several agreements one of which involves long term cooperation in research and exploitation of space for peaceful purposes.

Estonia's Supreme Soviet asserts the right to veto national laws affecting Estonia.

December Gorbachev visits New York to participate in the forty-third Session of the UN General Assembly, which he addresses on 7 December. His stay in New York is cut short by a devastating earthquake in Armenia and his visits to Cuba and Britain are postponed.

The talks on Southwest Africa continue in Brazil where the Brazilian Protocol is signed wherein the process of the decolonisation of Namibia is planned to begin 1 April, 1989.

1989

Events in 1989 switftly changed political leadership, military alliances, and economic policies of not a few countries. Therefore, this chronology for the year documents many of those events in detail, listed by country.

January

Czechoslovakia Demonstrations are held in Prague in honour of the twentieth anniversary of the Czechoslovakian student's suicide following the Soviet invasion in 1968. Police use water cannons to break up the demonstration by 2000 people. Dissident playwright Vaclav Havel is arrested and charged with inciting protests through comments quoted on foreign radio broadcasts. Police halt a train carrying demonstrators and arrest many people, bringing arrests to over 800 in one week. Havel is sentenced to nine months in prison.

East Germany Prime Minister Erich Honecker announces plans to reduce his country's armed forces by 10,000 troops, 600 battle tanks, and fifty combat aircraft – and military spending by 10% – by 1990, as a 'constructive contribution to disarmament.'

Hungary Freedom of assembly and freedom of association are passed by Hungarian parliament, allowing citizens for the first time since World War II to conduct peaceful demonstrations and form organizations independent of the communist Hungarian Socialist Workers' Party (HSWP).

Japan Emperor Hirohito dies after a sixty-two year reign.

Poland Prompted by continuing social unrest and a dismal economy, the Central Committee of the communist Polish United Worker's Party (PUWP) approves a resolution allowing the banned independent trade union, Solidarity, to undergo a two year trial period leading to the full legalisation of its activities. Representatives of the government, Solidarity, and the Roman Catholic Church meet in Warsaw and they jointly announce that a 'roundtable' meeting will be held to negotiate political and economic reforms and union pluralism. Interior Minister Czeslaw Kiszczak calls for participation of opposition groups in 'nonconfrontational' elections. Solidarity founder Lech Walesa demands freedom of speech and association and the establishment of an independent judiciary.

February

Hungary Party Central Committee, at end of two-day plenum, approves formation of independent political parties.

Iran Ayatollah Khomeini calls for the execution of author Solman Rushdie because Rushdie's new novel is an irreverent depiction of Islam.

Soviet Union The withdrawal of Soviet troops from Afghanistan is completed.

A protest is staged in Tbilisi by 15,000 Georgians to mark the sixty-eighth anniversary of Soviet Union's annexation of Georgia; more than 500, most of them members of National Democratic party of Georgia, are arrested.

Yugoslavia Albanian miners in Yugoslavia's ethnic Albanian-majortiy Kosovo autonomous province strike to protest increasing Serbian control of province; they demand resignation of top provincial leaders, allies of Communist leader Slobodan Milosevic. The officials resign. Yugoslavia's collective presidency orders federal troops into Kosovo to preserve order. Approximately 500,000 Serbs march on National Assembly building in Belgrade to protest the resignations.

March

Hungary Premier Karoly Grosz, briefing the HSWP Central Committee following his return from a visit to Moscow, reports that he and Soviet President Mikhail Gorbachev reviewed the history of 1956 invasion of Hungary and 1968 invasion of Czechoslovakia. He claimed Gorbachev spoke against foreign intervention in affairs of Warsaw Pact nations. This sends a strong signal to the world that, if the report is true, the Soviet Union will not use force to squash grass roots attempts to change existing political realities.

Soviet Union Communist Party Central Committee establishes a special commission to investigate whether Moscow Communist Party chief, Boris Yeltsin, deviated from party line by calling for entirely open parliamentary elections. Yeltsin supporters gather and 10,000 march to city hall in protest. The lack of action on the part of the police to break up the rally indicates the democratisation process has permeated layers of the Soviet society far below the governmental leadership.

In the first multi-candidate parliamentary elections held since 1917, scores of Communist Party officials, including party bosses in Moscow and Leningrad, suffer defeat providing a strong signal that the citizenry wants to seel a faster pace in economic, social, and political reform legislature.

United States The largest oil spill in US history occurs after the Exon Valdez tanker strikes a reef in the northern Pacific ocean.

April

England Ninety-five persons are killed by soccer fans eager to enter a stadium.

Poland The government and Solidarity reach agreement on a plan for political and economic reform. An agreement calls for strengthening the presidency whereby the president will be able to declare state of emergency, subject to legislative approval, but not have the power to dissolve the legislature. The current legislature is to be replaced with a lower house (Sejm) and an upper house (Senate).

Solidarity founder Lech Walesa meets with President Wojciech Jaruzelski in Warsaw, a clear recognition of Solidarity's strength.

Romania Leader Nicolae Ceausescu announces that his country's foreign debt, which in 1981 stood at $10 billion, has been repaid ahead of schedule, making Romania the only East bloc country with no foreign debt.

Soviet Union Gorbachev visits Ireland, Cuba, and Britain. In Cuba he warns that the Soviet Union 'categorically opposed. . . the export of revolution or counterrevolution and all forms of foreign interference in the affairs of sovereign states.' He announces his country will stop aiding Nicaragua if the US halts military aid to its Central American allies.

Soviet soldiers violently disperse a crowd of 10,000 Georgian nationalist demonstrators in Tbilisi. Twenty demonstrators are killed and many more are hurt. A 'Pravda' editorial denounces nationalist movements for attempting to undermine the USSR. Georgian press publishes Gorbachev's appeal to Georgia's Communists concerning the events in Tbilisi. Soviet human rights dissident Andrei Sakharov is chosen by Soviet Academy of Sciences for one of its reserved seats in the Congress of People's Deputies.

Eighty nations agree to ban production of chloroflurocarbon chemicals that endanger the ozone layer in the atmosphere.

May

Bulgaria Bulgarian Communist Party chief Todor Zhivkov announces land-reform plan that would break up large collective farms and allow farmers to lease land.

Hungary   Hungarians begin dismantling barbed-wire fence separating it from neutral Austria.

Havel is granted an early release from his prison sentence.

Poland   The parliament votes to give the Roman Catholic Church legal status and to return Church property seized in 1950s.

Soviet Union   In Moscow, Japanese Foreign Minister Sosuke Uno, on behalf of his government, invites Mikhail Gorbachev to visit Japan. The invitation is taken into consideration, but not accepted.

During this meeting with US Secretary of State James Baker in Moscow, Gorbachev informs Baker of additional proposals on reducing conventional weapons and forces, which the USSR plans to make during the Vienna Talks. The proposals concern radical cuts of armaments and armed forces of the Warsaw Treaty Organisation and NATO stationed in Europe by 1996-1997.

The First Congress of USSR People's Deputies convenes. Approximately 85% of the 2250 deputies represent the Communist Party; the remainder represent unofficial opposition groups including radical reformists and ethnic nationalists. Many deputies criticize the state of the nation and Gorbachev himself.

Gorbachev is elected by the new Soviet Parliament in a secret ballot as President of the Soviet Union, a position he already holds, but which was legally endorsed by this first-of-its-kind Soviet election. Gorbachev nominates Anatoly I. Lukyanov as Soviet Vice President which the deputies approve after four hours of debate. After giving his concluding acceptance speech, Gorbachev discloses, amongst other things, Soviet defense spending – the first time figures are made public – $128 billion for 1989.

Yeltsin finishes twelfth in balloting for eleven seats reserved for the Russian Republic in the Chamber of Nationalities. After Yeltsin supporters call for a national strike, Gorbachev rules that Yeltsin can take a seat in the Chamber if any member of the Russian delegation resigns; one deputy from Siberia resigns and Yeltsin is elected by a show of hands vote.

China   Gorbachev visits the People's Republic of China. As a result, Soviet-Chinese relations are normalised. Relevant agreements create a sound foundation for essentially a new stage in Soviet-Chinese relations.

Tens of thousand of people flock to Tinannamin Square in Bejing to herald Gorbachev's visit and openly support ideas of democratization. The gathering continues around the clock for several weeks after the Soviet leader's visit and is violently broken up by heavily armed military units.

June

Bulgaria Turkish Prime Minister Turgut Ozal vows to keep open his country's border for ethnic Turkish Bulgarians who want to emigrate.

Hungary A special event exhalting premier Imre Nagy who had been executed following the 1956 Hungarian uprising is celebrated throughout the country. Premier Miklos Nemeth attends the reburial ceremony.

Iran Khomeni, the political and religious leader, dies.

Japan S. Una is elected Prime Minister succeeding Takeshito who resigned due to scandal.

Poland After winning virtually all the seats contested, in the first open election in more than forty years, Solidarity is called on by Prime Minister Jaruzelski to join the Communists in a coalition government. Solidarity leaders refuse.

Soviet Union Social unrest flairs in Soviet Uzbekistan and security troops are sent in to restore order.

Premier Nikolai I. Ryzhkov announces the Afgahanistan war cost the government approximately $70 billion and the government's deficit of 6.2% of the GNP.

Gorbachev visits West Germany and signs several agreements expanding Soviet-West German cooperation. He reiterates Soviet support for a complete elimination of nuclear weapons in Europe.

July

Poland Solidarity leader Walesa announces support for Jaruzelski to be Poland's President which among other things signals Walesa's readiness to support a coalition government which includes Communists. However, in a joint session of parliament, virtually all of the Solidarity members vote against Jaruzelski and he resigns as General Secretary and is replaced by Premier Rakowski.

Soviet Union In a nationally televised speech, Gorbachev stresses that ethnic violence and nationalism pose 'enormous danger' to the Soviet Union and threaten reforms. He appeals for a keen sense of responsibility now and in the future and suggests that his countrymen do everything to resolve the issues of inter-ethnic relations on the basis of friendship and cooperation.

Gorbachev visits France and signs over twenty agreements aimed at expansion of bilateral ties and cooperation.

In a banquet speech at the Annual Warsaw Pact Summit Meeting in Bucharest, Gorbachev calls for 'tolerance' among allies and 'independent solutions of national problems.' Romanian leader

Ceausescu makes a speech complaining about alliance disunity. East German leader Honecker falls ill during the summit and returns to his country. The conference adopts a resolution calling for a secure Europe free of nuclear and chemical weapons, substantial cuts in armed forces, armaments, and military expenditures. Also, the communique recongnises that 'there are no universal models of socialism.' This is a clear signal to the West that the Soviet Union can not use the military might of the Warsaw Pact to inforce its political directives in Eastern Europe.

In an address before the Soviet Central Committee, Gorbachev says people are losing faith in the party and threatens to purge official who oppose *perestroika*. Leading Kremlin conservative, Yegor T. Ligachev, calls for restrictions on press and denounces the notion of multiparty democracy.

In a television interview, Gorbachev says that although the recent coal miner strikes are harmful to the economy, the strikers' demands are supportive of his reforms, thereby giving his support to grassroots efforts towards democratization.

The Supreme Soviet votes to approve resolution supporting Lithuania and Estonia's plans to develop autonomous free-market economic systems. Approximately 300 dissident members of Congress of People's Deputies, including Yeltsin and Sakharov, officially form the Inter-Regional Group of People's Deputies, a progressive faction within the body politic.

August

Czechoslovakia On the twenty-first anniversary of the Warsaw Pact invasion of Czechoslovakia 3000 demonstrators protest in Prague. The demonstration is broken up by security police, who arrest many.

East Germany The government accuses West Germany of interfering with its sovereign rights because of Bonn's refusal to expel East Germans seeking refuge at the West German embassy in Budapest. West Germany closes Budapest embassy to visitors in an effort to discourage refugees. Hundreds of East Germans flee into Austria during a joint Austrian-Hungarian friendship picnic held in the border town of Sopron and a few hundred more East Germans cross from Hungary to Austria a few days later. West German Chancellor Kohl requests a meeting with East German leader Honecker to discuss the unfolding human drama. Over one hundred East Germans from the Budapest embassy are flown to West Germany.

Japan The country gets it third Premier of 1989 when T. Kaifu is chosen to replace Uno.

Poland Premier Kiszczack who has replaced Rakowski struggles unsuccessfully to form a government, but eventually announces he is unable to do so. Solidarity, along with the United Peasants and Democratic parties, agree to Walesa's plan to unite as one cohesive voice. President Jaruzelski, meeting with Walesa in Warsaw gives approval to the proposed opposition government, asking only that PUWP be guaranteed control over the ministries of defense and interior. Kiszczack resigns the same day.

Jarulzelski releases a statement calling Solidarity activist, Tadeusz Mazowiecki, the best choice to head a coalition government. PUWP Central Committee adopts a resolution refusing to accept 'co-responsibility for future developments' if the party is not given enough representation in cabinet. Walesa accuses the party of 'blackmail'. Mazowiecki overwhelmingly wins parliamentary confirmation.

After telephone call from Grobachev to party leader Rakowski, the PUWP announces it will enter into 'partnerlike cooperation' with Solidarity.

South Africa President Pieter Botha resigns. He states in a nationwide address, 'I am being ignored by ministers serving in my cabinet.'

Soviet Union Estonia's Supreme Soviet approves legislation mandating a two-year residence requirement for voting and five-year residence requirement to hold local elective office. An estimated 20,000 ethnic Russians living in Estonia stage strikes to protest the legislation. The Soviet Ministry of Justice declares the law unconstitutional.

Soviet Politburo supports limited economic autonomy for the USSR's fifteen republics and urges that each republic be able to challenge national laws affecting it. But the Politburo reserves for the Soviet central government the sole authority over defense, foreign affairs, and internal security.

The Chairman of Soviet Central Committee International Policy Commission, Alexander N. Yakovlev, admits existence of secret protocols to the 1939 Nazi-Soviet nonaggression pact that allowed partition of Poland and permitted Soviet Union free hand in Estonia, Latvia and Lithuania.

Lithuania's Supreme Soviet declares illegal the 1940 Soviet annexation of Lithuania, and Lithuania's status as republic of Soviet Union. On the fiftieth anniversary of the nonaggression pact, 23 August, nationalist organisations in the Baltic republics, joined by some local Communist and government officials, issue statements in Talinn, Estonia, saying the USSR 'infringed on the historical right of the

Baltic nations to self-determination.' Large demonstrations are held in capitals of the Baltic republics to protest the pact. As many as one million form a human chain 400 miles long stretching from the Estonian capital, Talinn, through the Latvian capital, Riga, to the capital of Lithuania, Vilnius.

Turkey Prime Minister Ozal announces closing of borders to Bulgarians not possessing Turkish visas, effectively halting exodus of ethnic-Turk Bulgarians. Over 300,000 ethnic Turks have fled to Turkey since June, straining Turkey's ability to receive them.

The US announces that it is recalling its ambassador from Sofia to protest Bulgaria's treatment of ethnic Turks.

September

Hungary Interior Minister Istvan Horvath, in an interview published in the West German magazine 'Stern,' says none of more than 5000 East Germans in the Hungarian refugee camps will be allowed to emigrate until East and West Germany reach agreement on the issue. Foreign Minister Gyula Horn announces suspension of an agreement requiring Hungary to prevent emigration of East Germans to West Germany. Within thirty-six hours 10,500 East Germans pass into Austria and arrive in West Germany. An East German press agency calls the Hungarian action a 'violation of legal treaties.' Soviet spokesman, Gannadi Gerasimov, says Hungary's action is 'very unexpected' but 'does not directly affect us,' which is an announcement that Soviet armies will not interfere. By 1 October, nearly 30,000 East Germans have left Hungary for West Germany.

Hungary and Israel re-establish full diplomatic relations which had been broken off after the 1968 Mid-East War.

Hungarian government and opposition representatives reach accord to create a multiparty system in 1990. The programme calls for a unicameral legislature to be filled in free elections, the creation of a strong presidency with authority to choose the premier, a law legalising and granting rights to political parties, and a penal reform law.

East Germany Over one hundred East Germans voluntarily leave the West German mission in East Berlin after being promised assistance in seeking legal emigration from a prominent East German lawyer.

East Germany announces agreement to transport to West Germany thousands of East German refugees from Bonn's embassy in Prague.

Soviet Union The Ukranian Popular Movement for Perestroika, or RUKH, holds its founding congress in Kiev. Delegates call for the removal of the Ukranian Communist Party First Secretary, and for the transformation of the Soviet Union into a 'confederation' of autonomous republics.

Meeting in the US, Foreign Minister Shevardnadze and Secretary of State Baker adopt joint Soviet-American statements on chemical weapons and on the war in Lebanon.

On national television, Gorbachev takes note of 'threats of approaching chaos and talk of a threatened coup, and even civil war.'

Yugoslavia The Parliament of the Yugoslavia republic of Slovenia adopts amendments to its constitution giving the republic a right to secede from Yugoslavia. Tens of thousands of Serbs demonstrate in Novi Sad demanding a military takeover of Slovenia.

October

Czechoslovakia Protesters gather in Prague's Wenceslas Square to mark the seventy-first anniversary of founding of the Czechoslovakia Republic. When demonstrators ignore demands to leave the square, hundreds of riot police charge into the crowd, beating protesters and arresting more than 300 persons.

East Germany Over 5,000 additional refugees have entered the Prague embassy grounds, and as many new emigres have crossed from East Germany into Czechoslovakia.

The government bans unrestricted travel to Czechoslovakia. Trains bound from Prague to Hof, West Germany, via East Germany are boarded by 11,000 East Germans. Police clash with an estimated 10,000 protesters in Dresden who attempt to halt and board the refugee train.

East Germany marks its fortieth anniversary. Visiting Soviet President Gorbachev visiting East Germany stresses the country should adopt Soviet-style reforms and says policy for East Germany is made 'not in Moscow but in Berlin.' Gorbachev declares to Eric Honecker, the long-time Communist hard-line leader 'Life punishes those who delay.' Protesters calling for more freedom and chanting 'Gorby, Gorby,' fill the streets and cities throughout the country. Demonstrations in East Berlin, Dresden and Leipzig are broken up violently by security police. More than 50,000 protesters march in Leipzig with no interference. State Security chief Egon Krenz is reported to have flown to Leipzig and personally countermanded Honecker's instructions, in which reports later claimed Honecker ordered security forces in Leipzig to use deadly force if necessary to put down those demonstrations.

The Politburo meets in emergency session. Socialist Unity Communist Party (SED) chief ideologist Kurt Hager says that it is necessary for the party to study 'change and renewal.' The regime releases hundreds of demonstrators who had been arrested. Honecker announces the leadership's willingness to confer with 'all citizens.' In Leipzig 100,000 demonstrate peacefully for reform, and thirty thousand march in Dresden.

As pressures for reform in East Germany increase, Honecker steps down. His successor Egon Krenz, voices support for limited reforms.

Demonstrators estimated to number between 200,000 and 300,000 protest in Leipzig on one occasion and nearly that many on a following day, and 100,000 protest in Dresden. East Germany announces amnesty for citizens who have fled country and for those facing prosecution for demonstrating.

East German leader Krenz visits Moscow at the end of the month and meets with Gorbachev on 1 November.

Hungary The Congress of the Hungarian Socialist Workers Party votes to change the name of their party to the Hungarian Socialist Party (HSP), to restructure the party hierarchy, and to adopt a new party programme renouncing Marxism in favour of democratic socialism. During the Congress Reszo Nyers is names HSP president and the position of party General Secretary is dropped. Congress also votes to divest the party of much of its property holdings, to disband the Workers' Militia and to disestablish party cells in factories.

The National Assembly votes to make changes in the constitution, deleting references to the communist party's 'leading role' in society, and allowing free formation and functioning of political parties, establishing separation of government's executive, judicial, and legislative branches, codifying civil and human rights, and renaming the country – from the People's Republic of Hungary to the Republic of Hungary. The National Assembly passes a law formally legalizing opposition parties and votes to disband the Workers' Militia. 23 October the thirty-third anniversary of the 1956 uprising, President Matyas Szuros, speaking before rally of 80,000 in Budapest, formally declares Hungary a free republic.

As result of a petition circulated by the opposition party, Alliance of Free Democrats and signed by 250,000 citizens, the Hungarian National Assembly sets 26 November as the date for a referendum on the method of choosing the nation's president. Voters are to choose between a popular presidential vote to be held 7 January, 1990, or a parliamentary presidential vote to occur after free multiparty parliamentary elections are held later in 1990.

Poland Solidarity-led government announces anti-inflation measures, including a limit on indexing of wages to inflation and the reduction of state subsidies, promising the 'full introduction of market mechanisms and institutions' in 1990-91.

Soviet Union   The Soviet legislature approves a bill giving workers right to strike, the first time since the Bolshevik Revolution. The bill severely restricts conditions under which strikes can be called and forbids strikes in transportation, communications, defense and power-supply sectors. Most of the 26,000 thousand miners in Arctic city of Vorkuta defy the legislation and stage a one-day strike to demand implementation of concessions won by miners in strikes held earlier in the year.

Shevardnadze arrives in Warsaw for a summit of Warsaw Pact foreign ministers. He meets with Polish Premier Mazowiecki and with President Jaruzelski and calls for dissolution of Warsaw Pact and NATO military alliances. A joint communique is issued calling for non-interference in the affairs of sovereign nations.

November

Bulgaria   A pro-democracy demonstration is held by 9000 environmentalists in Sofia.

Bulgarian leader Zhivkov unexpectedly resigns as President and party General Secretary.

Czechoslovakia   Premier Adamec announces that Czechoslovakians will no longer need formal exit visas to travel to Yugoslavia.

Rally in Prague, attended by 20,000 students, marking the fiftieth anniversary of an anti-Nazi protest held prior to the outbreak of World War II, turns into an anti-government protest. Czechoslovakia security forces attack students who attempt to enter Wenceslas Square arresting some, hospitalising others. The next day 2000 people gather in Prague to protest the rumored death of a student in a protest the day before. An anti-government demonstration is staged the following day and 10,000 attend. Czechoslovakia dissidents, including playwright Vaclav Havel, meet in Prague and agree to form an umbrella opposition organisation, Civic Forum. A peaceful rally is held in Prague attended by more than 200,000 demanding free elections and resignation of Communist Party leader Milos Jakes while smaller demonstrations are held in cities throughout Czechoslovakia. Premier Adamec holds a closed-door meeting with Civic Forum leaders in Prague. Later Havel announces before a crowd of 150,000 that Adamec promised not to impose martial law and to investigate charges of brutality against security forces, and that Adamec expressed support for bringing non-communists into the Czech government.

Alexander Dubcek, Czechoslovakian leader during the 'Prague Spring' uprising in 1968, reemerges from official disgrace to address a crowd of 200,000 in Prague. At an emergency session of the party Central Committee, Jakes and the entire upper level of government leadership resign. Havel tells a Prague crowd, estimated at 800,000, that the government shake-up was a 'trick'. Premier Adamec announces resignation, but stays on as caretaker. Central Committee announces that it will call a special Communist Party congress in January to discuss the party's future. Millions of workers throughout Czechoslovakia stage a two-hour work stoppage in support of the pro-democracy movement.

Adamec opens official power-sharing talks with Civi Forum negotiators headed by Havel. He agrees to form a government with non-communist representation and states support for removal from the constitution of the clause which guarantees the Communist Party's 'leading role' in society, and to do away with Marxist-Lennist curriculum in schools. The Czechoslovakian parliament removes the 'leading role' provision from the constitution. The government announces that its border with Austria will be opened and all remaining restrictions on travel to the West will be dropped.

East Germany Borders with Czechoslovakia are re-opened. More than five thousand East Germans camped at the West German embassy in Prague depart for West Germany. Five members of eighteen member East German party Politburo resign, including Ministers of State Security and Interior. A huge pro-democracy demonstration is held in East Berlin. The Premier, his entire cabinet, and other top officials resign or are removed.

The breaching of the Berlin Wall begins as it becomes known that East German curbs on travel are ending. Throngs of East Germans cross to West Berlin, and most return to East Berlin. On the next day, East German soldiers begin tearing down sections of the wall.

West German leaders, including Chancellor Helmut Kohl and former Chancellor Willy Brandt, gather in West Berlin to applaud the opening of the Berlin Wall. The Volkskammer (parliament) confirms Modrow as premier. During a demonstration held in Leipzig 200,000 people demand free elections. Modrow disbands the Ministry of State Security (state police), renaming it the Office of National Security and promising to reform it.

Hungary A national referendum is held to determine whether the country's President should be chosen by direct elections or by the new parliament. Voters support parliamentary election of the President by a margin of 51% to 49%.

Romania The fourteenth Congress of Romanian Communist Party opens in Bucharest. Romanian leader Ceausescu delivers five-hour keynote address, calling the Communist Party the 'vital centre' of

Romanian life. Congress votes unanimously to re-elect Ceausescu to another five-year term as party General Secretary.

Soviet Union Gorbachev publishes a manifesto insisting that Marxism will be revived in the Soviet Union, and under the leadership of the party. The document, spread across two pages of 'Pravda,' is apparently intended to reassure the party faithful that Communism is not collapsing, and thus to counter conservatives. Gorbachev describes his goals as 'humane socialism,' echoing the 'socialism with a human face' promoted by the Communist liberalisers in Czechoslovakia during Prague Spring rebellion in 1968.

Soviet state security chief, Vladimir A. Kryuchkov, admits in a televised speech that the KGB, was one of the 'mechanisms of repression' used by Joseph Stalin. Kryuchkov pledges that such abuse will never happen again.

Gorbachev declares that German unification 'is not a matter of topical politics.' Even discussing it, he says, is interfering in the internal affairs of the Germans.

December

Bulgaria Nine independent opposition groups in Bulgaria, including Eco-Glasnost, merge to form the Union of Democratic Forces. A demonstration is held in Sofia by 50,000 pro-democracy protestors. Mladenov, in a speech before Central Committee plenum, announces support for free elections and end to party's 'leading role' in society. He also reports that Bulgaria's foreign debt is more than $10 billion. Tthe parliament building in Sofia is surrounded by 20,000 protesters demanding an immediate end to the Communist Party's political monopoly.

The government and opposition forum agree to open negotiations on the country's political future. At a demonstration 10,000 people call for faster reform. The Central Committee announces that full civil rights will be restored to ethnic Turks 'immediately'.

Czechoslovakia The new party Politburo declares that the 1968 Warsaw Pact invasion of Czechoslovakia was 'not justified.'

Adamec announces new cabinet containing non-communist members; opposition Civic Forum rejects the cabinet. A demonstration by 200,000 protestors is held in Prague demanding a more broadly based government. The Czech republic, along with Slovakia one of country's two constituent republics, announces formation of a new cabinet, the majority of whose members are non-communists. Adamec threatens to resign unless new cabinet is allowed to take office. Civic Forum delivers to Adamec a list of persons it would like to have named to new cabinet and then Adamec resigns in protest. President Husak names a communist minister, Marian

Calfa, to succeed Adamec. A new cabinet is formed and Husak resigns.

Dissident Havel and former leader Dubcek announce their candidacy for the presidency as 150,000 people celebrate in Wenceslas Square.

Newly appointed Foreign Minister Diensthier says at a press conference that the October 1968 agreement allowing Soviet troops to be stationed in Czechslovakia was signed under duress and is invalid. Calfa goes to Moscow and meets with Gorbachev. They agree to open negotiations on issue of Soviet troops in Czechoslovakia. The Communist Party votes to disband the People's Militia.

Dubcek and Havel are unanimously elected parliament chairman of the national parliament, and president, respectfully.

East Germany East German Volkskammer votes to revoke the constitutional guarantee of SED's leading role' in society. Special parliamentary committee issues a report concluding that former leader Honecker and associates lived in luxury and engaged in embezzlement, bribe-taking, and currency speculation. At emergency session of SED Central Committee, party members suspected of involvement in corruption, including Honecker, are expelled from the party.

Premier Modrow announces his intention to form a special investigatory commission, including opposition members, to look into the corruption scandal, and several arrests are made. Airline flights from East Germany to Romania are suspended, apparently to prevent suspect officials for shipping out incriminating documents. Modrow goes to Moscow for a meeting of Warsaw Pact leaders and has a 'conversation' with Gorbachev.

East Germany agrees to lift all restrictions to travel to East Germany by West Germans, effective 1 January, 1990. Krenz resigns as president and chairman of council of national defense. Manfred Gerlach, head of SED-allied Liberal Democratic Party, is named interim president. Roundtable talks between SED, allied parties and opposition groups including the New Forum agree to set 6 May, 1990 as the date for free general elections.

Congress elects Gregor Gysi as new party chairman, votes to abandon traditional politburo/central committee structure in favour of 100-member commission headed by an executive board, rejects German reunification, but votes to support the notion of some form of confederation with West Germany. In a demonstration in Leipzig 200,000 people demand German reunification.

Romania Hundreds of Romanians battle security forces in Timisoara when police attempt to evict and deport Rev. Laszlo

Tokes, who has protested for the human rights of Romania's ethnic Hungarians. As many as 10,000 are reported to protest in Timisoara against the rule of Ceausescu. The security forces, acting on Ceausescu's orders, open fire, reportedly killing several hundred. Ceausescu departs Romania on a state visit to Iran. Clashes continue in Timisoara, with reports that protesters are shot from helicopters and army tanks surrounding the area.

Ceausescu returns to Bucharest and makes a television speech denouncing Timisoara demonstrators as 'fascist reactionary groups.' Ceausescu is shouted down during a public speech in Bucharest and government forces there clash with approximately 10,000 protesters, killing some, but failing to disperse the crowd. Widespread violence breaks out throughout Bucharest and Ceausescu declares martial law. The defense minister refuses to enforce it and is killed by security forces. When protesting crowds storm the Central Committee building, key arm forces leaders join the uprising. Ceausescu and his wife flee by helicopter to Tirgoviste, forty-five miles northwest of Bucharest, but are captured later that same day.

During the uprising, former Foreign Minister Corneliu Manescu appears on television to declare he is heading the Council of National Salvation and taking leadership of the country until free elections can be held. The security police who remain loyal to Ceausescu stage a counterattack against the army in Bucharest.

Mass graves containing what are alleged to be bodies of hundreds of demonstrators are unearthed in Timisoara. The Soviet government hails overthrow of Ceausescu regime as 'the will of the Romanian people' and Gorbachev says he will confer with the Warsaw Pact allies on providing 'assistance' to the new government of Romania. All the while, the shooting between the two sides continues. Secretary of State Baker announced that the US would not object if the USSR and other Warsaw Pact nations rendered military assistance to support the uprising.

Ceausescu and his wife are tried before an 'extraordinary military court' on charges of genocide and attempting to flee the country to collect more than $1 billion secreted abroad. They are condemned to death and executed, all of which is shown on national television. The fighting in Bucharest slackens.

The Council of National Salvation names Ion Iliescu interim president until elections scheduled for April, 1990. Dissident engineering professor Petre Roman is named Prime Minister and a new cabinet is appointed.

Soviet Union Gorbachev visits Italy, signs Joint Soviet-Italian

Declaration and several agreements on cooperation. He also visits the Vatican and meets with Pope John Paul II and among other things stresses, 'We need spiritual values, we need a revolution of the mind. This is the only way toward a new culture and new politics that can meet the challenge of our time.'

Gorbachev and Bush meet off the coast of Malta. They proclaim that the cold war is over. Their talks show that the relationship between the superpowers has reached a new level of consensus.

The Communist Party in Lithuania breaks with Moscow. Party leaders in Moscow support Gorbachev's denunciation of the Lithuanian party's defiance, but a two-day meeting of the national leadership ends without a consensus on how to deal with the Lithuanian party's decision to form an independent Communist organisation apart from Moscow. While tolerating and supporting the decisions in Eastern European countries to allow multi-party systems, Gorbachev has firmly resisted similar moves at home and efforts to dilute the power of the central Communist Party.

Officials in the Soviet Ukraine announce they will legally register congregations in Ukranian Catholic Church.

Amid continuing nationalist unrest in the Baltic republics, Lithuania adopts a multiparty system in defiance of Gorbachev and the Soviet constitution. Its Communist Party breaks with the Soviet Party.

Pravda prints front-page article suggesting possibility that Article Six of Soviet constitution, guaranteeing that the Communist Party has a 'leading role' in society, might eventually be dropped. Gorbachev, before a meeting of the party Central Committee, threatens to resign if conservative opposition to his reform programme continues. The Soviet parliamentary opposition coalition, Inter-Regional Group, cancels plans for general strike supporting free parliamentary debate on abandoning Article Six. The second session of Congress of People's Deputies opens in Moscow. Gorbachev tells the legislature that it is not yet time to discuss abandoning Article Six and the Congress votes 1,138-839 to postpone this debate.

Andrei Sakharov, a leading dissident and member of Congress of People's Deputies, dies of heart attack in Moscow. More than 150,000 queue in the freezing cold to view Sakharov's body as it lies in state.

The Congress of People's Deputies approves an economic reform package of price reforms and other market innovations. The opposition members propose a vote of no confidence in the government, but are defeated 1m685-199.

The Lithuanian Communist Party Congress, meeting in Vilnius, votes overwhelmingly to declare independence of the party leadership from Moscow, and party leader Algirdas Brazauskas announces the party's intention to establish an 'independent democratic Lithuanian state.' Gorbachev announces that he views the action with 'alarm,' and in another address that the efforts of secessionists will 'sow discord, bloodshed and death.'

Gorbachev makes a report ot the Party plenum entitled 'The Destiny of Perestroika is in the Party's Unity.' The Congress votes to condemn the Nazi-Soviet nonaggression pact signed before World War II and the secret protocols dividing Eastern Europe into spheres of influence.

Latvia's parliament votes to delete from the republic's constitution reference to the Communist Party's 'leading role.'

Yugoslavia Leaders of the republic of Sebia vetoes Markovic's plan to introduce drastic free-market measures into the economy. A half million workers stage a brief strike against radical economic reform.

1990

January Bush and Gorbachev exchange televised New Year's greetings. Bush calls for a 'new century of peace and freedom.'
Gorbachev visits Lithuania in an effort to convince the legislature to rescind its calls for independence from national legislation.

General M. Noriega of Panama surrenders to US officials after American military forces invade the country to apprehend him.

Havel travels to East and West Germany and states that a united Germany 'must free its neighbours of fear.'

Mitterand calls for a confederation of Eastern and Western European states to ensure peace on the continent.

Romania outlaws its Communist Party.

February Poland's United Worker's (Communist) Party votes itself out of existence and reforms as the Social Democracy Party. M. Rakowski states, 'The main weakness of the communist movement and the source of its failing was the abandonment of political democracy.'

The four major World War II Allies and East and West Germany agree on a framework for negotiating the reunification of Germany.

Kuwaiti police use force to dispense pro-democracy protesters.

South African black nationalist leader Nelson Mandela is freed after more than twenty-seven years in prison.

Famous Soviet-born cellist M. Rostropovich plays his first concert in the USSR in sixteen years.

In addressing the US Congress Czechoslovakia President Havel refers to the rise of democracy in the USSR and Eastern Europe as a 'historically irreversible process,' and that now nations 'will be able to create. . . the 'family of man.'

March The communist party in Nicaragua is defeated in elections. Ortega pledges to hand over power.

Soviet troops begin phased withdrawal from Czechslovakia.

The KGB issues a report that 786,098 people had been shot to death as enemies of the state during the reign of Stalin.

Lithuania formally declares independence from the USSR.

The Congress of People's Deputies repeals Article Six of its constitution which guarantees the Communist Party's leading role in society opening the way for a multi-party system, and finalizes the legal foundation creating a western-style executive presidency. Gorbachev hails the creation of an executive presidency as 'the most important decision in the history of our state.'

McDonald's fast food restaurant opens in Moscow serving 30,000 on its first day.

Gorbachev says NATO membership is 'absolutely out of the question' for a united Germany.

South Africa's seventy-five year rule over Namibia ends. President Nujoma declares, 'Africa's last colony is, from this hour, liberated.'

April Moscow places an embargo on crude oil and natural gas being sent to Lithuania to pressure the republic to rescind legislation calling for independence from the Soviet Union.

Pepsi-Co Inc. and the USSR sign a ten-year agreement under which Pepsi-Cola soft drink would be bartered for Soviet ships and vodka. The deal is valued at $3US billion.

More than seven hundred eminent American scientists, including forty-nine winners of the Nobel Prize issued a petition calling global warming, 'the most serious environment threat of the Twenty First Century.'

May South Korean President Roh Tae Woo and Gorbachev exchange messages and agree to normalize relations between their countries.

Gorbachev says the Soviet Union will review its policies on European arms if a united Germany becomes a member of NATO.

The Latvian Parliament votes in favour of independence from the Soviet Union.

The South African government and the ANC hold their first formal talks which are aimed at future negotiations on ending white minority rule and the apartheid system of racial separation.

May/June Gorbachev and Bush hold their second summit in Washington, and sign significant accords on arms, chemical weapons, and trade.

June Gorbachev approves a law on freedom of the press that is intended to end decades of government censorship and allow individual citizens to start newspapers.

Speaking before delegates from the Russian federated republic, he strikes back at critics declaring that his five years of power had accomplished 'what whole generations were striving for and could not achieve. . . Many things in *perestroika* are now hampered by the fact that the public conciousness is unprepared and marked by conservatism and narrow-minded attitudes, which formed for decades within totalitarian ideology.'

In a heated defense of Gorbachev's policies in Eastern Europe, Shevardnadze states in an interview, 'It is time to understand that neither socialism nor friendship, neither respect nor good relations can rest on bayonets, tanks, or bloodshed.'

The first post-communist goverment of Hungary is instructed by Parliament to negotiate the country's withdrawal from the Warsaw Pact.

Thatcher visits the Soviet Union stressing support for the beleaguered leadership of Gorbachev.

The leaders of the Warsaw Pact declared an end to the idea of the West as an 'ideological enemy.'

Mandela visits several countries in the West and is greeted like a hero.

July The official economic and social merger of the two Germanys becomes effective.

The Soviet Union drops its objection to a united Germany's membership in NATO.

It is announced that as of 1 August, Soviet citizens will be free to hold hard currency, and to open foreign currency accounts without having to justify the origin of the money.

During a meeting in Moscow between Daisaku Ikeda and Gorbachev, the Soviet leader announces his decision to make his first visit to Japan in the spring of 1991.

The Soviet government lists its economic embargo of Lithuania after the small republic's Parliament places a moratorium on the declaration of independence it had announced a few months earlier.

The Twenty-Eighth Congress of the Communist Party convenes amidst various differences of opinion between the delegates. Yeltsin walks out of the congress and quits the party.

August Iraq invades Kuwait, takes control of the government, and announces annexation of the territory. Thousands of foreigners are indefinitely detained within the two countries.

The United States, answering requests by Saudi Arabian leaders, commences a massive military buildup within that country on the borders of Iraq and Kuwait.

The Soviet Communist Party abandons the so-called *nomenklatura* system which empowered Communists to control virtually every important job in the country.

September Bush and Gorbachev meet in Helsinki and discuss ways their countries will work together in an effort to pressure Iraq to move its military presence out of Kuwait. The superpower leaders hold an unprecedented joint press conference and in so doing, they express unity in their efforts to support economic sanctions against Iraq instituted by the United Nations earlier in the month.

October The Nobel Prize committee announce the award of it's peace prize to Mikhail Gorbachev; the committee cited President Gorbachev for "his leading role in the peace process".